AF541831

Political Environment and its Impact on Tourism

Political Environment and its Impact on Tourism

Varinder Singh Rana

RANDOM PUBLICATIONS
NEW DELHI (INDIA)

Political Environment and its Impact on Tourism

ISBN 978-93-5111-878-7

Published in 2016 in India by

RANDOM PUBLICATIONS

4376-A/4B, Gali Murari Lal, Ansari Road
New Delhi-110 002
Phone : +9111-43580356, 011-23289044, 011-43142548
e-mail: sales@randompublications.com,
info@randompublications.com, randomexports@gmail.com

Reprinted 2019

Type Setting by : Friends Media, Delhi-110089
Digitally Printed at: Replika Press Pvt. Ltd.

Preface

Politics is the practice and theory of influencing other people. More narrowly, it refers to achieving and exercising positions of governance - organized control over a human community, particularly a state. Furthermore, politics is the study or practice of the distribution of power and resources within a given community (a usually hierarchically organized population) as well as the interrelationship(s) between communities.

Tourism is travel for recreation, leisure, religious, family or business purposes, usually for a limited duration. Tourism is commonly associated with international travel, but may also refer to travel to another place within the same country. The World Tourism Organization defines tourists as people "traveling to and staying in places outside their usual environment for not more than one consecutive year for leisure, business and other purposes". Tourism has become a popular global leisure activity. Tourism can be domestic or international, and international tourism has both incoming and outgoing implications on a country's balance of payments. Today, tourism is a major source of income for many countries, and affects the economy of both the source and host countries, in some cases being of vital importance.

Change is normal in politics as it is in tourism. Yet, historically, the relationship between politics and tourism has been a relatively small sub-field of the social science of tourism, even though there are an immense number of examples of the way that political change has affected the patterns, processes and directions of tourism development. In trying to draw the interconnections between political change and change in tourism this chapter will outlines some the elements of politics and public policy that are determinants or at least influences on tourism, as well as the interrelationships between them. It then goes on to highlight the importance of temporality to understanding public policy change.

– Author

Contents

1

Globalization and Democracy

AN OVERVIEW

Today's world is a democratic world. Sartori has called it a world of 'democratic confusion' because democracy is the most confused concept of political theory. It is not simply a form of choosing and authorizing government, it has also been defined as 'a type of society and a manner of life', as an ideal or as an end in itself. Every state, whether it is liberal, socialist or communist, boasts itself of being democratic and does not hesitate to call its opponents undemocratic, with the result that the concept has been the victim of contradictory interpretations.

Dictatorships have been established in the name of democracy. According to Hagopian, democracy is 'one of the most defused and pervasive concepts of history'. Similarly, according to Macpherson, there is a good deal of muddle about democracy and this is due to 'a genuine confusion as to what democracy is supposed to be, for the word democracy has changed its meaning more than once and in more than one direction.' Moreover, the term cannot be divorced from ideological considerations. There was a time when democracy used to be a bad word. Democracy, in its original sense of 'rule by the people or government in accordance with the will of the bulk of people', was considered a bad thing—something dangerous to nobility and civilized living.

However, its full acceptance as a respectable form of government became apparent only by the time of first world war, a war which was fought by the Western liberal-capitalist countries to make the world sale for democracy. Since then, the question of merits and demerits of democracy or whether democracy is the best form of government has been relegated into oblivion, so much so that everybody claims to be democratic. National liberation movements against imperialism and colonialism were attempts to assert the democratic right of self-determination of the peoples of Asia and Africa. Similarly, revolutions were made against the Western type of liberal democracy in the name of proletarian democracy or peoples' democracies. Such movements have changed the face of democracy and have made it the most ambiguous term of political theory. In

1949, UNESCO sponsored an inquiry into the conflicts and ideals associated with the concept of democracy. The questionnaire was sent to scholars of many countries and two points emerged:

- There were no replies averse to democracy. Probably for the first time in history, democracy was claimed as the proper ideal description of all systems of political and social organizations advocated by influential proponents.
- The idea of democracy was considered ambiguous and even those who thought it was clear or capable of clarity were obliged to admit certain ambiguity either in the institutions or devices employed to effect the idea or in the cultural or historical circumstances by which the word, idea and practice are conditioned.

Contemporary democracy is not the monopoly of western world. It cannot be equated exclusively with the unique western liberal democracy. The erstwhile non-liberal systems of communist countries such as USSR and East European countries, and the somewhat different semi-liberal systems of most of the under-developed countries of Asia and Africa have also a genuine historical claim to the title of democracy. All of them evolved their unique characteristics of democracy. In this chapter, we shall discuss various theories of democracy in the modern nation-states which have come into existence during the last 200 years.

DEVELOPMENT OF THE IDEA OF DEMOCRACY

For the greater part of human history, democracy was treated by intellectuals and political leaders with contempt. Democracy originally meant rule by the common people, the plebians. It meant rule by the untrained, ignorant mob. Its egalitarian character was contrary to the naturally hierarchical character of society. Democracy considered what is right by the counting of heads rather than by any standard of truth or justice. Plato defined it as 'the worst form of government, less than tyranny'. In democracy, freedom degenerates into license and equality into insolence. Aristotle considered it as the rule of the poor, regardless of whether the poor were a majority or minority.

He emphasized three elements of democracy: i) intellectually, democracy meant equality, ii) constitutionally, it meant rule of the majority, and iii) socially it meant rule of the poor at the expense of the rich. On the other hand, Greek philosopher Cleon defined democracy as the rule 'of the people, by the people and for the people'. A classical theory of democracy was developed in Athens. It was justified on the grounds that citizens should enjoy political equality in order to be free to rule and be ruled in turn. The key features of this democracy were: i) direct participation of citizens in the legislative and judicial functions, ii) assembly of the citizens being sovereign and had the power to legislate on all common affairs of the city, iii) public offices were filled through direct election, lot or rotation, and had short duration. However, this type of democracy was limited to small city-states, and had a slave economy which created 'free' time for citizens.

And more importantly, citizenship was restricted a to relatively small number of people. In the middle ages, one could not expect any theory of democracy or any demand for a democratic franchise. When feudalism prevailed, power depended on rank, whether inherited or acquired by force of arms. It was only in the seventeenth and eighteenth centuries that democracy became a respectable term. It were movements like Reformation and Renaissance that made the case for democratization of state, society, economy and politics. The initial theoretical thrust came from English puritans of the left such as Diggers and Levellers.

The classical democratic element was provided by John Locke who sought to free the individual from arbitrary government and establish him as an independent sovereign being guided by his conscience and right reason. Government, according to him, must derive its authority from the free consent of the governed. The equalitarian element of democracy was provided by Rousseau who sought to re-introduce elements of direct democracy through his theory of 'General Will'. However, while these philosophers provided the foundation of a plausible concept of democracy, they did not push their thought to logical conclusion. Their views were far away from the fact that people actually rule.

During eighteenth century, the American revolutionaries and constitutionalists such as Jefferson and Madison tried to lay down the institutional basis of democracy. In England, Bentham and James Mill advocated right to vote and representative government. J.S. Mill elaborated the aims, ideals and institutions of democracy which later on came to be known as classical-liberal democracy. Implicit in his writings was the view that democracy was desirable not only because it produces public policies but also makes participation in a common undertaking rewarding. He saw democracy as participatory, developmental, educative and constructive. This type of democracy was endorsed by many subsequent liberal writers such as T.H. Green, Harold Laski, R.M. MacIver, John Dewey, W. Wilson etc.

During the latter half of twentieth century, classical liberal theory of democracy was challenged not only by liberalism itself which produced a new theory known as Elite theory of Democracy, but also by two other non-liberal variants of democracy: the Marxist-communist or peoples' democracy, and a host of theories evolved by the underdeveloped countries. The major thrust of the elite theory of democracy was that democracy as a government by the people was a myth and political power, far from being wielded by the people, was competed among the elitist/pluaralist groups. A new theory of democracy known as Participatory Democracy which has evolved in Europe and America during the last twenty-five years is trying to free democracy from the elitist elements. A powerful critique of liberal democracy and a radically different image of good society was provided by Marxism. Marxism rejected the whole idea of liberal democracy, terming it as 'class democracy' since capitalist society was a class-divided society.

Instead, it proposed a new theory of democracy to be established by the working class after overthrowing the capitalist state. This is known as the proletarian democracy or 'Dictatorship of the Proletariat'. Again, after the second world war, a large number of Asian and African countries got independence from colonial rule either through revolutionary struggle or without any actual use of force.

These revolutions were made by the leaders who were able to get support for their vision of building a future society. A part of this vision was democracy. However, these leaders arrived at their own theories of democracy by the conscious selection of those elements in both liberal and Marxist theories which they found applicable to the problems of their own people.

Thus we find that though democracy is a legitimate and universally appropriate form of government, different structural foundations or social pre-conditions produce quite different but possible democratic systems. However, in all kinds of democracies, the ultimate ethical principle at the most general level has been the same: to provide conditions for the free development of human capacities and to do this equally for all members of society. However, serious differences arise when we move from the general to the particular level in different societies. The different theories of democracy are nothing but different attempts to achieve this goal.

MEANING OF DEMOCRACY

Seen from the above account of the development of the idea of democracy, it is next to impossible to give any universal definition of democracy. Cranston writes that democracy is nothing but different doctrines in different people's mind. C.D. Burns also complains: Tew words have been more loosely and variously defined than democracy.

It has almost literally meant all things to all people'. The UNESCO questionnaire had also pointed out the vagueness of the term: voices of complaints on the looseness and vagueness of current use of the word democracy have been heard at least since the days of the French Revolution'. One can agree with Laski that 'Democracy has a context in every sphere of life and in each of these spheres it raises its special problems which do not admit of satisfactory or universal generalization'.

The difficulty with giving any precise definition of democracy lies also in the fact that the term has been understood not only as a form of government but also as an ideal or a way of life. The latter meaning takes a broader view of democracy which includes the ideals of democratic man, democratic society, democratic economic system and democratic morality. A number of definitions have appeared from time to time associating democracy with the process of government, some of which are as follows:

- *Lincon:* Democracy is 'a government of the people, for the people and by the people'.
- *Seelay:* Democracy is a form of government in which everyone has a share'.
- *Sartori:* A democratic political system is one that makes the government responsive and accountable and its effectiveness depends first and foremost on the efficiency and skill of its leadership'.
- *Lipset:* Democracy...may be defined as a political systems which supplies regular constitutional opportunities for changing the governing officials and a social mechanism which permits the largest possible part of the population to influence major decisions by choosing among contenders for political office'.
- *Macpherson:* '...democracy is merely a mechanism for choosing and authorizing governments or in some other way getting laws and political decisions made'.
- *Schempeter:* 'The democratic method is that institutional arrangement for arriving at political decisions which realizes the common good by making the people itself decide issues through the election of individuals who are to assemble in order to carry out its will'.

From the various definition of this controversially interpreted political concept, the following ideas may be selected which are commonly associated with this democracy:

- A high level of political participation in the selection of public policies and public officials at regular intervals. It is the right and duty of all citizens to get involved in elections, public discussions and other aspects of political process.
- Meaningful and extensive competition among individuals and organizations for effective positions of government.
- Availability of civil and political liberties, sufficient to secure integrity of political competition and participation such as constitutional state, guarantee of basic rights such as right to vote, freedom to form organizations, free and fair elections, decentralization of political power etc.

In short, democracy is associated with Participation, Competition and Civil and Political Liberties. Historically, it has been defended on grounds of fundamental values such as equality, liberty, moral self-development, social utility, satisfaction of wants, efficient decisions etc.

THEORIES OF DEMOCRACY

As mentioned above, democracy means rule by the people. However, to define democracy as the rule of the people raises more questions rather than helping to clarify its meaning. There is a lot of disagreement on both what constitutes 'people' and what is meant by 'rule'. If 'demos' means people, then the question is who constitute 'people', what is the scope and extent of their participation; what are the conditions which are conducive to participation.

Similarly, if 'crats' means rule, then what is the scope of that rule; does rule mean control of the people over law and order, control over the economy and the public policies? What is the mechanism for those who do not want to participate? Just as there are innumerable questions, numerous answers have been given by different thinkers to these questions. While some thinkers believe that all should directly participate in the decision-making, others believe that people can also participate through their representatives. Still others believe that rulers should be chosen by the people and should be accountable to them.

The rulers should be accountable to the representatives of the people. Some believe that if the rulers act in the interest of the people, this will suffice. The different theories of democracy answer these questions in a systematic manner. For the purpose of our study, the following theories can be identified:

- Classical-liberal theory of democracy
- Elitist theory of democracy
- Pluralist theory of democracy
- Participatory democracy
- Marxist theory of democracy or peoples' democracy

While the classical-liberal and Elitist/Pluralist theories are representative democracy, the participatory theory and the peoples' democracy try to blend elements of direct democracy so as to make the participation of the common man in the decision-making process a reality. Let us now discuss these theories in detail.

REPRESENTATIVE DEMOCRACY

Modern democracies are representative democracies. Though the rise of democracy in Athens in associated with the direct participation of citizens in the affairs of the state, the rise of modern nation-state made the institution of direct democracy irrelevant. The industrial revolution, creation of towns and cities, migration of population and capitalist economy created a number of problems such as the scope and extent of participation, participation vis-a vis the requirements of skilled administration. The increase in population and other geographical and physical limits made direct democracy not only impossible but also unnecessary and undersirable.

The ideal form of democratic state in the modern period was found in Representative Democracy in which people exercise their power through deputies or representatives periodically elected by them. The concept of representative democracy was systematically put forward by J.S. Mill in his book Considerations on Representative Government. According to him, a representative system along with freedom of speech, press and assembly provides a powerful mechanism whereby government can be watched and controlled.

Through electoral competition, it is able to harness leadership qualities for the maximum benefit of all. Echoing Aristotle's views, he writes that when the government is controlled by all citizens, there is a constant danger that the wisest and ablest will be overshadowed by the lack of knowledge, skill and experience of the majority. Again, there is a difference between controlling the business of government and actually doing it. Control and efficiency increase if people do not attempt to do everything. The business of government requires skilled employment. The more the electorate muddle in this business, the greater the risk of undermining efficiency and reducing overall benefit to all.

Thus the benefits of popular control and efficiency can only be had by representative democracy which separates functions and control. Representative democracy combines accountability with professionalism and expertise. It can combine the advantages of bureaucratic government without its disadvantages. The different forms of representative democracies value both democracy and skilled government

CLASSICAL-LIBERAL THEORY OF DEMOCRACY

Liberalism supported the democratic ideas right from the beginning. In fact, it was only with the rise of liberalism in England and Europe that the path was cleared for democracy and it became a respectable concept. Democratic ideas were nothing but a logical requirement of the governance of a society which had freed itself from absolute power of the kings and religious traditions. The ideas of liberty, equality, rights, secularism and justice became the cornerstone of liberalism and democracy became a means of achieving them. The liberal democracies that we know were liberal first and democratic afterwards. According to Macpherson, before democracy came in the western world, there came a society and politics of choice, a society and politics of competition, and a society and politics of market. It was the liberal state that was democratized and in the process, the democracy was liberalized.

Early traces of classical-liberal democratic ideas are found in the writings of Thomas Moore's Utopia (1616), Winstanely's The Law of Freedom (1652) and English Puritanism as well as in the thinking of Levellers. However, it was the social contract theory which became crucial in establishing the foundation of democracy because the contract could be made only when all men were assumed to be equal. Thomas Hobbes in Leviathan (1651) elaborated the democratic principle that the government is created by the people through a social contract. It was John Locke who provided the formula that government must be by the people and aim solely at their good. The essence of his argument was that:

- Ultimately all political power inheres in the people,
- The legitimate power of the government is a limited one; the government should not violate certain rights of the people, otherwise, the contract between the government and the people is dissolved, and
- Individual rights are a part of man‘s nature. Ultimately, a government is dedicated to the needs of the individual and not vice versa.

Locke‘s ideas about politics were complemented by Adam Smith in the realm of economics. He opposed mercantalism promoted by the state and argued that the best economic decisions should be made by the people themselves.

Freedom to produce, buy and sell, free and open competition, free economic exchange would give advantage to the best endeavours and most industrious proportionate opulence. The French philosopher Montesquieu elaborated the theory of separation of powers which had a great democratic appeal and influenced the making of American constitution. On the American continent, Jefferson. Madison and Hamilton tried to give institutional shape to the ideas of Locke, Adam Smith and Monesquieu.

VIEWS OF BENTHAM AND J.S. MILL

Jermy Bentham was the first modern liberal thinker who prepared the ground for the attitude towards democracy. He along with James Mill and J.S. Mill justified democracy on utilitarian grounds. He said that individuals require protection from the governors as well as from each other, and an assurance that those who govern pursue policies that are in consonance with the interests of the individual. Thus for him the problem was how to make sure that governments follow the wishes and interests of the community in matters of law and policy. In other words, the problem was how to find a system of choosing and authorizing government which would make and enforce the laws needed by the society.

The solution to this problem was representative democracy, constitutional government, regular elections, secret ballot, competition between parties and leaders, majority rule etc. Thus Bentham came to see democratic franchise as essential to the goal of the greatest happiness of the greatest number. The only way to prevent the government despoiling the people was to make the governors frequently removable by the majority decision. However, his views on democratic franchise were not consistent. Till 1802, he advocated limited franchise, in 1809 he called for a householder franchise limited to propertied class, in 1817 he talked about universal franchise for men.

However, broadly speaking, liberal democracy with universal franchise and constitutional government was seen as the best protector of individual rights and laisses faire capitalist economy. It was J.S. Mill who set the course of democratic thought in the nineteenth century. Through his writings he sought to defend a concept of politics which increased individuality, representative government, efficient administration and non-interference in the economic affairs. While accepting the views of Bentham on democracy as a means of protecting the citizens from the oppression of the rulers, he supplemented it with another dimension—the moral worth of democracy for the improvement and development of mankind as a whole. His emphasis was more on what democracy could contribute to human development. Macpherson has called Mill's views on democracy as 'Developmental democracy'.

According to Mill, man is capable of developing his powers and capacities and a good society is one which permits and promotes these activities. Liberal democracy or representative government was important because it was an effective means for the free development of individuality. Democracy drew people in the operations of government by giving them a right to vote which could bring a fall in government. Participation in political life such as voting, involvement in local administration and jury service was vital to create a direct interest in developing citizenry.

Like Rousseau, Mill conceived democracy as a prime mechanism of moral self-development and highest and harmonious expansion of individual capacities. However, while accepting participation in the elections as an essential means of human development, Mill did not favour universal franchise or the principle of one-man-one-vote. He was fearful that the working class being in majority, one-man-one-vote may lead to legislation in the interest of one particular class at the expense of other classes as well as of posterity. Instead, he recommended a system of plural voting for the members of the smaller classes so that neither of two classes should outweigh the other and impose class legislation. While everyone should have vote, some should have several votes.

In his later book, Representative Government (1861) he argued for plural vote for some along with the exclusion of others such as people receiving poor relief, bankrupts, illiterates, those not paying taxes etc. While participation in the political process was necessary to improve people's quality, participation with equal weight was deemed to reinforce low quality. Hence those who had already attained superior quality, through education or property must not be made to yield their power to the rest. As he wrote 'It is not useful but hurtful that the constitution of the country should declare ignorance to be entitled to as much political power as knowledge'.

Thus, although from a purely arithmetical point of view, Mill could not be ranked as a full egalitarian yet his moral dimension was more democratic because it wanted to move towards a society of individuals more humanly developed. On the whole, he drew the conclusion that a representative democracy, the scope and powers of which are tightly restricted by the principle of liberty and laissez faire in economic relations is the best guarantee of free community and brilliant prosperity. The above ideas of classical-liberal democracy found further support in the writings of T.H. Green, Hobhouse, Lindsay, Barker, Laski, MacIver, John Dewey, W. Wilson etc.

With the evolution of the party system in the twentieth century, the classical-liberal theory was further strengthened. The contradiction which Mill had seen between universal franchise and the class interest turned out to be unfounded. Franchise was extended to all adult population. In fact the early twentieth century liberal thinkers felt that the democratic party system had overcome the dangers of class government. For example, MacIver saw the party system as an effective way of reducing the multitudinous differences of opinion to relatively simple alternatives. Similarly, John Dewey felt that democracy was the best method to organize the scattered, mobile and manifold public.

CHARACTERISTICS OF CLASSICAL LIBERAL DEMOCRACY

From the above discussion, we can sum up the characteristics of classical-liberal theory of democracy as follows:

- The classical liberal theory of democracy from John Locke onwards, enshrines supremacy of the people.
- It takes individual as the basic unit of democratic model, assuming that he is rational, ethical, active and self-interested. It emphasizes individual freedom and the right of the individual to pursue his own good with minimum of state interference.
- It hated the tyranny of the old regimes of monarchies and aristocracies, stressed the role of vigilance and participation in protecting the hard won rights against the sinister interests of the government. Hence participation in political life was felt necessary not only for the protection of individual interest but also for the creation of an informed, committed and developing citizenry. Political involvement was considered essential for the development of the individual.
- Participation was deemed a virtue. Through this opportunity, it was believed that the horizon of the individual would be widened, his knowledge extended, his sympathies made less parochial, his practical intelligence developed. It would serve as a means of intellectual, emotional and moral education, leading towards the full development of the capacities of the individual.
- At institutional level, it advocated representative government with elected leadership, regular elections, secret ballot, constitutional state,

independent judiciary, individual rights and civil liberties including freedom of thought, feeling, taste, discussion, publication etc.

- It made a clean demarcation between elected representatives and the bureaucracy. The benefit of popular control and efficiency can be had only be recognizing that they have quite different functions.
- At economic level, it was built upon economic inequality and political equality. It believed in competitive market economy, private possession and control over the means of production and laissez faire economy. According to Macpherson, democracy was to maximize the liberty of citizens and above all secure their property and the working of the capitalist economy. Liberal democracy neither destroyed or weakened the state, it strengthened both the state and the capitalist society.

CRITICISM

- Inspite of being a comprehensive theory of democracy, the classical-liberal theory was vehemently criticized and found inadequate to meet the needs of highly industrialized and technological states which emerged during the inter-war period and the second world war. The main grounds of criticism are as follows: The classical theory rests on a view of man as rational, active, informed and ready to take active part in the political process. Lord Bryce, Graham Wallas and later the empirical writers maintained that man is neither as rational, as disinterested, as informed or active as it is assumed to be. The classical theory either ignores, underplays or simply condemns the role of organized groups, leaders or emotions in political affairs. As Davis writes, 'the reality of irrational mass emotions, self-interest, group egoism and the prevalence of oligarchic and hierarchical social and economic organizations need no longer be denied in the name of democratic values'.
- The classical democracy is centred around the proposition that 'the people' hold a definite and rational opinion about every individual question and they give effect to this opinion by choosing their representatives who will see to it that their opinion is carried out. However, it fails to provide definition of such terms as 'people' or 'rule' which are obviously central to a conception of government as the rule of the people. Public opinion as the basis of government is a 'democratic myth'. In actual practice, public opinion does not make the government; rather it is the government which moulds the public opinion.
- The classical theory is based on the assumption that there exists a common good (such as human self-development) which is always

simple to define and which every normal person can be made to see by means of rational argument. However, as was pointed out by Schempeter, there is no such thing as a uniquely determined common good on which all people could agree or be able to agree by rational argument. Common good is bound to mean different things to different people.

- Public policy is not necessarily the expression of the common good as conceived by the people alter widespread discussion, debate, consultation and consent. Such a description of policy-making is held to be dangerously naive because it overlooks the role of demagogic leadership, mass psychology, group coercion and the influence of those who control concentrated economic power. According to Walker, classical democracy is unrealistic because i) it employs concepts of the nature of man and the operation of society which are Utopian, and ii) it does not provide an adequate operational definition of its key concepts.
- With the advent of the party system, democracy has been reduced essentially to a competition among the elites rather than the masses. These elites are the driving force and they formulate issues. What we are confronted with in the analysis of the political process is not a genuine but a manufactured will, manufactured in ways similar to commercial advertising. People neither raise nor decide issues but the issues that shape their fate are normally raised or decided for them. The wishes of the electorate are not the ultimate ideas nor the electorate‘s choice flows from its initiative. Rather it is shaped by the elite.
- The classical theory takes an over-simplified view of the complex procedure and decisionmaking process in politics. It lacks a satisfactory treatment of the problems caused by simultaneous affirmation of majority rule and minority right. The complex and technical nature of the political process is beyond the understanding of an average man who is too much engrossed in his own activities. As Davis writes, ‘The highly technical and complex process of policy making is over-simplified and misunderstood (by the classical theory)‘.
- The classical theory of democracy was based upon political equality (equality before law) and economic inequality. While the early liberals such as Bentham, James Mill and J.S. Mill tried to absorb the working class aspirations through limited political participation, the theorists of the first half of the twentieth century increasingly lost sight of the class character of liberal democracy and its exploitative consequences upon the working-class. The neoliberals like Lindsay, Barker, MacIver, Dewey felt that democracy with its regulatory and welfare

state could be the best way of bringing a good society. Although they were not insensitive to the concentration of economic power in a few hands, yet they did not find fundamentally anything wrong with the capitalist relations of production. They hoped that with some redistribution of rights between the classes, the democratic process could adjust the differences of various interests through peaceful and rational give and take. For example, Barker wrote that such redistribution would be 'a matter of constant adjustment and read justament, as social thought about justice grows and as the interpretation of the principles of liberty and equality broaden with its growth'. And this could be done through voluntary class cooperation aided by the state. However, as been pointed out by Macpherson, such a redistribution still remains a dilemma of liberal democracies.

ELITIST THEORY OF DEMOCRACY

The classical theory of democracy which gave central place to the idea of political equality and individual participation in the affairs of the government was challenged in the twentieth century by a number of thinkers determined to bring democracy face to face with the empirical reality. For them, the problems were: how realistic is it to expect the individual to directly participate in the day-to-day politics? can the ordinary citizen bear the strain of playing public role? will liberty be not destroyed if the masses are allowed to bring a variety of impulses unaided by an externally imposed discipline? In other words, is self-government possible? The answers to these questions led to models of democracy very different from the classical-liberal theory of democracy.

These models are popularly known as i) Elitist Theory of Democracy and ii) Pluralist Theory of Democracy. What led the realists to revise the classical theory of democracy? Historically, a number of factors during the inter-war period created favourable circumstances for such a change. Primarily, they were: large scale warfare, international rivalry in economic growth, economic depression, rise of fascist governments in Italy and Germany which led to the general enhancement of the importance of leadership, an increased need to remove political decisions from the democratic responsiveness, and the belief that only the experts could save the democratic system.

What became overwhelmingly clear was that the industrial organization of society demanded so much specialization, hierarchical and bureaucratic control that the demands for democratic participation in the decision-making were simply unrealistic. On the whole, the drive away from equality of control in the modern society became extraordinarily powerful. Not demanding much from individual citizens, the revisionists defined democracy in terms of 'system maintenance'. They encouraged their readers to appreciate the value of orderly, constitutional government, political stability, and an electoral system that successfully makes elites accountable to the more visible parts of the body politic. The elitist theory of democracy can be studied on the following lines:

- Meaning of the concept of Elite
- Elite theory of democracy
- Characteristics of the elite theory of democracy
- Criticism

MEANING OF THE CONCEPT OF ELITE

The term elite is usually used to mean a minority group distinguished from the mass of the people by some factor or factors that put it in a more advantageous position than the mass with regard to certain important aspects of social life.' According to Suzanne Keller, elites are those 'minorities which are set apart from the society by their pre-eminence in the distribution of authority, achievement and reward'.

The kind of elites with which we are concerned are the political power elites and are often categorized as 'governing elites', 'political elites,' 'power elite', 'ruling elite' etc. Such elites have as one of their distinguished feature the position of special access to or special ability to gain political power. According to Lasswell, 'the political elite comprises of the power holders of the body politic. The power holders include the leadership and the social formation from which leaders typically come and to which accountability is maintained during a given period'. Similarly, Presthus defines political elite as 'minority of specialized leaders who enjoy a disproportionate amount of power in the community's affairs.

In short, the elite is a group of people who hold political power because of their higher ability and provide leadership in all affairs of the society. An elite holds political power because it is an elite. The elitist tradition of political thought has a long history. In a sense, Plato was an elitist. But modern organizational elitism has arisen in the last 50 years or so, achieving its most notorious expression in the works of classical elitists like Vilfredo Pareto, Geatano Mosca, Robert Michels and J.O. Gassett. In USA, the theory found expression in the writings of James Burnham and C. Wright Mills!

The elite theory is based upon the idea that the society consists of two broad categories of people—the selected few and the vast masses. Pareto, in his book Mind and Society. wrote that every society is ruled by a minority that possesses the qualities necessary for its accession to full social and political power. Those who get to the top are always the best. They are the 'elites'—persons who rise to the top in every occupation and stratum of society. He also believed that the elites generally came from the same class, those who are wealthy and are also intelligent. Thus society consists of two strata of population: (i) lower stratum or the nonelite, and (ii) a higher stratum or the elite which is divided into governing elite, and non governing elite. Pareto also gave the concept of the circulation of elites which was further developed by Mosca.

According to Mosca, two classes of people appear in every society: a class that rules, and a class that is ruled. The former is less numerous, performs all political functions; monopolises power and enjoys the advantages that power brings; the latter more numerous, is directed and controlled by the first in a manner that is now more or less arbitrary and violent. 'The domination of an organized minority over unorganized majority is inevitable'. It is always the minority organized as a group which rules over the unorganized majority. Similarly, Robert Michels, whose name is associated with the 'iron law of oligarchy' asserted that the majority of human beings in a condition of eternal tutelage are predestined to submit to the domination of a small minority and must be content to constitute the pedestal of an oligarchy'. Leadership is a necessary phenomenon in every form of social life. The majority of human beings are 'apathetic, indolent and slavish and permanently incapable of self-government'. In short, the theory holds that:

- Division of society into dominant and subordinate classes is a universal tact. People are unequal in their ability and capacities;
- The elites exercise power and influence because of their superior quality such as intelligence, ability, administrative capacity, military power or moral authority;
- The elites are open groups and there is circulation of elites. Some new elites are admitted and some old go out. Sometimes a whole set of elites is replaced by a new one through revolution.
- Since, the majority of the masses are by and large apathetic, lazy and indifferent, society needs leadership in every walk of life. Elites provide this leadership.
- In the present century, the ruling elites consist of three kinds of people—intellectuals, managers of the industries and bureaucrats. C Wright Mills who used the term 'Power elite' discussed three major elites—economic, military and political.

ELITE THEORY OF DEMOCRACY

A generation of theorists of political elitism flourished around the second world war who tried to attempt a theory of democracy which could be reconciled with the theory of political elites. Considering the existence of political elites as inevitable phenomenon of modern political life, these democrats welcomed elitism and evolved what they called an 'Elitist Democratic Theory'—a kind of democracy in which elites were seen as the bulwark of democracy, protecting it from the dangers of totalitarianism'. They evolved a concept of democracy as a political system in which political parties in the form of elites complete for votes of the mass of electorate, the elites are relatively open and are recruited on the basis of merit, and people are able to participate in ruling the society at least in the sense that they could exercise a choice among the rival elites. The elite theory of democracy was deeply influenced by the classical elitism of Pareto, Mosca and Michels.

In the English speaking world, the theory was systematically formulated by Joseph Schempeter in his book Capitalism, Socialism and Democracy (1942). Since then it has been built up by many political scientists and has been supplemented by a host of writers such as Bernard Berlson, G. Sartori. Robert Dahl, Eckstein, Raymond Aron, Karl Mannehium, Almond and Sydney Verba etc.

The elite theory of democracy begins by attempting to assess realistically what is meant by 'rule by people' in a complex industrial society. Relying on the arguments presented by elite theorists, it was claimed that popular rule means very little indeed. It could be demonstrated conclusively that any large scale organization (such as the state) is of necessity organized on hierarchical lines. There are certain people who possess more power than others. Any organization can be divided into two groups—the elites who make the decisions, and masses who follow it. The reasons are obvious. Every member cannot be expected to know the full details involved in running the government. People are normally concerned with earning their livelihood for themselves and pursuing their individual interests. To expect an ordinary citizen to be a full time participant in the political process is simply absurd.

The complexities of modern society demand that we adopt a specialization whereby some people become expert in running the organization. In other words, the basic assumption of the elite theory of democracy was that most men are incapable of understanding the complexities of government decisions, adhering to liberal values or even continuing to have an enthusiasm in the democratic procedure. Secondly, the elite theory of democracy feared the participation of the people in the political proces and wanted to restrict their entry. The fear originated as a reaction to the totalitarian and fascist movements and regimes which sought to mobilize mass support as a means of achieving power and then destroying the democratic system itself.

Whereas for the classical liberal democracy, the enemies were the kings, aristocrats and plutocrats, for the elite theory of democracy, the new enemy was the people. Any deep incursion by them into politics and rapid mobilization of their numerical strength was a sign of authoritarian trend. Democratic and liberal values could be saved only by keeping the masses away from politics. Whereas the classical-liberal theory of democracy believed that people hold a definite and rational opinion about national issues and they give effect to their opinion by selecting their representatives, the Elite theory of democracy reverses this process. That is to say, the role of the people is only to elect the representatives who in turn produce a national executive or government. 'Democracy is simply a mechanism for choosing and authorizing governments, not a kind of society nor a set of moral ends.' The voter's role is not to decide political issues and then choose representatives who will carry out those decisions, it is rather to choose the men who are responsible for choosing the policies and enacting legislation. The mechanism consists of a competition between two or more self-chosen set of political parties (elites) for the votes which entitle them to rule until the next elections. The individuals who compete are politicians. The citizens' role is simply to choose between sets of politicians periodically at elections time. The citizens' ability thus is to replace one government by another which protects them from tyranny.

In short 'the democratic method is that institutional arrangement for arriving at political decisions in which individuals acquire the power to decide by means of a competitive struggle for the people's votes'. Similarly, Giovanni Sartori, is his book Democratic Theory writes, 'the democratic theory of elites is, in the light of present day factual knowledge, the core of democracy itself. He cautions that democracy is terribly difficult. It is so difficult that 'only experts and accountable elites can save it from the excess of perfectionalism, from the vortex of demagogy...adequate leadership is vital to democracy. He rejects the idea of self-government demos as either deceptive myth or a demagogic device and accepts elites as necessary evil.

Democracy can be defined as a system 'where the majority designates and supports the minority (elite) which governs.' Political democracy is a method or procedure by which, through a competitive struggle for sanctioned authority, some people are chosen to lead the political community. Democracy is the product of effects that results from the adoption of this method. Similarly, Plamenatz writes, 'In democracy, those who govern acquire the right to do so by competing for the people's votes' All elite theorists deny that there can be in any real sense government by the people. Raymond Aron writes 'it is quite impossible for the government of a society to be in the hands of any but a few...there is government for the people, there is no government by the people'.

In any society which is large and complex, democracy can only be representative, not direct and the representatives are a minority who clearly possess greater political power than those whom they represent. Democracy means rule of the political elite which has been elected by the people. We have democracy when competition for power between various competing elites goes on and the people vote to decide who will enjoy political power. In what sense the Elite Theory is democratic?

Firstly, the simple and important point that the theory believes in plurality of elites. The existence of choice for the people as to which elite (s) shall hold political power is the key democratic feature. Although there is at any one time rule by a minority but over a period of time, there is an alternation or some other form of changing the elites. Secondly, while the power is held by elites, the choice as to which elites shall hold power remains in the hands of people. It is this decision-making by people, together with the dynamic relationship between elites and masses which makes the elite theory democratic.

Thirdly, the process of moving in and out of power involves elite competition: they compete for the position of power, which gives the people the ultimate power. The result of competition among the elites is democracy because the power of deciding between the competitors is in the hands of the demos. Fourthly, people's ultimate power consists in the capacity to remove one set of elites from power and appoint new ones. This feature of elite democracy ties it with the general idea fundamental to all theories of democracy that there should be a meaningful choice for electorate. Thus the electoral process holds key place in the elite theory. It is a mechanism which gives people ultimate control over the elites. The elites in power have a duty to give an account of themselves and their action to the people who have a right to remove them if the account is unsatisfactory. The elite theory of democracy has two sides: the elite side and the democratic side. The elitist side is the stress on the importance of leadership and the need for specialization; the democratic side consists in the 'openness of the elites'. The masses can become members of the elites. There is a possibility of the rise of new elites from out of the masses. According to Bottomore, the elitist democratic system implies the following conditions:

- The elites are relatively open
- They are recruited on the basis of merit,
- There is a continuous and extensive circulation of elites,
- The mass of population is able to participate in ruling society to the extent that it can exercise choice in selecting between the rival elitist groups,
- The democratic elites have a mass background,
- The distance between the elite and the masses is minimum.

CHARACTERISTICS OF ELITE THEORY OF DEMOCRACY

- At the heart of elite theory of democracy is the presumption of an average citizen's inadequacies. The concept of an active, informed democratic citizen is a myth. The theory believes that the political inactivity of the average citizen is more or less a permanent aspect of his behaviour. It considers political inactivity as a sign of satisfaction with the operation of the political system. It is considered as a form of passive consent. As a result, a democratic system must rely on the wisdom, loyalty and skill of its political leaders and not on the population at large.
- The elite theory conceives democracy primarily in procedural terms:

it is seen as method of making decisions, a mechanism for choosing and authorizing governments, and not a kind of society nor a set of moral ends. The mechanism consists of competition between the two or more self-chosen elites arrayed as political parties, for the votes which will entitle them to rule till the next election. The voter‘s role is not to decide the political issues but to choose representatives who will make decisions which ensure efficiency in administration and policy-making. The average citizen has some measure of political power because of his right to vote in regularly scheduled elections. The theory expects that the political leaders in an effort to gain support at the polls, will shape public policy to fit the citizens‘ desires.

- The elite theory of democracy calls for an agreement on democratic values among the elites which it considers as the only main bulwark against the breakdown of constitutionalism. It calls for a consensus among the elites—political parties, leaders, trade union executives, and leaders of voluntary associations to defend the fundamental procedures of democracy in order to protect their own positions from the irresponsible demagogues. Agreement among the political leaders is more important than consensus among the common citizens for achieving stability.
- Several elite theorists have suggested that democracies have good reason to fear increased political participation. They argue that a successful democratic system depends on widespread apathy and general political incompetence. The idea of democratic participation is thus transformed into a nobel lie, ‘designed chiefly to ensure a sense of responsibility among political leaders.‘ If the uninformed masses participate in large numbers, democratic self-restraint will break down and peaceful competition among the elites—the central theme of the elite theory— will become impossible.
- The principle aim of the elite theory was to make democracy more realistic and to bring it closer to the empirical reality. The elite theorists were convinced that the classical liberal theory does not account for ‘much of the real machinery‘ by which the system operates. But in the process of bringing it closer to the reality, they have transformed democracy from a radical theory into a conservative political doctrine, stripping away its distinctive emphasis on popular political activity so that it no longer serves as a set of ideals towards which society ought to be striving.
- The elite theory of democracy has shifted the emphasis of democracy from individual participation in decision-making to the needs and functions of the system as a whole. The central question for the elite theory is not how to design a political system which encourages

individual participation and enhances the moral development of the citizen but how 'to combine a substantial degree of popular participation with a system of power capable of governing effectively and coherently'. The elite theory allows the citizens a passive role in political activity. The overriding concern of the elite theory is with maintaining the stability of the democratic system. Political participation has been substituted by stability and efficiency as the prime goals of democracy.

CRITICISM AND EVALUATION

The elite theory of democracy has been criticized by a number of writers, prominent among whom are C.B. Macpherson, Greame Duncan, Barry Holden, Bottomore, Plamenatz, Christian Bay, J.L. Walker, Robert Dahl etc. The main lines of criticism are as follows:

- The elite theory of democracy is excessively arbitrary and does not pay attention to the recognized characteristics of democracy. According to Barry Holden, if we define democracy as the making of political decisions by the electorate, then elite theory is not democratic. The appointment and removal of elites by means of elections is held as the key to the democratic process. If it means that the electorate only appoint and remove governors and do not decide upon issues and policies, then this is not an instance of democracy. If the electors are only to choose the representatives, this means that they have no voice in running the country.
- The heart of the classical theory of democracy was its moral purpose. The elite theory deliberately empties out the moral content from the democratic phenomenon. There is no nonsense about democracy as a vehicle for the improvement of mankind. Elite democracy changes the means and the locus of the contributions of the government to human development. Politics may play a part in the pursuit of the ideal but it no longer has the paramount role which it had before. The most significant realms for responsible personal activity lie beyond the limits of politics—economics, education, arts etc. Elite democracy, though not denying the traditional democratic hopes for moral progress, conspicuously excludes them from the list of essential features in the definition democracy.
- For elite theory of democracy, participation is not a value in itself. All elite theories deny that there can in any real sense be government by the people. Popular government in the classical democracy meant active participation of most adult citizens in the determination of public policies. In the elite theory of democracy, the popular rule means only the popular choice at periodic elections of governors who make

policy-decisions. The extent of popular participation, which is essential for political democracy, is more than that. However, according to Bottomore, this is an undemocratic element which becomes 'more apparent when the representative principle is applied in a system of indirect elections whereby an elected elite itself elects a second elite which is endowed with equal or superior political power.

- Responsibility of the government, according to the elite theory, refers to the accountability of the creative and governing elite to those who have been the object of its policies. Citizens must have minimum involvement in the affairs of the state. They have to judge the governors, their records and their promises largely as passive objects. That is, they are to judge the world they never made. If a high degree of social solidarity and a sense of community are necessary for the effective functioning of any sort of democratic government, then it must come largely from some other source than the political activity of the citizens.
- An important unsatisfactory element in the theory is its concept of passive apolitical common man who pays allegiance to his governors and to the sideshow of politics while remaining primarily concerned with his private life, evening of television with his family, or the demands of his job. Only when the average citizen finds his demands threatened by the action or inaction of government that he may vigorously strive to influence the course of public policy.
- The primary concerns of the elite theory of democracy have been the maintenance of democratic stability, the preservation of the democratic procedure and the creation of machinery which would produce the most efficient administration and coherent public policies. With this the social movements have been pictured as a threat to democracy or as political extremism. Whereas the social movements also serve as the 'creators and carriers of public opinion', the elite theory fears that the social movements put the system out of gear and disrupt the mechanism designed to maintain the due process of law.
- By replacing the classical theory of 'democratic humanism' by that of 'democratic mechanism', the elite theory of democracy has stripped democracy of much of its radical elan and has diluted its Utopian vision, thus rendering it inadequate as a guide to the future. As Davis Lane writes: 'The institutional idea of contemporary democracy lacks the radical bite of classical theory. It is bound by the limits of political reality. It is less a guide to future action than a codification of past accomplishments. The theory generally accepts the prevailing distribution of status in society and finds it not only compatible with

political freedom but even a condition of it.' It provides democracy with something of a system to be preserved rather than an end to be sought. Those who wish a guide to the future must look elsewhere.

PLURALIST THEORY OF DEMOCRACY

Apart from Elite Theory of Democracy, modern democratic theory has another dimension which has been developed primarily by the American political scientists since the second world war. This is known as the Pluralist Theory of Democracy. The elitist and the pluralist theories of democracy are distinguished as two types of democracy but there are important inter-connections between the two and the writings of some theorists contain an amalgam of both. Both theories point to the power of groups other than people as a whole and as such both run counter to the classical-liberal democracy. Both see democracy as consisting of plurality of power holding groups and their relationship to one another and the mass of the people. Nonetheless, there are enough differences to outline them as two separate theories. In the Elite Theory of Democracy, the concern is with the elites that control or seek to control the government.

In the pluralist theory, the focus is on the groups that seek to influence rather than control the government. This is understood by distinction between political parties and pressure groups. Another difference is the different role given to the electoral process in the two types of theories. Elite theory is centred upon elections: it is by virtue of competition for the peoples' votes that the elite model is held to be democratic. In the pluralist theory, although elections may be seen as a necessary condition for the existence of the democratic process, that process is itself constituted primarily by the inter-election activity of the groups. To a very great extent, the pluralist theory of democracy was a reaction against the nondemocratic character of elitism.

The pluralist theory of democracy was formulated as part of the rejection of the elitist analysis of politics. Whereas elite theory believed that the masses were incapable of making decisions on major issues, the pluralist democracy, recognizing the inadequacies of the electoral process, called for other means of eliciting the will of the people.

MEANING OF THE CONCEPT OF PLURALISM

Although the origin of pluralism lies far back in history, it became part of the liberal creed in the twentieth century. Pluralism can be characterized by its' view that power is and ought to be decentralized and scattered among a number of groups and associations. In USA, pluralism manifested itself especially in the group theory of politics. Some writers treat 'group theory of politics and pluralism as synonymous. It was the group theory of politics associated with Bentley and Truman that provided the immediate intellectual basis for the pluralist theory of democracy. Group theory entered into pluralism in two ways. Firstly, it provided the view that the society is basically composed of various interest groups. Such groups engage the interests of the population and act as a chain between the masses and the elites. Secondly, groups provide the foundation of what is known as the 'pressure group' theory which represent the masses in a much more meaningful way because they articulate and make effective the specific demands of the citizens. On the whole, groups provide for some real participation and they advance the perceived interests of the masses. The modern concept of pluralism believes that in the industrial/ technological societies, power is highly fragmented; it is so amorphous, shifting and tentative that only a few are said to have more than others over a period of time. Power is broadly shared among a group of competing public and private groups; those in high places appear to have more power but in fact they are mediators among conflicting interests for whose power and support they always bargain.

As Durkheim maintains: 'Collective activity is always too complex to be able to be expressed through a single and unique organ of the state...A nation can be maintained only if between the state and the individual, there is inter-related a whole series of secondary groups near enough to the individual to attract them strongly in their sphere of action and drag them in this way into the general torrent of social life'. Through their leaders, such groups mediate between individual and all organized forms of power, thereby ensuring the representation of affected interests. They give private citizen a voice in the government and ease consensus.

Even though industrial and political integration and technological demands have made power concentrated in a few hands, the competition among fewer but larger interest groups goes in favour of public interest. The competition among big business, labour and government keeps each interest from misusing its power. Though there are inequalities in wealth, education and power, the presence of associations and groups provide the broadest possible representation of private interest that make democracy viable.

Pluralism insists that government is not merely the responsibility of politicians and officials but also that of individuals and social groups of any kind who have their part to play and make their influence felt in indirect ways. Modern pluralism agrees that some form of elite rule by highly educated and interested groups is the essential requirement of our system. However, pluralism exists if no single elite dominates decision-making in every substantive area. If bargaining and opposition among three or four elite groups persists, pluralism remains. Here pluralism comes near the elite theory.

PLURALISTIC THEORY OF DEMOCRACY

The pluralist theory of democracy has been supported by a number of American political scientists such as S.M. Lipset, Robert Dahl, V. Presthus, F.

Hunter, R.E. Agger etc. According to these writers, political power is divided among diverse interest groups, associations, classes and organizations in the society and the elites which lead them. These groups raise their demands directly or through the mediating agencies of political parties on the political system. Pluralist democracy means 'a political system in which policies are made by mutual consultation and exchange of opinions between various groups so that no group or elite is so powerful as to dominate the government to such an extent that it may implement all its demands completely. The theory believes that power should be shared by all groups in the society and all organizations and groups must have their share in the policy making.

No social class should really control the machinery of the government to the total exclusion of other competing classes or groups. According to Presthus, pluralist democracy is 'a socio-political system in which the power of the state is shared by a large number of private groups, interests, organizations, and individuals represented by such organization...pluralism is a system in which political power is fragmented among the branches of government, it is moreover, shared between the state and a multitude of private groups and individuals. Duverger defines it as 'a plurality of decision centres'.

According to Truman, twentieth century democracy consists of a pluralistic struggle among diversified interest groups. Writing in the context of USA, he felt that United States was a democracy by virtue of the fact that no small set of the multifarious interests controlled a dominant share of public policy decisions.' For the pluralist democracy, the behaviour of the individual citizens per se is not crucial since the virtues of groups would make up for the failures of individual citizens to conform to the popular democratic image. If the citizens are ignorant of the political issues that affect their interests, the relevant interest groups would protect them. If the individual citizen lacks the resources to make his wishes known, the relevant interest groups would pool their resources, aggregate their separate concerns and articulate them to the appropriate decisions makers.

The key character of this model of democracy is that no single group or minority coalition groups dominate in all important areas of political decisions. For group theorists like Dahl, modern democracy itself could be defined as 'a process of governance by which minorities— plural—rule'. In order to effect such a rule, the theorists postulate an open political system in which all citizens have the legal opportunity and the economic resources to organize and to pursue their interests in the political arena. Such an opportunity is vital because it provides an instrument by which support and opposition towards a proposed measure may be expressed.

The pluralist theory believes that normal politics consists in the resolution of conflicts among groups. As most citizens lack the competence to govern directly, democracy works better when citizens are governed indirectly through membership of or identification with a group that supports their interests. Individuals should actively participate in and make their will felt through groups of many kinds. The democratic quality of the pluralist theory is preserved not only by the great diversity of competing groups but also by the greater commitment to the democratic principles among the group leaders and activists. A consensus must exist on what is called 'democratic creed'.

All groups must have faith in the democratic methods of voting, organizational membership and other political activities. They must believe that elections are a viable instrument of mass participation in political decisions. In the political community there must be different centres of power, influence and competition. Also a lively competition among individual elites and groups possessing different basis of power is a critical factor in the pluralist theory of democracy. Here pluralist theory comes very near to the elite theory. As has been pointed out earlier, the line between the elitist and the pluralist democracies can become blurred or non-existent. The greater the emphasis on the importance of plurality of elites and the dispersal of power, the nearer elite theory comes to the pluralist theory. Indeed, the two have been merged by Robert Dahl in his 'pluralist-elitist' theory of democracy.

Dahl's Polyarchy

Robert Dahl has explained thc theory of democracy in his books A Preface to Democratic Theory and Polyarcy. In his democratic theory, Dahl has combined the elite concept of government and the electoral competition with the pluralist stress on the dispersal of power. The plurality of elites is regarded in the same light as that of the plurality of groups. According to him, people act both through the electoral system and the group process. In his type of democracy which he calls 'Polyarchy', there are several places where decisions are made— merchants, industrialists, trade unions, farmers' associations, consumers, politicians, voters.

A number of groups and association influence policy making in the government. No one succeeds in obtaining full satisfaction of their demands. Some groups may be more influential than others, though it is difficult to measure the different degrees of this influence exactly. Moreover, the groups have greater power to resist policies which are not wanted and relatively less power to get desired policies implemented by the government. He defines the normal political process a polyarchal democracy by which he means 'a political system in which all active and legitimate groups in the population can make themselves heard at some crucial stage in the process of decisions.

Dahl argues that in polyarchal democracies, it is the minorities—plural—which rule. This argument is based on two lines of reasoning: i) even superficial observation suggests that in USA, decisions are made by endless bargaining; perhaps in no other national political system in the world is bargaining so basic a component of the political process, and ii) all groups share the political power and minorities rule'. If minorities do not exercise political influence effectively, they at least are accorded sufficient political status to prevent revolutions stemming from the disregard of their intense preferences by the majority. According to Dahl, the formulation of elites is natural in the industrial democratic societies but he rejects both the notion of the 'power elite' and the 'ruling class'.

In his book Who Governs, he came to the conclusion that the city was governed by a combination of elites in the cultural and economic fields but none of which could be described as a ruling elite. He firmly believes that the political elite in USA is a democratically competing pluralist elite leadership drawn from a large number of elites in different fields of society. The laws passed by the government are the result of a compromise between the forces of labour, capital and the organized power of other intermediatory groups.

Thus although minorities rule in both democracy and dictatorship, the characteristic of polyarchy greatly extends the number, the size and diversity of minorities, whose preferences influence the outcome of government decisions.

CHARACTERISTICS OF PLURALIST THEORY OF DEMOCRACY

- It believes that democracy is a political system run by competitive minorities because only they can secure political liberty of the masses.
- No single group should dominate the decisions-making process. Power should be decentralized, shared, contested and bartered among various groups in the society.
- To keep a check on the concentration of power, there should be a system of checks and balances between legislature, executive, judiciary and administrative bureaucracy.
- The function of the government is to mediate and adjudicate among different groups.
- There should be different centres of power, influence and competition with wide resource base of different groups.
- There must be consensus among different groups on political procedures, range of policy alternatives and legitimate scope of politics.

CRITICISM AND EVALUATION

The pluralist theory of democracy presumes that the group process and its outcome constitute the popular will and the general interest. However, as Holden points out, this is based on a general fallacy since that which results from the pursuit of particular interests may not be that which is desired by anybody. Firstly there is a mistake of supposing that the outcome of the clash of interests will necessarily bear a relevant relationship to those particular interests. For example, the result of the clash of interests among the groups of property developers, inhabitants, architects, local authorities, and the environmentalists over a policy of slum clearance might well result in that nothing is done. This would be an outcome that nobody wants. Secondly, it is also misleading that the individuals want only what is incorporated in their various interests. Indeed what an individual wants may run counter to what is involved in the pursuit of group interests. For example, as a wage earner, many people may want higher wages, but if asked at the elections, they might well say that as individuals they want a sound economy and an end to inflation even if this may mean a wage restraint. Critics remain unconvinced that the procedural safeguards that assure competition form an adequate foundation for democracy. For example, Micheal Mavgolis points out that the pluralist theory of democracy, inspite of assuring competition among elites, does not give a satisfactory explanation on the following grounds:

- It does not devise ways for the elected legislature, the central institution of liberal democracy, to control the huge bureaucracy;
- It does not limit military's control of the budgetary resources and technical information that allow it to manipulate public policy in its favour;
- It lacks the capacity to limit or control the great concentration of wealth, income and employment opportunities found in large private corporations;
- The theory does not devise ways to increase or redistribute society's resources so that traditionally underprivileged groups like racial minorities, women and those of lower socioeconomic status get sufficient share to allow them opportunities to participate in politics with their compatriots on a substantial footing;
- It could not devise ways to achieve all the above within the limits of natural resources available for development at reasonable economic and environmental cost.

Thus in order to improve upon the pluralist theory of democracy, many American political scientist have developed possible restatements of democratic theory that may meet many of the above criteria. Rober Dahl, for example, has suggested socialization of private corporations either through public ownership or public control. He has argued that the private decisions of these corporations concerning economic investment and planning have so much impact on the public sector that the public must have some say in them, if the polity is to call itself a democracy'. On the other hand, Ithiel de Sole Pool and Duncan have stressed on the necessity of making relevant information available to responsible decision makers. It has been suggested to enhance citizens' control through public access to the otherwise proprietary files of a large bureaucracy both public and private by means of a nationwide computerized information network.

Such information can form the basis of direct participation by citizens in the public policy formulation. Similary, Frederich Thayer has suggested that democracy can only be achieved if the hierarchical authority to make decisions binding upon others is replaced by a cooperative network of individual decision makers. However, the task of linking principles of democratic theory to the practices of democratic governance has always been difficult and it has been rendered even more difficult in recent times by the ever expanding scope of welfare state.

The pluralist-elite theorists have attempted to make a virtue out of the shortcomings of these institutions. They supplement the presumed linkages between citizens and representatives, realized through the electoral process, with indirect linkages realized through interest groups, political parties and leadership elites. Their critics have pointed out that governments based upon such practices violate too many democratic principles. However, they have failed to develop an alternative that remains true to democratic principles.

PARTICIPATORY THEORY OF DEMOCRACY

The theories of democracy during the last 200 years have assumed that a proper system of government must provide opportunities for political participation by ordinary citizens in the affairs of the state. While the opportunity to vote in periodic elections is the minimum qualification for democracy, participatory democracy believes that comprehensive opportunities and forms of political participation are the essence of democracy. The participatory theory of democracy justifies participation both as an ideal i.e. why people should participate, and as a functional requirement, i.e., how to and how much to participate in the affairs of the state. Though the term 'Participatory Democracy' is frequently used to cover a variety of models from classical Athens to Marxist tradition, the type of participatory democracy with which we are dealing here is a new model of democracy developed by certain Left Wing political writers from 1960s onwards. It was the result of the political upheavals, student movements, internal debates within the left wing ideology and dissatisfaction with liberal and Marxist ideas on democracy. Many writers have contributed to the development of this new model of democracy, but primarily it is associated with three names: Carole Pateman, C.B. Macpherson and N. Poulantzas. This theory was also developed as a counter model to Legal Democracy propounded by Hayek and Nozic. Although many writers have advocated participatory democracy as the appropriate response to twentieth century challenges, yet theory and practice of this model remains quite limited.

WHAT IS PARTICIPATORY DEMOCRACY

Participatory Democracy has developed as a reaction against the Elitist/ Pluralist theories of democracy. It is the common man's reaction against the 'expert'. In Elitist/Pluralist theories, power of decision-making is the monopoly of certain -elites or groups and the role of the masses is reduced only to the selection of elites once in few years. The participatory democracy seeks to distribute decision-making power more equitably.

The helplessness of the individual against the growth of the functions of the state and the concentration of decisionmaking power in a few hands led to a number of movements calling for the direct involvement of ordinary people in the decision-making. While adhering to equality and majority rule, participatory democracy wants to extend this political equality by some sort of grassroots decision-making of an authoritative nature. According to Cook and Morgan, participatory democracy has two broad features: i) decentralization of authoritative decision-making so as to bring it closer to the people affected by the decisions, ii) direct involvement of common man in making the decisions.

Participatory democracy agrees with the classical liberal idea that democracy is not only a form of government but also a means of equal right to self-development. Such a development can be achieved only in a participatory society—a society which cares for collective problems and helps in the formation of politically active citizens who take a continuous interest in the governing process. It believes in direct participation of citizens in the regulation of key institutions of society, making political parties more open and accountable, and maintaining an open institutional system to ensure the possibility of experimentation with new political forms of participation. Since Participatory Democracy wants to restore common man's participation, the natural questions are:

- Why is there a need for participation, and
- How to and how much participation?

NEED FOR PARTICIPATION

As stated above, Participatory Democracy means involvement of common man in the authoritative decision-making. The early liberal thinkers like J.S. Mill had defended participation both on grounds of protecting the citizens from the oppression of the rulers and as a means of improvement and development of mankind as a whole. It were the elitist/pluralist theories which discouraged participation. The theorists of Participatory Democracy want to restore participation once again.

According to Carole Pateman, the free and equal individual is found rarely in the contemporary democracies. The formal existence of rights (though not unimportant) is of little value if they cannot be actually realized. Freedom can be assessed from the concrete liberties and opportunities available to the individual in the society to participate actively in the political and civic life. Drawing upon the central notions of Rousseau and Mill, Pateman argues that participatory democracy fosters human development, enhances a sense of political efficacy, reduces the sense of estrangement from power centres, nurtures a concern for collective problems and contributes to the formation of an active citizenary capable of taking a more acute interest in government affairs.

If people know that opportunities exist for effective participation in decision-making, and that participation is worthwhile, they would definitely like to participate actively. Similarly, Macpherson writes that liberty of the individual can be fully realized only with the direct participation of the people in the regulation of the affairs of the state. Participation is a learning process. Participation changes the psychology of man since it socializes people into new beliefs, attitudes and values. According to Cook and Morgan, it increases the political efficacy or a person's sense of effectively manipulating his environment.

In an age when people find themselves helpless in the administrative complexity, a change in the decision-making through participation can overcome this sense of powerlessness and the resultant apathy. Participation can lead to acquisition of more information on public affairs. Participants become aware of possible alternative solutions to problems. Participation can revive the feeling of community solidarity and increase the ability to cope up with the tensions of modern life. Participation also results in better decisions. Participatory democracy is everyman's revolt against the expert. Even ordinary people are experts in certain matters.

They are better than elected representatives. Collective wisdom may be specially relevant to our times of rapidly expanding higher education in the industrial and technological societies. The more man knows collectively the better. Also the best protection from tyranny is through the dispersal of power. Participatory democracy can rescue the individual from apathy, ignorance and alienation. Thus participation is the essence of democracy and without the involvement of common man in the decision-making, it is meaningless.

METHODS AND SCOPE OF PARTICIPATION

Now, if participation in the affairs of the government is a precondition for self-development, the question is what are the possible means available to the common man. Inspite of disagreement among various theorists regarding the means and extent of participation, one can pinpoint a number of means in the modern democratic state. Some of these are: voting in local or national elections; canvassing or otherwise campaigning in the elections, active membership of a political party; active membership of a pressure group; taking part in political demonstrations; industrial strikes with political objectives or other activities aimed at changing public policy; various forms of civil disobedience such as refusing to pay taxes; membership of consumer councils for publically owned industries, involvement in the implementation of social policies; various forms of community development programmes such as women development, family planning, environment issues etc; taking part in referendum, recall etc.

The participatory democracy finds a number of shortcomings in the representative democracy and wants it to be supplemented by a number of measures by permitting the ordinary citizens to participate in the decisionmaking process. Opinions, however, differ as to how the people can directly and effectively participate and a number of alternatives have been and can be proposed. The classical-liberal democracy had evolved a number of participatory means such as elections, universal adult franchise, individual rights and civil liberties, freedom of thought and belief, participation in local government, public debates and jury service etc.

However, the recent supporters of participatory democracy consider these means inadequate. According to them, modern mass democracies produce alienated, isolated citizens, and that the governments in reality lack legitimacy. The inequality in power and resources have limited the means of life, liberty and equality, thereby restricting the capacity of the individual to effectively participate in political life. The state being a part of the productive process, produces a number of inequalities in daily life through its laws. Elections are not always an adequate mechanism to ensure the accountability of the representatives.

Hence peoples' control over the democratic process becomes an urgent matter. According to Poulantzas, since the state has grown in size and power, institutions of direct democracy or self-management cannot simply replace the state because this will leave a vacuum which will be filled by bureaucracy. However, participation of people can be enhanced through two sets of changes: i) the state must be democratized by making parliament, the state bureaucracies and political parties more open and accountable, and ii) new forms of struggles at local level through factory-based politics, women's movements, ecological groups must ensure that society as well as the state are democratized. But how the two are to be interrelated is a big question mark. Macpherson also admits that the problem posed by size and number of modern states are formidable and it is very difficult to imagine a political system in which all citizens can be involved in a face-to-face discussion every time a public issue arises. However, it does not mean that there is no scope for change.

This can be achieved through a combination of competitive parties and organizations of direct democracy. There will always be issues and different interests around which political parties might form. Moreover, only competition between political parties guarantees a minimum response of government to the people. However, this party system can be organized on less hierarchical principles making political administrators and managers more accountable to the people. A substantial basis would be created for participatory democracy if i) parties are democratized according to the principle of 'direct democracy', ii) if these genuinely participatory parties operate within the parliamentary structure, iii) if they are supplemented by fully-managed organizations in the work-place and local community. Only such a political system can realize the democratic value of 'equal right to self-development'.

According to Carole Pateman, participation can be increased by making democracy count in people's everyday life. This can be done by extending democratic control over those institutions which affect the daily life of the people. For this, democratic rights need to be extended to the economic enterprises and other institutions of society. The political rights of the citizens must be supplemented by a similar set of rights in the sphere of work and community relations.

There is no doubt that the institutions of direct democracy cannot be extended to all political, social and economic spheres because of a number of constraints. Also many of the liberal democratic institutions like competitive parties, political representatives, periodic elections are unavoidable elements of participatory society. But direct participation and control over immediate local issues, complemented by party and interest group competition in government spheres can most realistically advance the principle of participatory democracy. Also the opportunity of participation at work place can radically alter the nature of national politics. Individuals would be able to learn more about the key issues in resource creation and hence would be better equipped to judge national questions, the performance of the representatives and participate in decisions of national importance when the opportunity arises. Through such methods, the representative democracy can be extended to change into participatory democracy.

CHARACTERISTICS OF PARTICIPATORY DEMOCRACY

On the basis of the above discussion, the chief characteristics of Participatory Democracy can be enumerated as follows:

- It believes that democracy is not only a form of government but also a means of selfdevelopment. An equal right to self-development can be achieved through participatory society—a society which fosters a sense of political efficacy, nurtures a concern for collective problems and creates a kind of citizen who takes continues interest in the governing process.
- Apart from representative institutions, it calls for direct participation of citizens in the regulation of key institutions of society such as work place and local community.
- It wants to reorganize the party system so as to make the representatives directly accountable to the people.
- Only 'genuine' accountable political parties should operate the parliamentary system.
- It wants to maintain an open institutional system to ensure the possibility of new forms of democratic control.

- It wants to make a direct improvement in the poor resource base of individuals and social groups by extending economic rights and redistribution of material resources.
- It wants to minimize the hold of unaccountable bureaucratic power in both public and private life.

PROBLEMS OF PARTICIPATORY DEMOCRACY

According to David Held, while the participatory democracy recognizes many difficulties associated with the previous models of democracy (classical-liberal, earliest/pluralist etc.) and represents an advance upon them, it leaves many questions unresolved. There is no doubt that we learn to participate by participating and that it does help foster an active and knowledgeable citizenship, still it does not mean that an increased participation per se will automatically bring a new revolution in human development. There is no guarantee that people generally become more democratic, cooperative and dedicated to the common good.

As Burnheim points out, it would probably be wiser to presuppose that people will not perform better either morally or intellectually than they do at present. There is every possibility that participation will lead to consistent strifes and clashes, leading to contradictions between individual liberty, distributive justice and democratic decisions. Secondly, the participatory democracy is based on the belief that people in general want to extend the, sphere of control over their lives. However, it is one thing to recognize a right, and another to say that we must, irrespective of choice, must participate in public life. What if they do not want to do so? What if they do not really want to participate in the management of social and economic affairs.? What if they do not wish to become creatures of democratic reason? Or if they wield democratic power undemocratically, who is to check them? Thirdly, participatory democracy consider democracy not only a form of government but also a way of life and human self-improvement.

According to David Held, although participatory theorists are right in pursuing the implications of democratic principles for the organizational structure of society and state, yet they have not clearly resolved the highly complex relation between individual liberty, distributional matters and democratic process. By focusing on the desirability of collective decision-making, they leave these relations to be decided by democratic negotiations. But the basic problem is: Should there be limits on the power of the people to change and alter political circumstances; should the relation between liberty and equality be left to the whims of democratic decisions. Participatory theorists are vague on these points.

Fourthly, according to Cook and Morgan, as a system of government also, participatory democracy has not been able to build a systematic theory.

Participation of ordinary citizen in the decision-making process both at local level and national raises a number of problems which have not been adequately dealt with at theoretical level. Some of these problems are: i) What would be an appropriate unit for this kind of decision-making?, ii) What should be the proper size and function of the participatory unit, iii) The involvement of a large number of citizens may affect the efficiency and competence of the decisions, iv) How the decisions taken at the local levels may be coordinated with the political decisions at other levels and with the overall interest of the society at large. Such innumerable problems have created a variety of difficulties for the implementation of participatory democracy but have also a lot of criticism from the New Right school of thinkers.

MARXIST THEORY OF DEMOCRACY OR THE CONCEPT OF PEOPLES' DEMOCRACY

Democracy is not the monopoly of the western liberal world. The concept was equally accepted by Marx, Engles and the subsequent Marxist writers, though with an altogether different connotation. As discussed above, the liberal world associated democracy with political institutions like elected legislatures, universal adult franchise, several political parties competing for power, freedom of thought, expression, association and assembly. Marxism, on the other hand, adjusted democracy in the overall philosophy of socialist revolution.

It associated democracy with the dictatorship of the proletariat or peoples' democracy and the establishment of a socialist society, and its abolition as a form of state in the higher stage of communism. As a form of political organization, Marxism considers democracy to be ultimately determined by the relations of production in a given society. In a class divided society, democracy exists practically for the members of the dominant class. In the bourgeois society, democracy is a form of dictatorship of the bourgeoisie.

It frames constitutions, forms parliament and other representative bodies and introduces adult franchise and formal political liberties. But the bureaucratic machinery of the bourgeois state is so patterned that the political activities of the working class keep them out of the decision-making power. The rights are proclaimed formally and are not guaranteed, the representative bodies are no more than an instrument of policy of the ruling class. Hence the fight of the working class for democracy acquires a major significance as a condition and component of the proletariat's struggle for the socialist transformation of society. Socialist democracy, according to Marx, is the highest form of democracy because it is genuine democracy for the majority of the people.

It is people's democracy. Economically, it is based on the social ownership of the means of production. Politically, it will involve the masses directly in the administration of the state and social affairs. It is in this context that Marx defined democracy as 'an association in which the free development of each is the condition for the free development of all'. In the higher state of communism, democracy as a form of government will wither away and it will become a habit or a way of life. Lenin, another Marxist writer, laid stress on the class character of democracy and defined democracy as nothing but a form of state which is essentially a class rule. However, the concept of democracy as interpreted by the Marxist writers bred in the European tradition such as Bernstein, Rosa Luxemburg, Kautsky and the Austo-Marxists laid less emphasis on the class concept of democracy and did not agree with the criticism of the bourgeois democracy per se.

The working of peoples' democracy in USSR and East European countries brought into open serious contradictions in the theory and practice of Marxist theory of democracy. The state, in these countries, far from withering away strengthened its hold upon the society. In the seventies, the Eurocommunists made an attempt to blend communism and liberal democracy. We can study the Marxist concept of democracy or peoples' democracy on the following lines:

- Criticism of the bourgeois concept of democracy
- Marxist concept of peoples' democracy or dictatorship of the proletariat.
- Characteristics of Peoples' Democracy
- Change made by Lenin and Stalin
- Other Marxist writers on democracy
- How far the Communist states were democratic.

CRITICIMS OF BOURGEOIS CONCEPT OF DEMOCRACY

During 1840s, Marx and Engles associated themselves with democracy which they saw as an egalitarian movement leading to socialism. Marx wrote twelve essays during this period to express the principle tenets of his democratic convictions. 'Organ of Democracy was the subtitle of the journal which he edited. Marx was fully convinced that only democracy could help in establishing the state on a rational basis. He criticized the aristocratic, hereditary domination of landed interests, and property qualification for franchise.

He wanted the popular will to permeate the executive and legislative branches of the government. Similarly, he also attacked the nondemocratic bureaucracy. During this period, all his criticism of the despotic institutions was based upon his concept of humanism. His devotion to the goal of human freedom, respect for law as a human need, his concern for the separation of powers in a democratic state and his defence of the rights of the individual were all a part of the western liberal tradition. In the Paris Manuscripts of 1844, Marx put forward his concept of democracy which could accomplish general human emancipation..

Although he was critical of the rights granted by the bourgeois state, yet he realized the historical importance of these right in so far as they provided an opportunity to the working class to organize themselves against the oppression of the dominant class for general emancipation. Similarly, he regarded the bourgeois freedom as only one step in the direction of man's total freedom. Marx was still to develop the class concept of democracy but his commitment to communism was quite clear i.e. it was to be classless and based upon the absence of exploitation of man by man.

The first great democratic battles which Marx and Engles experienced were a series of uprisings that exploded across the major cities of Europe in 1848. However, the happenings of 1848 led them to reject the view that communism and democracy were synonymous. This was because while the democrats wished to overthrow feudalism and establish representative institutions within the capitalist society, they were not ready to allow power to descend to the working class. After the failure of revolutions in France and Germany, Marx saw the unreliability of the petty bourgeois democrats.

Democracy was a progressive demand against autocracy but it was also the highest form of the capitalist state, and as such 'stands condemned if seen as an ultimate aim'. However, the meaning of democracy was not different from that of the liberal notion i.e. constitutionalism, civil liberties, representative institutions and universal adult franchise. For liberals, this provided a satisfactory means of ascertaining and implementing the will of the people. However, for Marx, it made a mockery of its aim because the selfish and corrupt politicians misused democratic structure for their own personal ends. 'The formal values of liberal constitutionalism were wrong in a number of ways.

Firstly, the basis of bourgeois democracy was the economic system in which the means of production were vested in the capitalist class. The state sanctioned the existence of private property, personal ownership of capital, profit motive in production, free competition, free contract and free market. In a classdivided society where bourgeoisie controlled and owned the means of production, it also controlled and dominated the state apparatus. The state power, rights and privileges were exclusive to it and were defined in such a way that the working class did not possess them.

Secondly, the state bureaucracy, courts and police, the army apparatus and maintenance of law and order were not neutral but served the interests of the dominant class. Here, we have the core of Marxist critique of bourgeois democracy. It is that 'the state parliament and the entire political sphere do not occupy neutral ground in which success is obtained purely on the basis of arguments and numerical appeal. On the other hand, for the working class, it was an enemy territory.

These are simply the devices to delude and deceive the masses into believing that the power of the state belonged to them while in reality this was controlled and exercised by the bourgeois minority'. Parliaments talked without being listened to. Parliamentary influence could not bring any fundamental change in the basic social and political power which is in the hands of the bourgeoisie. Hence, democracy was nothing but a convenient form for the maintenance of class rule, to be used as and when and in so far as it serves the class interest.

In short, the liberal bourgeois democracy hides its intentions, is a class state instead of a natural arbiter; it offers paper freedoms for real political freedoms; and it offers only political freedoms instead of general human emancipation‘. However, while maintaining that bourgeois democracy was not real democracy for the working class and that working class cannot come to power through democratic means, Marx and Engles held the view that this kind of democracy could be used by the working class to organize itself, to raise the level of political consciousness and to achieve the level of proletarian revolution. The main feature of the bourgeois democracy was universal suffrage which provided a 'school of development‘ for the working class and offered definite but limited possibilities for the revolutionary movements.

The question of suffrage was also connected with the 'transition to socialism‘. Marx was willing to allow that there might be some isolated cases where the transition would be achieved by nonviolent means, though he was very sceptical about such a process and took it for granted that it would not be the common pattern. Nevertheless the notion that a revolutionary party has no interest in the bourgeois parliament finds no confirmation in the writings of Marx and Engles. For them, the revolutionary and the parliamentary paths were not opposed but complementary to each other. They accepted parliamentary tactics as one part of class struggle. But theirs was a vigorous, radical and suspicious parliamentarianism, and involving no renunciation of other forms of struggle'.

PEOPLES‘ DEMOCRACY OR DICTATORSHIP OF THE PROLETARIAT

Marx and Engles accepted the Enlightenment ideal of democracy as a participatory activity. However, he saw this notion of democracy as incompatible with the parliamentary model of bourgeois democracy which viewed politics as a specialised activity restricted to a relatively harmless sphere. For Marx, genuine democracy, as distinct from the sham bourgeois democracy, comes into existence only after the proletarian revolution.

The Paris Commune of 1871 provided an actual indication of 'the political form at last discovered under which to work out the economic emancipation of labour. For Marx, the significance of the Paris Commune was that it had begun to dismantle the state apparatus and given power to the people. The whole initiative hitherto exercised by the state was laid into the hands of the Commune, whose municipal council was elected by universal suffrage and a majority of whose members were working men or acknowledged representatives of the working class. The Commune was to be a working, not a parliamentary body, executive and legislative at the same time'. It got rid of the police, suppressed the standing army and replaced it by armed people. Like the rest of the public servants, magistrates and judges were to be elected, responsible and revocable, and all public services had to be done at workmen's wages. In short, in the Commune, Marx saw an attempt to give power to the working class and to bring into being a regime as close to direct democracy as possible. Marx and Engles pointed to the Paris Commune as illustrating what they meant by people's democracy as the Dictatorship of the Proletariat.

However, the term Dictatorship of the Proletariat as understood by Marx and Engles and as it was interpreted by Lenin in the context of Russian Revolution deserves careful consideration. According to Selucky, the term was used by Marx not more than five times while Hal Draper finds this phrase used by Marx and Engles not more than eleven times. The study of the concept in the context of its appearance proves adequately the democratic credentials of Marx and Engles. In The Class Struggles in France, Marx referred to the class dictatorship of the proletariat as the inevitable transit point to the abolition of class differences generally. In The Critique of the Gotha Programme (1875), he wrote, 'Between the capitalist and the communist society lies the period of the revolutionary transformation of the one into the other. There corresponds to this also a political transition period in which the state can be noting but the revolutionary dictatorship of the proletariat'.

After the seizure of power by the workers in the Paris Commune, Marx further elaborated the idea of democracy. This view of democracy cannot be understood without reference to the Dictatorship of the Proletariat. Democracy and Dictatorship of the Proletariat were not mutually exclusive concepts but this dictatorship permitted a clear distinction between the bourgeois democracy and the proletarian democracy. Marx and Engles conceived of every state as the dictatorship of the ruling class. They used the term dictatorship in the sense of rule of a particular social class and not as a government of a single party.

For them the concept was not primarily a political concept but a social one. The opposite of this phrase was the 'dictatorship of the bourgeoisie' which signified the different forms of bourgeois governments such as absolute monarchy, constitutional monarchy, democratic republics. Similarly the Dictatorship of the Proletariat was used to signify the different forms of proletariat governments. Marx and Engles were more concerned with the content rather than the form of post-revolutionary state. Democracy meant no more no less than rule by the majority. Since Marx and Engles were certain that at the time of socialist revolution, the proletariat would be in the majority, this very notion of democracy merely suggests that 'the dictatorship of the proletariat meant to be the rule of the majority by the majority and for the majority.'

It was peoples‘ democracy in the real sense of the terms. According to Marx and Engles, revolution could be violent or peaceful depending upon the presence of democratic political possibilities. However, whether peaceful or not, the socialist revolution must be democratic. Although, at the time of Communist Manifesto, there was no possibility of bringing any social change through peaceful, parliamentary means, yet the Manifesto declared that ‘the first task after the revolution would be to raise the working class to the level of democracy‘.

Inspite of being deficient and incomplete, both Marx and Engles positively assessed the historical importance of political emancipation of man (political right), universal suffrage and right to representation and association granted by the bourgeois democracy. Marx and Engles, as is well known, anticipated the possibility that socialism could be introduced peacefully by parliamentary means in countries like England and United States. Towards the end of his life, Engles explicitly declared that ‘dictatorship of the proletariat‘ would express itself under the political form of bourgeois parliamentary republic. He wrote, ‘If one thing is certain, it is that our Party and the working class can only come to power under the form of democratic republic. This is even the specific form of dictatorship of the proletariat as the great French revolution had already shown.‘

CHIEF CHARACTERISTICS OF PEOPLES‘ DEMOCRACY

- Democracy is essentially a participatory activity by the working class in the affairs of the state through direct democratic means. It is a rule by the majority, of the majority and for the majority.
- Peoples‘ democracy can be established only after the proletarian revolution and raising the working class to the level of political decision-making. It requires the defeat of the bourgeoisie and their class privileges and the unity of the working class.
- At economic level, peoples‘ democracy means social ownership of the means of production, appropriation of all large-scale private capital, central control of production in the hands of the state, rapid increase of productive forces, state control of transportation and communication, equal liability of All citizens to work, and public direction of employment.
- At political level, democracy means integration of executive and legislative functions; all government personnel to be directly elected and subject to recall; election and recall of magistrates; replacement of army and police force by people‘s malitia; full local autonomy; public officials to be paid no more than workmen‘s wages.
- At social level, there will be no inheritance; free education for all children; heavy graduated taxation, reunion of town and country

through more equitable distribution of population over the whole country; integration of work and non-work environments; sustained development of forces of production so that all basic needs are met and people have sufficient time to pursue non-work activities.

- People's democracy is a transition stage between capitalist democracy and communism. After the abolition of classes and the establishment of socialist society will start the higher stage of communism. It will be a society based upon abolition of scarcity and private property, elimination of markets, exchange and money, end of social division of labour. Here government and politics will be replaced by self-regulation, all public affairs will be governed collectively, administrative tasks will be done by rotation or election; and all public questions will be decided on consensus. Thus communism will herald not only the end of politics but also of democracy as a form of government. It will become a part of habit and a way of life. It will turn into self-rule in the real sense of the term.

CHANGES MADE BY LENIN AND STALIN IN THE CONCEPT OF DICTATORSHIP OF THE PROLETARIAT

The Marxist concept of democracy as the Dictatorship of the Proletariat as developed by Lenin and Stalin, and the establishment of peoples' democracies in USSR and other communist countries introduced major variations in the original concept. Lenin called DP as the major idea of Marx regarding the state, the main content of socialist revolution and necessary for workers for their victory. However, he gave different interpretations of this concept at different times.

In 1918, he called revolutionary dictatorship of the proletariat as the 'rule won and maintained by the use of violence of the proletariat against the bourgeoisie, rule that is unrestricted by any laws'. In 1919, he shifted emphasis from the use of force to the organizational task of building socialism. In 1920. he made clear that the dictatorship of the proletariat can be exercised neither by the proletariat class as a. whole nor by a mass proletariat organization but only through its vanguard—the Party, on behalf of the proletariat.

The question of democracy was examined by Lenin in relation to three phases: Capitalist Democracy, Socialist Democracy, and Communist Democracy. Defining democracy, he wrote, 'Democracy is a form of state, one of its varieties'. In a class divided society, government is both democracy and dictatorship. It is democracy for one class and dictatorship for the other class. For example, the bourgeois democracy is the dictatorship of the bourgeois class over the working class; it is the dictatorship of the bourgeoisie.

It is a democracy by an insignificant minority. It is democracy for the rich where the capitalist class controls not only the political institutions but also structures other institutions in such a way as to guarantee their overall control on the society. Since it does not serve the working class interest, it has to be destroyed and replaced by a radically different form of state, by a different set of institutions to serve the proletarian interests. Regarding the socialist democracy, Lenin frankly accepts that the new socialist state established after the revolution will be an instrument of power and repression quite as much as the capitalist state.

In it, the proletariat, 'organized as a ruling class creates its own appropriate apparatus of violence to enforce its class purpose on the non-proletarian and other elements'. The victory over the bourgeoisie requires a long persistent battle which can be carried through only by strong determination and use of force. During the transitional period from capitalism to communism, class struggle will continue and it will aim at the complete overthrow of the bourgeoisie. During this period, 'the state must inevitably be a state that is democratic in a new way (for the proletariat and the propertyless in general) and dictatorship in a new way (against the bourgeoisie)'.

DP is also class state but with a difference. The difference consists in the fact that all hitherto existing class states have been dictatorship of an exploiting class minority over the exploited majority, whereas the dictatorship of the proletariat is the dictatorship of the exploited majority over the exploiting minority'. The twin purpose of the dictatorship of the proletariat is i) to defend the revolution and ii) to organize the new social and economic order.

These functions, according to Lenin, are carried out by the Party which is the guide and leader of all the exploited classes. Thus in the hands of Lenin, the dictatorship of the proletariat became 'the dictatorship of the Party'. He advocated that the transition from socialism to communism will be carried out by the party which will not only suppress the exploiters but also discipline the workers and the whole population. Reduced to simple terms, Lenin's argument was that any state is an instrument of class domination.

Where there is dominance, there is neither freedom nor democracy. It is only in the communist society when the class struggle has ended and a classless society has been created that it will become possible to speak of freedom. 'Only then' according to Lenin 'will there become possible and realized a truly complete democracy, democracy without any exception whatever. And only then will democracy begin to wither away....Communism alone is capable of giving really complete democracy and the more complete it is, the more quickly will it become unnecessary, and wither away of itself. In other words, communism will cause even the truly complete democracy to wither away.

He categorically states that 'it is constantly forgotten that the abolition of the state means also the abolition of democracy; that the withering away of the state means the withering away of democracy'. The more complete the democracy, the nearer the moment when it begins to be unnecessary. Thus in the context of bourgeois democracy, democracy does not exists; in the context of dictatorship of the proletariat there is more democracy than before in the sense that the proletarian majority, rules over the minority, but all the same real democracy still cannot exist; in the context of communism, democracy should not exist because it is superfluous. While for Marx democracy as such is a stateless society; for Lenin democracy is a form of state and therefore, a stateless society cannot be a democracy. With Stalin, the dictatorship of the proletariat came to be associated with autocracy and reign of terror. A new turn was given to the theory of revolution; the party was converted into a centralized and all powerful bureaucracy. DP meant further centralization of power and greater use of repressive and arbitrary power.

It became a regime in which one man had absolute power of a kind which Lenin had never imagined. Stalin used that power to the full, herding into camps millions upon millions of people and liquidation of countless others including the vast number of people who were part of the upper and uppermost layers of society. Thus whereas Lenin reduced the DP to the dictatorship of the party; Stalin further reduced the dictatorship of the party to the dictatorship of one person. It was taken for granted that the Party and the working class formed a perfect unity and that the former represented the latter.

OTHER MARXIST WRITERS ON DEMOCRACY

The concept of democracy as understood and interpreted by some Western Marxist writers has been quite different from that of Lenin and Stalin. Edward Bernstein, for example, not only challenged Marx's analysis of capitalism, he also claimed that socialist revolution and the dictatorship of the proletariat were neither necessary nor desirable. He believed that political democracy and liberal freedoms extended to the working class are much more important than a militant class struggle which could bring only crude communism.

Another writer, Karl Kautsky, however, defended the basic tenets of Marxism but criticized the Marxist concept of democracy of DP as put forward by Lenin. Kautsky held that Lenin was wrong in claiming that UP was a particular form of government opposed to democratic form. For Marx and Engles, democracy had also social content. Also unless the proletariat represents a majority of population, no socialist revolution can be successful, and if they represent the majority, no dictatorship is necessary. He gave importance to democracy than to socialism and by merging the democratic tradition with the Marxist socialist doctrine, Kautsky laid the foundation of achieving socialism through democratic means.

Another Marxist revolutionary, Rosa Luxemburg also criticized the anti-democratic policy of Lenin, for suppression of free political life, of establishing the dictatorship not of the masses but over the masses. She agreed with Lenin that the party should seize power but rejected the social democratic principle that the party must first gain majority and only then think of taking over power. But this does not mean that the party should seize power despite the majority of population, should maintain itself by terror and reject all normal forms of political freedom and representation. Democratic institutions were not perfect but to abolish them was wrong because it would paralyse the political life of the masses. There must be unlimited democracy, a free public opinion, freedom of election and the press, the right to hold meetings and form associations. Otherwise the DP would be replaced by the dictatorship of the clique.

Dictatorship is not a matter of abolishing democracy but of applying it correctly. Also it must be of the class and not of the small leading minority. She wanted that the masses must participate actively in political life and in shaping the new order. For her socialism and freedom were inseparable. After the first world war and the collapse of the Second International, all key concepts of Marxism such as class struggle, DP, proletarian democracy became subjects of intense debate. It led to a variety of Marxist thought and different views on the nature of democracy.

Moreover, the devastation of the economy after the war led to the rise of welfare state in Europe which made structural changes in the capitalist economy. As result, the working class in these countries instead of being the agents of revolution became a part of the capitalist system. A number of European communist parties quietly abandoned the goal of revolution and socialist democracy. During the second world war, the communist parties of Europe not only see their sight on constitutional changes but also shared power with political parties of opposite ideologies. While they declared that their purpose was the establishment of a socialist society and proclaimed their allegiance to Marxism, they nevertheless accepted constitutionalism, parliamentary democracy, electoral process and representative institutions of bourgeois democracy.

Palmiro Togliatti, an Italian communist, for example, stated firmly: We always start from the idea then socialism is a regime in which there is the widest freedom for the workers, that they in fact participate in an organized manner in the direction of the entire social life. Togliatti‘s ideas later on led to the ‘historical compromise‘ among the communist parties of France, Italy and Spain which gave rise to the concept of Eurocommunism. These parties criticized the concept of DP as developed in Russia and stated that socialist transformation can be brought about only through peaceful democratic means.

Thus the Western Marxist concept of democracy has been evolved in direct opposition to the Leninist concept of democracy as the DP. It firmly believes that the socialist transformation in the advanced capitalist societies can only be brought about by using the bourgeois democratic institutions. Socialism can be brought about by peaceful means. It implies parliamentary democracy, multiparty system, civil liberties, rights of freedom of expression and trade union activities. Democratic features are not the monopoly of the bourgeois regimes but a part of the Enlightenment tradition of the Western civilization. The revolutionary methods of seizure of power by the proletariat are not possible in the advanced capitalist societies.

HOW FAR THE COMMUNIST STATES WERE DEMOCRATIC

Unfortunately, the historical experience of the DP has not been in keeping with the concept of proletarian democracy as developed by Marx and Engles. The goal of Marxism has been the establishment of a proletarian state and society in which men, free from the fetters of capitalism' would learn to organize production for the common good. The revolution in Russia failed to achieve this because it was proletarian in a new sense provided by Lenin and later on by Stalin.

As stated above, the concept of DP was transformed into a minority, 'government of a small number' under the leadership of Lenin. Under Stalin, DP became a means of autocracy and reign of terror. The 1936 constitution admitted the exclusive domination of the Communist Party.

The party, with restricted membership, never became a mass party. The effort was to make the party less proletarian and less democratic and convert it into a centralized bureaucracy. The denunciation of Stalin by Khrushchev at the 20th party congress in 1956 had a profound repercussion on the communist movement. Khrushchev condemned the cult of individual and called for a restoration of Leninist principles of socialist democracy. The Communist Party was no longer the vanguard of the proletariat but became the party of the whole people.

However the constitution of 1977 reinforced the power of the party, uniting the secretaryship of the party with the Presidency of the state. It dropped the talk about the dictatorship of the proletariat and used the term 'state of the whole people'. However, the lack of political and civil liberties and the establishment of state socialism or 'socialism from above' were criticized by many Marxist writers and Soviet dissidents such as Edward Kardelj, S. Stjanovic, Roy Medvedev. S. Stjanovic, for example, attacked the undemocratic nature of the Soviet socialist system where the concept of government by the working class was missing.

The continuous increase in the power of the state gave birth to a new class and a bureaucratic socialist society. Similarly, Roy Medevdev called for decentralization of power, freedom of expression and freedom to form other political parties, democratization of social life, functioning of the Party on democratic lines, safeguards to the opinion of minorities, dissidents, freedom of press etc. Whether the communist states were democratic depends upon the meaning of democracy. According to Macpherson, if we define democracy in the narrow sense, meaning a system of choosing and authorizing government, then the communist states being the vanguard states were governments for the people but not governments by the people. Again the vanguard state can be democratic if there is full intra-party democracy and the party membership is open. Even from this point of view, these states could not be called democratic. But there is a broader meaning of democracy which contains an ideal of human equality, an equality that can be realized only in a classless society. In this broad sense, the communist states could be termed democratic. But on the whole, whereas Marx's negative critique of bourgeois democracy was maintained, its positive alternatives were barely contemplated.

THEORIZING POVERTY, INEQUALITY, AND DEMOCRACY

Opening the conference's first session, Professor Nancy Bermeo presented a paper examining the nature of inequality and its relation to democracy. Focusing on the period between 1990 and 2005, Bermeo observed that, although the number of democracies rose dramatically and economic growth accelerated at a rapid pace, economic inequality remained constant or even increased in some cases. Taking this disjunction as her starting point, Bermeo attempted to explain it and explore its implications. Bermeo dealt first with some conceptual matters pertaining to the definitions of inequality and poverty.

She defined inequality as the condition of having different, and therefore unequal, command of resources valuable for well-being. From an empirical point of view, one cannot define inequality without a modifier—political inequality, gender inequality, economic inequality, and so on. Democratization diminishes political inequality by creating an even field for all citizens, but it does not directly affect the private realm of family or the market. Poverty, on the other hand, refers to levels of income that are inadequate for well-being, or to deficits in capability that derive from an insufficiency of economic means.

Thus, economic inequality is a matter of the distribution of economic resources that arises when economic units are ranked according to the wealth they earn or possess. Whereas inequality exists on a gradient, poverty is intrinsically dyadic, dividing the population between poor and non-poor. As two distinct phenomena, economic inequality and poverty are not necessarily correlative.

Having made this clarification, Bermeo asked if democracy diminishes inequality. Democracy presumptively leads to a demand for greater economic equality, and many scholars indeed think of democracy as a "game of redistribution." Yet as measured by Gini coefficients, income inequality in the majority of democracies has either remained constant or increased. Reversing the question, Bermeo asked if economic inequality affects the quality of democracy. The harmful effects of inequality could hypothetically include a disproportionate influence of the wealthy, political detachment on the part of a large sector of the population, support for populism, support for personalist rule, corruption, and low levels of accountability. While cautioning about the reliability and comparability of some data, Bermeo reported a strong negative correlation between income inequality and measures of voice and accountability— evidence of the threat that inequality poses to the quality of democracy.

Third, Bermeo investigated whether democracies are at risk, and concluded that economic inequality by itself will not be a cause of democracy's collapse since the breakdown of democracy requires "coup coalitions"—critical masses of counter-elites who have the capacity to topple regimes. Coup coalitions are not easy or likely to form for a number of reasons. For one, international actors have raised the cost of coups. Also, wealthy classes that once backed coups have come to believe that they have more power in an electoral democracy than in an authoritarian regime. In addition, democracy enjoys powerful appeal across regions, in many cases offering opportunities for radical change that are less risky than seizures of power. So, in spite of its deleterious effects, inequality does not pose an imminent risk for democracies.

COMPARING SOCIAL POLICIES

While Bermeo's paper emphasized the relationship between inequality and democracy, the paper by Professors Stephan Haggard and Robert Kaufman focused primarily on the different strategies that new democracies have employed in dealing with poverty and other social welfare issues. They noted that there are two principal kinds of strategies that states have pursued. The first emphasizes universal policies of social assistance, while the second seeks to target assistance more narrowly to make sure that it benefits the poor.

Comparing the experience of Central and Eastern Europe with that of Latin America, Haggard and Kaufman examined the effects of democratization on social policy. Democracy generates electoral incentives for politicians to compete by advocating redistribution and expanded welfare commitments. It also guarantees freedom for previously excluded groups to organize. To ascertain the actual impact of democratization, however, one has to pay close attention to the authoritarian legacy in each of these regions.

The effects of authoritarianism linger, conditioning the characteristics of present-day democracies. Critical realignments and political coalitions produced distinctive authoritarian models, which, in turn, created constituencies that influenced the course of social policy in new democracies. In Latin America, for example, the reform coalitions that pushed and implemented the transition from oligarchic rule that took place from 1910 to about 1950 were comprised not only of labor unions, but also of dissident factions of the oligarchy. These cross-class reform coalitions excluded rural peasants and unorganized urban workers, perpetuating their political marginalization.

While post-war importsubstitution industrialization strategies accommodated welfare entitlements for the organized urban working class, they largely failed to address the impoverishment of these politically excluded classes. In short, these political realignments and ISI strategies resulted in a highly skewed welfare system that benefited the middle class and upper echelons of the blue-collar working class. In Central and Eastern Europe, where the authoritarian legacy is that of communism, critical alignments in the transition to communist rule repressed all other parties and tightly controlled labor. Statesocialist welfare systems were founded on a social contract that produced a fundamentally different social welfare trajectory.

Communist development in Central and Eastern Europe was characterized by central planning, including manpower planning and effective employment guarantees; nationalization that led to state provision of social insurance and services, particularly pensions and health insurance but also family allowances; and collectivization of agriculture that extended the system into the countryside and universalized guarantees. There were intra-regional variations, of course, but the convergence of Central and East European state-socialist welfare systems was much greater than that of welfare systems in Latin America. In his presentation, Haggard presented data on government spending in the last two decades of the twentieth-century to demonstrate the enduring effects of welfare legacies on contemporary social policy.

Reflecting the state-socialist legacy, social security spending from 1980 through 2000 in Central and Eastern Europe and Central Asia represented about 13 to 14 percent of GDP. By comparison, in Latin America social security spending represented only between 6 and 9 percent of GDP, while in East and Southeast Asia it represented merely about 1 percent of GDP. Health spending follows the same pattern as social security spending. Central and Eastern Europe and Central Asia spend about 4 percent of GDP on health while Latin America spends a lower percentage, and East and Southeast Asia even less.

Education spending, however, follows a different pattern. East and Southeast Asian countries spend on the order of 4 to 4.5 percent of GDP on education, whereas Central and Eastern Europe, Central Asia, and Latin America exhibit much lower rates. Haggard and Kauffman demonstrated that the effects of democracy on social policy are clearly conditioned by the distribution and organization of interests. They highlighted the importance of historical legacies, drawing attention to the constraints that these place on countries in terms of the social policies they can pursue.

CENTRAL AND EASTERN EUROPE

In their paper, Professors Béla Greskovits and Dorothee Bohle asked what remedies for poverty and inequality have been adopted by Central and East European states and to what degree they have been successful. Greskovits and Bohle explored the strategic differences between the model adopted by the Visegrád group plus Slovenia and the model followed by the Baltic group, despite the common features of their transition from communist rule. The authors also examined how these postcommunist states integrated themselves into the global economy.

Both groups of countries exited their previous economic system through a process of export-oriented development that was very successful in attracting foreign investment. Their economic policies, generally speaking, were biased in favor of international corporations and tended to neglect small and medium-sized domestic enterprises. "Jobless growth" was a function of the private sector's limited employment capacity, and depressed wages were insufficient for survival in some sectors. The Visegrád-4 and Slovenia reindustrialized along the lines of what might be called "core-like" specializations, emphasizing such sophisticated products as cars, electronics, machinery, and chemicals.

This reindustrialization created a dualism between the transnational corporations' workers, who live in the more developed regions, and workers in more traditional sectors of the economy. In contrast, the Baltic States, as well as Bulgaria and Romania, followed a more "semi-peripheral" path of reform involving de-industrialization, de-skilling, and the development of less advanced specializations. These semi-peripheral sectors tend to produce lower wages, a function of the low-cost, union-free sweatshops run by the highly mobile transnational corporations that proliferated following the fall of Soviet enterprise.

The costs of this precarious transnationalization were paid by the sweatshops' working poor. The two different models of welfare capitalism adopted by the Visegrád and the Baltic countries are reflected in differences in the relative size and volume of social benefits, public-sector employment, and education spending, as well as in the treatment of minority ethnic groups. Social spending in the Baltic countries averaged between 12 and 13 percent of GDP, whereas the Visegrád-4 plus Slovenia spent much more, 19 to 23 percent—though this amount is still below that of the EU-15 countries.

In terms of the cost of social benefits per person between 2004 and 2006, the Baltic States spent approximately □1,500. The Visegrád-4 countries spent a significantly greater amount, □2,661, while Slovenia, a more economically advanced country, spent □4,470. Spending per person in the EU-15 is approximately □6,700. As for public-sector employment, one can observe a much higher level in the Baltic-3 than the Visegrád-4. Additionally, in the Baltic States, the at-risk-of-poverty rate after social transfers is 20 percent, while only 14 percent of the population in the Visegrád-4 countries is at risk, and only 12 percent in Slovenia—rates much better than the 16 percent in the EU-15. Poverty and inequality in Central and Eastern Europe have a strong ethnic dimension.

In Estonia and Latvia, many of the working poor are ethnic Russians. Similarly, in the Visegrád-4 countries, a considerable segment of the long-term unemployed are ethnic Roma. The high number of unemployed minorities carries significant political implications since it is particularly difficult to build redistribution coalitions on the basis of sectors that are considered foreign by the majority of the population. The ethnic dimension of poverty further compounds its alienating effect.

The question of why the Baltic and Visegrád models are so different is intriguing given that both groups of states inherited similar industrial and welfare legacies and had similar transformative visions built on "returning to the West." The answer, according to Greskovits and Bohle, is that popular consent for policy and social legitimacy was sought via different sorts of appeals. In the case of the Visegrád countries, consent was sought on the basis of a welfarist model— assuring the population that its socioeconomic welfare would be taken care of. In the Baltic States, by contrast, the basis of legitimacy was more nationalist. The new social contracts in the Baltic States, which had been Soviet colonies, emphasized the recovery of national independence rather than the welfarist promises that were central in the Visegrád-4.

TURKEY

Later at the conference, Öykü Uluçay discussed the case of Turkey. Turkey has one of the highest levels of poverty among OECD countries, but by the standards of most developing countries its level of poverty is very low, affecting only 12 to 13 percent of the population. A looser definition of poverty yields a rate of 31 percent, but pensions and social transfers reduce it to 25 percent.

This is a very modest result when compared to the performance of the EU-15, where pensions and transfers reduce the level of poverty by 15 percentage points. Turkey has a very complex welfare system grounded not only in state services, but also in social structures independent of the state. Alongside the state system, Turkey has a traditional welfare regime—a safety net that is based more on societal than government-provided services, and includes the diversification of economic activities within extended families, urban-rural linkages, informal housing, and extended networks of kinship.

EAST AND SOUTH ASIA

Professor Jaeyeol Yee gave a presentation on East Asia, emphasizing the cases of Korea and Taiwan. With Gini indexes of.24 and.34, respectively, Taiwan and Korea have extremely low coefficients of inequality compared to countries such as Argentina (.51), Bolivia (.68), Brazil (.59), Botswana (.63), and Zambia (.53). Yet the amount of social spending in Korea and Taiwan is also low, an apparent contradiction that needs further exploration. Things may be changing in East Asia, however, where the Gini index has been increasing since 1992.

Yee averred that inequality is deepening in both Korea and Taiwan, especially in the former. Between 1991 and 2006, the ranks of the middle classes decreased by 13 percent while the low-income and highincome classes increased by 7 and 5 percent, respectively. Moreover, in 1996, 41 percent of Koreans perceived themselves as being middle class, whereas now that percentage is only 28 percent. With respect to India, Partha Mokhopadhyay traced the evolution from the anti-poverty policies started by Indira Gandhi in the mid-1970s to the more universal policies of the present. Suhas Palshikar pointed out in his remarks that politics in India is becoming less focused on identity issues and more on public welfare.

LATIN AMERICA

Alberto Díaz-Cayeros presented a paper that focused on the panoply of targeted programs known as conditional cash transfers, which have been quite successful in reducing poverty in Latin America. In Brazil, for example, more than 11 million people benefit from the Bolsa Familia program. In Colom Alberto Díaz-Cayeros presented a paper that focused on the panoply of targeted programs known as conditional cash transfers which have been quite successful in reducing poverty in Latin America. In Brazil, for example, more than 11 million people benefit from the Bolsa Familia program.

In Colombia, about 5 percent of the population benefit from similar targeted programs. In Mexico, there are 5 million families—about 25 million people—who benefit from such programs. In Peru, there are some 230,000 families—about 1 million people. The prevailing way of addressing poverty in Latin America has been not to reform the overall welfare system, but to develop specific anti-poverty policies. Poverty in Latin America has dropped significantly over the past five years from about 42 percent to about 36 percent. The effect of the current economic crisis remains to be seen. Significantly, centrist governments were the first to begin to apply these kinds of programs. Rightist governments followed suit, while leftist governments adopted these policies much later.

AFRICA

Professor Larry Diamond gave a presentation on the case of Africa. Inspired by Peter Lewis's "Growth Without Prosperity in Africa," which appeared in the October 2008 issue of the Journal of Democracy, Diamond noted that African states have the highest percentages of poverty, with about 51 percent of Africans living below the poverty line. Africa also has the greatest levels of economic inequality: The richest quintile of the population captures 65 percent of the national income while the lowest quintile shares in only a very small percentage of the wealth. As Diamond commented, if CCT programs were to be applied in Africa, they would have to cover the overwhelming majority of the population.

Diamond pointed out that African states are unique in terms of governance as well. In most of the cases the conference addressed, the presumption is that the state acts with a desire to advance the collective public good, but such an understanding does not exist in many African states where primordial structures hinder effective governance based on universalist concerns. Instead, the norm too often is pursuit of particularistic concerns within hierarchical sociopolitical structures. Suggesting that effective policies must move the concerns of African states from the particular to the universal, Diamond criticized foreign aid schemes that pay insufficient attention to governance and accountability.

COMMON THREADS AND CONCERNS

The discussions at the conference manifested a number of common threads and concerns. One was the impact of historical legacies, in regard to which two distinct patterns can be discerned. In the first, as exemplified by the cases of East Asia and of Central and Eastern Europe, new democracies came into being with lower levels of poverty and lesser degrees of inequality. In the case of Central and Eastern Europe, these were the legacy of the former communist regimes.

In East Asia, they were a product of post- World War II reform, especially land redistribution. The second pattern, as manifest in the cases of Latin America and Africa, is characterized by high levels of poverty and inequality, the lingering legacies of colonialism and oligarchic rule. Another common thread uniting these different regional experiences is the structure of constraints that limited the choices available to governments. These limitations in choice are also a function of countries' historical legacies. Countries with high levels of poverty, such as those in Latin America, tended to prioritize targeted policies, while other countries focused on reforming or strengthening the overall welfare system. Such policy decisions are determined by the constraints under which policymakers operate. A third common thread is the matrix of consequences resulting from market policies. Although these policies helped achieve macroeconomic stability and opened up economies, they also had unintended consequences, often weakening already frail welfare systems. In Latin America, two paths opened as a result of government policies toward poverty.

Countries reluctant to address poverty fell prey to populist authoritarian forces while governments that addressed these issues successfully have been able to build more stable democracies. In South and Southeast Asia, governments that have addressed the challenges of poverty have fared well. The popularity of Thailand's ousted prime minister Thaksin Shinawatra can in part be attributed to his anti-poverty policies and introduction of a universal healthcare system.

As Nancy Bermeo noted in her paper, Thailand has exhibited an exceptional record of reducing inequality. In India, the recent electoral success of the

Congress Party can also be partly attributed to its effective antipoverty policy. India is a success story not only in terms of democracy, but also in terms of reducing poverty from 50-to-55 percent to current levels of about 20-to-25 percent.

This success is a function of the implementation of a consistent, sustained, and effective anti-poverty policy that has been in place since the 1970s, as well as of the tremendous economic growth India has experienced in the past 10 to 15 years. Central and Eastern Europe has experienced a similar success story, though today the Visegrád countries seem to be handling the economic crisis better than the Baltic States. In Turkey, the continued success of the Justice and Development Party can in part be attributed to its social welfare policies.

CONCLUSIONS

High levels of poverty and inequality not only lower the quality of democracy, but may pave the way for the emergence of authoritarian populists and democratic backsliding. Therefore, addressing the social question, which warrants attention in its own right, is critical to the sustainability and quality of democracy. There are different ways to confront the challenge of poverty and inequality, depending on historical legacies, the structure of constraints, and the impact of previous economic policies. There is no single recipe, yet the comparative analysis presented at the Bratislava conference, and the four conference papers that will appear in the October 2009 Journal of Democracy, shed considerable light upon the advantages and drawbacks of these different approaches.

2

Tourism and Economy

TOURISM: AN INDUSTRY

Tourism industry is the one that deals with the tourists as consumers, the money spent by them, and the resources rendering various goods and services which facilitate the composition of the tourism product. This industry has been named as a 'smokeless industry' because unlike other industries it is invisible and non-polluting. The tourism industry is an extraordinarily complex integration of many industries spread over many sectors.

Tourism is an umbrella industry containing a set of inter-related business participants. For example, industries like Transport, Accommodation, and Travel Companies, Recreation and Entertainment Institutions, Handicrafts business, etc and the provision of the many goods and services demanded by tourists. Interestingly, most of the component industries also get related to varied commercial and non-commercial activities over and above providing their services to the tourists.

Over the years, there has been a growing awareness of tourism as a human activity, an industry, and a catalyst for economic growth and development. Like any other industry the tourism industry draws resources from the economy, adds value and produces marketable products. The only difference here is that no tangible product is produced like in the case of a manufacturing industry. The product in this case is intangible and joint or composite in nature. The tourism industry impacts various auxiliary and ancillary industries as well. Tourism today is undergoing a rapid transformation towards a new industry having far-reaching implications for organizations in the travel and tourism industry in particular, and consequences of import for developing and developed countries in general, growing increasingly dependent on the tourist dollar. The forces driving the change in this industry are many.

In olden times people travelled mainly for commercial and religious reasons and leisure travel was for the rich. Today people travel for a variety of motivations, including business, leisure, religion, culture, visiting friends and relatives, education and health. The means of transportation have become varied and faster and as the transport becomes faster, new travellers emerge and people travel greater distances. Another important force driving the growth within the industry is the growth and expansion of the middle class and an increase in their disposable income. The travel industry is complex in nature and challenging to manage. This is for three main reasons- their process type, cost structure and market features.

In terms of process, most operations are a combination of customer processing operations, material processing operations and information processing operations. There is a mix of cost structures based around provision of service, food, accommodation, sightseeing, airfare etc. Forecasting and packaging are some key market features. Originally segmentation in the industry was based on social class however, currently many factors influence segmentation in the industry.

Now there are products that are specially marketed to specific groups of people or market segments based on lifestyle. Due to segmentation more choice is created for consumers and branding has emerged, major companies are developing brands that are easily recognizable, for example, Thomas Cook holidays, Star Cruises, etc. Tourists are now a sophisticated lot. They are demanding and constantly looking for new variations in the products and newer destinations. In addition, there is growing environmental awareness and travellers are increasingly prepared to shun over-commercialized and polluted destinations for newer and less popular ones. Parallel to all these changes in the market place, there is deregulation of the airline industry, an explosion of technology both for automated reservations and for travel management, and an increasing trend towards concentration of the industry reflected by the large numbers of mergers, takeovers and acquisition of the industry from 'old' to 'new' tourism.

New tourism is a transition from the existing to the tourism of the future typified by:

- Enhanced tourism experiences
- Flexible tourist products
- Management of the tourist industry
- Segmentation
- Thrust towards diagonally integrated organizations and

There are clear and apparent manifestations that the tourist industry is beginning to take on newer dimensions. The emerging new practice is the creation of a number of factors including the system of new information technologies in the tourism industry, deregulation of the airline industry, environmental pressures; technology compensation; changing consumer tastes, leisure time, work patterns and income distribution.

The economics of new tourism is quite different from the old. From system gains, segmented markets, designed and customised holidays the focus now is also on, profitability and competitiveness in tourism. The new tourists show greater care and have a concern for conservation of the natural environment. There has been a shift towards eco tourism, green tourism, rural tourism, farm tourism, sustainable tourism, etc. with perpetual opportunities of benefit from this new tourism. Competitive Strategies for success have to be employed today for survival.

There are new techniques and trends to be followed by the industry players. To gain competitive advantage, the players and participants of the industry will have to

- Be customer friendly,
- Be quality conscious,
- Innovate new and better products,
- Make meaningful value additions.

And for tourist destinations to be competitive, certain key principles need to be incorporated into the policy framework.

Some of these are:

- Be environmentally sensitive,
- Encourage private sector participation,
- Make tourism a leading sector,
- Strengthen the distribution channels in the market place.

Today tourism is sensitive to the environment as well as inhabitants of the region or area, tourism is sustainable, and tourism is capable of transforming tourism-dependent and vulnerable areas' economies into viable entities. Tourism is in a stage of revolutionary change and a new kind of tourism is emerging fast. New tourism promises flexibility, segmentation and diagonal integration. It is driven by information technologies and changing consumer requirements. Today this industry can produce an entire system of value addition and wealth generation.

The objective today is 'tourism should be planned in a manner that it benefits the community as a whole, has benefits for the locals, and optimizes the expectations of the tourists besides taking care of the environment.'

TOURISM IS A GROWTH INDUSTRY

In the 21st century the global economy will be driven by three major service industries–Technology, Telecommuni-cations and Tourism. Travel and tourism will be one of the world's highest growth sectors in the current century. Tourism, just as to experts is expected to capture the global market and become the largest industry in the world. The statistics and projections point to an era of unprecedented growth of tourism around the world. From 70 million international tourist arrivals in the year 1960 the WTO has estimated that international tourism arrivals worldwide would be 1.5 billion by the year 2020. The latest report from the World Travel and Tourism Council "in the year 1999

Travel and Tourism generated about 3.5 trillion US dollars of GDP and almost 200 million jobs across the world economy: approximately.

World travel and tourism GDP is forecast to increase in real terms at 3% per annum in the decade 2000-2010. During the same period employment in travel and tourism is expected to grow at about 2.6% per annum."

World Travel and Tourism Council has summarized some of the highlights concerning worldwide travel and tourism industry as follows:

- The Travel and Tourism Industry contributed 11.7% towards world GDP in 1999;
- Travel and Tourism has emerged strongly from the South- Asian crisis with leisure tourism rising by 4.7% in 1999 and business travel by 4.4%;
- Tourism related spending by international visitors amount to 8% of world exports in 1999 with a further impact by export of Travel and Tourism related goods;
- Travel and Tourism related GDP is forecast to increase at 3% per annum in real terms;
- In the coming years, over 8% of all jobs worldwide will depend upon Travel and Tourism;
- Travel and Tourism will support the creation of over 5.5 million jobs per year over the next decade.

Thus, tourism today is a shining sector and a great economic force. Its status as a major economic activity has been recognized by almost all the nations of the world. During the 1960s there was emphasis on tourism as an earner of foreign exchange, a catalyst of development, and a security against the uncertain fluctuations of commodity prices. Today however, its impact is not only economic but social and cultural as well.

Cultural tourism is a fertile ground for exercising creative talents, fostering special kinds of relations between visitor and the host populations. It enables the tourist to form a view of his present world and a global concept of the historic past. Thus, tourism has wider implications encompassing not only economic benefits but also social and cultural benefits as well.

TOURISM AND DEVELOPMENT

Development can be viewed from various dimensions, however, for the purpose of this current session, we use the following definition of economic development: Economic development is a process of economic transition that involves the structural transformation of an economy and a growth of the real output of an economy over a period of time. It is a long run concept. Structural transformation is achieved through modernization and industrialization and is measured in terms of the relative contribution to gross domestic product of agriculture, industry and service sectors. The potential of tourism to contribute to development is widely recognized in the industrialized countries, with tourism playing an increasingly important role and receiving government support. Tourism along with some other activities like financial services and tele-communications is a major component of economic strategies. Tourism has become a favoured means of addressing the socio- economic problems facing rural areas on one end, while enhancing development of urban areas on the other.

TOURISM AND NATIONAL DEVELOPMENT

Tourism emerged as a global phenomenon in the 1960s and the potential for tourism to generate economic development was widely promoted by national governments. They appreciated that tourism generated foreign exchange earnings, created employment and brought economic benefits to regions with limited options for alternative economic development. National tourism authorities were created to promote tourism and to maximize international arrivals.

However, an awareness of the negative environmental, social and some other impacts also increased. The importance of economic benefits at the local level, environmental and social sustainability was also widely accepted. It was observed that tourism presents excellent opportunities for developing entrepreneurship, for staff training and progression and for the development of transferable skills. Tourism development focuses on national and regional master planning. It also focuses on international promotion, attracting inward investment. The primary concern has been with maximizing foreign exchange earnings. These earnings enable the government to finance debt and also to finance some investment in technology and other imports for economic development.

NO TRADE BARRIERS TO TOURISM

Unlike many other forms of international trade, tourism does not suffer from the imposition of trade barriers, such as quotas or tariffs. Mostly, destination countries have free and equal access to the international tourism market. This position has become strengthened by the inclusion of tourism in the General Agreement on Trade in Services, which became operational in January 1995.

REDISTRIBUTION OF WEALTH

Both internationally and domestically, tourism is seen as an effective means of transferring income, wealth and investment from richer, developed countries or regions to less developed, poorer areas. This redistribution occurs as a result of both tourist expenditures in destination areas and also of investment by the richer, tourist generating countries in tourist facilities. Thus it appears as if, the developed countries support the economic growth and development of less developed countries.

TOURISM AND POVERTY REDUCTION

Tourism can contribute to development and the reduction of poverty in a number of ways. Economic benefits are generally the most important element, but there can be social, environmental and cultural benefits and costs as well. Tourism contributes to poverty reduction by providing employment and various livelihood opportunities. This additional income helps the poor by increasing the range of economic opportunities available to them. Tourism also contributes to poverty alleviation through direct taxation of tourism generated income. Taxes can be used to alleviate poverty through education, health and infrastructure development. Some tourism facilities also improve the recreational and leisure opportunities available for the poor themselves at the local level. Tourism is not very different from other productive sectors but it has four potential advantages for pro-poor economic growth:

- It has higher linkage with other local businesses because customers come to the destination;
- It is relatively labour intensive and employs a large proportion of women workers;
- It has high potential in poor countries and areas with few other competitive exports;
- Tourism products can be built on natural resources and culture, which might sometimes be the only assets that people have.

The contribution of tourism to the local economy is also important to note. It has five kinds of positive economic impacts on livelihood, any or all of which can form part of a poverty reduction strategy:

- Collective income which may include profits from a community run enterprise, land rent, dividends from joint ventures. These incomes can provide significant development capital and provide finance for corngrinding mills, a clinic, teachers housing and school books
- Dividends and profits arising from locally owned firms and business units
- Earnings from selling goods and service or casual labour
- Infrastructure gains, for example, roads, water pipes, electricity and communications.
- Wages from formal employment

At this point it must also be mentioned that there are some disadvantages of tourism as well. For example, leakages and volatility of revenue. These are also common to other economic sectors. However, tourism may involve greater trade-offs with local livelihoods through more competition for natural resources, particularly in coastal areas.

STRATEGY FOR DEVELOPING COUNTRIES

Tourism plays a very important role in the economies of many countries. Earnings from tourism-related activities contribute a considerable portion to their GDPs. Tourism is now being viewed as a significant tool and an important strategy in achieving economic growth in these countries. The WTO is convinced that tourism has considerable potential for growth in many developing countries and Less Developed Countries where it is a significant economic sector and promising high growth rate; and that it has advantages when compared with other economic sectors. This case can be summarized as follows: Comparative Advantages of Tourism as a Development Strategy for Developing Countries.

- Access to international markets is a serious problem for developing countries particularly in traditional sectors like food, agriculture and textiles where they confront tariff and non-tariff barriers. This is not the case for the tourism sector, where barriers would involve visa restrictions and related taxes only. The example of Cuba is instructive in this regard. Whilst Cuba has struggled to find export markets for its sugar and tobacco, it has been much more successful in maintaining a dynamic tourism industry.
- In many developing countries, for example South Africa, China, Philippines and India, domestic tourism is growing rapidly and like international tourism brings relatively wealthy consumers to areas where they constitute an important local market. Domestic tourism can be accessed by people with lower budgets and is often equally valuable to the economy.
- Most export industries depend on financial, productive and human capital. The tourism industry not only depends on these, but also on natural capital and culture, which are sometimes the only assets owned by the poor.
- Tourism has particular potential in many countries with few other competitive exports.
- Tourism is a much more diverse industry than many others and can build upon a wide resource base. This diversity results in wider participation of the informal sector, for example a farming household produces and sells local handicrafts.
- Tourism is consumed at the point of production. This results in great opportunities for individuals and micro-enterprises, in urban or marginal rural areas, to sell additional products or services to the potential consumers.
- Tourism is often reported to be more labour intensive than other productive sectors. Data from six countries with satellite tourism accounts does indicate that it is more labour intensive than

nonagricultural activities, particularly manufacturing, although less labour intensive than agriculture.

- Tourism provides various employment opportunities especially to women as compared to some of the other sectors.

Perceived Disadvantages of Tourism as a Development Strategy:

- Foreign private interests drive tourism and it is difficult to maximize local economic benefits due to the high level of foreign ownership, which means that there are high levels of leakages and few local linkages. But that might not be the case many times.
- Many small enterprises and individual traders sustain themselves around hotels and other tourism facilities and these small companies are not foreign owned. There is often confusion about levels of foreign ownership as local ownership is often masked by franchise agreements and management contracts. WTO is studying this issue in collaboration with UNCTAD as part of its poverty elimination research.
- Tourism can impose substantial non-economic costs on the poor. For example, loss of access to resources, displacement from agricultural land, social and cultural disruption and exploitation.
- Many forms of development bring with them disadvantages that need to be managed. The economic and non-economic negative impact needs to be determined and the issues addressed. It is for this reason that the WTO supports a holistic livelihood approach to assessing the impact of tourism-positive and negative–on the poor. Issues like environmental management and planning at local level need to be addressed through the good governance agenda.
- Tourism is a vulnerable industry. It reacts immediately to factors like changes in economic conditions in the originating markets, levels of economic activity in tourism in the destination markets. Thereby affecting international visitor arrivals. It is also very vulnerable to civil unrest, crime, political instability and natural disasters in destination countries.
- It has been observed that the volatility of export markets for tourism is not significantly greater than other commodities. Many times tourism has the advantage noted that it is not subject to tariff or other non-tariff barriers and that the destination has some control over civil unrest, crime and political instability
- Tourism requires highly sophisticated marketing. International tourism marketing is expensive, although there are more efficient and less costly forms of marketing available today. Many government agencies at the national level, tie ups of domestic hotels and resorts with international participants, word of mouth publicity, target marketing are some of the methods used.

Tourism in many developing countries and many LDCs has been growing strongly in recent years and there are strong reasons to think that these trends will continue. Many developing countries have comparative advantages in tourism where tourism constitutes one of their better opportunities for development.

The disadvantages, which are often identified in relation to international tourism in developing countries, are few when tourism is compared with other sectors of the economy. WTO believes that tourism is considered alongside other industries as a development option and that where tourism presents the best opportunity for local economic development and antipoverty strategies, development banks, bilateral and multilateral development agencies should back it with determination.

LINKAGES AND LEAKAGES

The term leakage in used to refer to the amount spent on importing goods and services to meet the needs of tourists. Leakages take place across national boundaries that can have impact on the balance of payments of the countries. It results from the economic exchange between the two countries. It also occurs when the local economy is unable to provide reliable, continuous, supplies on the basis of competitive prices of the required product or service and of a consistent quality to meet the market demand.

From a tourism and poverty perspective it is generally more productive to focus on the other side of the coin-linkages. When the local economic linkages are weak, the revenue received from tourism in the local economic area leaks out. In order to reduce such leakages, it becomes necessary to deliver consistently at an appropriate quality and at competitive prices, at the same time, engaging the local suppliers who use local capital and resources.

LEAKAGES

From the perspectives of local economic development and poverty reduction, we are not concerned how much a tourist spends outside the country, but how much he is not spending in the local economy, which means, limiting the benefit to local communities and the poor among them.

Leakages, which have negative impact on the development of local tourism, are:

- Advertising and marketing efforts abroad
- Impact skills, expatriate labour
- Imported commodities, goods and services
- Imported technology and capital goods
- Increased oil imports
- Repatriation of profits
- Transporting tourists to the destination country

However developing local sources of supply, encouraging local ownership and enhancing linkages to the local economy can improve this. The last two of these can create more jobs and opportunities for small and medium enterprises at the same time.

LINKAGES

There are many ways in which local communities can be benefitted by these propositions. The best way is to increase the extent of linkages between formal tourism sector and the local economy. By formal tourism sector we mean hotels, restaurants, lodges, and tour and transport agencies. To the extent linkages to the local economy can be increased, the extent of leakages will be reduced.

The increased integration can further develop strong linkages between tourism and other economic sectors. Not only do agriculture, fisheries, manufacturing, construction and domestic industries get integrated, the auxiliary and ancillary industries are also strengthened.

This in turn provides additional revenue and jobs, which reduces the import content and foreign exchange leakages from the tourism industry. Government and development agencies should create local linkages as part of their overall tourism development strategy in the planning, construction and operational phases.

There are three sets of factors, which are important in enhancing the extent of local linkages:

- The creation of employment at all skill levels and particularly where there is existing capacity.
- The Anti-poverty tourism development strategies have suggested 'new attractions'. The tour operators at the ground level should integrate these. The critical areas include creating mutually beneficial business linkages between the formal and informal sectors. Small and emerging entrepreneurs are often neglected. Local government should ensure that microenterprises and emerging entrepreneurs are promoted while taking local tourism marketing initiatives. Visitor attractions, parks, cultural sites and hotels should be encouraged to provide information about local products and services provided by the poor.
- There is need to understand tourist expectations thoroughly. Also, small enterprises to meet the credit needs and marketing needs are also required. Small enterprises sometimes face difficulties in meeting the requirements of health and safety, licensing and other regulatory requirements. There is a need to systematically educate and train the poor in such a way that they are able to integrate themselves with the growing requirements relating to regulations.

The local market should be geared up to deliver qualitatively reliable and competitive goods and services to tourists. The local business community should be actively involved in the process through partnership approaches. This requires continuous efforts, which is possible through long-term partnership to benefit from linkages. Once planning commission concessions are being granted, private sector companies can be asked to make the development of such linkages part of their bid.

Tourism can help in diversifying other sectors of the local economy and can create new ones, offering additional community livelihood opportunities. Local economic benefits and ownership are likely to be greater, if local communities participate in diversified business activities. Now with the growing awareness governments are adopting policies, to encourage and facilitate participation by the local communities. The participation by the poor in the development of tourism projects may result in increasing employment and growth of complementary products. These benefits can further be maximized through partnerships at the destination level. There is a tremendous possibility of bringing about sustainable development for the local economy if Hotels and tour operators work together with local communities, local government and NGOs.

This can help in reducing poverty and can provide a richer experience to domestic and international tourists. Such partnerships will benefit both the host communities and the tourism industry. This will also help them earn more tourism dollars, euros or pounds without any leakages. This can further be utilized for community development. Through affirmative policies, enterprises can contribute significantly to economic development, in both their constructional and operational phases. Some practical strategies for developing local economic linkages.

Market Access and Enclave Tourism

There is practically no link between local people and tourism market. Tourists are not accessible to the local community when they are within their hotels, coaches, and safari vehicles or inside sites and attractions such as museums. These are all enclave forms of tourism. The local community people who wish to sell their products to tourists don't have access to them. They end up hawking and touting at entry points.

The problem is still more difficult in case of Cruise ship passengers and tourist on "all inclusive" hotel or resort packages where local entrepreneurs hardly interact with them. Access to the market plays major role in involving entrepreneurs in the tourism industry. This is particularly true in the case of the informal sector; where the return on local skills and services is often maximized and where the scale of capital investments is low. There is a need to keep this aspect in mind at the time of tourism planning, as access to tourists for the informal sector is often neglected. Some tourists prefer all-inclusive packages, as they do not always feel safe in a new destination and are happier in a protected environment. They feel protected from the poverty and hassle from beggars, touts and hawkers in some destinations. But there is a way to solve this problem. This requires partnership approach between Hotel and informal traders.

This allows informal traders to provide such an environment where tourists feel secure in moving beyond the enclave and to approach "hassle-free" crafts markets. Local guides can also help in establishing contact between tourists and traders by rotation for which they may have agreement among themselves.

This also requires observing certain code of conduct by the local traders and guide. There should be a design to link the informal sector with formal sector so that poor members of community can be helped and tourist market becomes accessible to them. This can help them gain the economic benefit from it. There are a number of strategies that can be used to enhance overall economic benefits and can further reduce poverty.

Growth and Selection

Attracting more of the most appropriate market Segments It has been observed that the tourism sector in the poorest countries is generally highly dependent on international markets, as they do not have significant domestic markets. However, it has also been noted earlier that a significant number of developing countries have strong domestic tourism sectors as well as significant outbound tourists. It becomes imperative that the domestic market should always be considered first by the poorest countries, but in order to maximize foreign exchange revenues, the primary focus continues to be on international arrivals.

There is a challenge to attract larger numbers of those international and domestic tourists who are most likely to benefit the poor, those predisposed to visit local markets and to seek first hand experiences of nature, culture and daily life which are most likely to be provided by poor people. It is worth mentioning the importance of intra-regional tourism in this regard; WTO reported intra-regional tourism as growing in most regions of the world. It is significant that 40% of Africa's tourism comes from neighbouring African countries. This opportunity can be grabbed by opening up the roads and improving the modes of transport between countries in Africa, which would greatly enhance the movement of people and contribute in reducing poverty. Intra-regional tourism is especially valuable for pro-poor tourism and local economic development.

This is because of the fact that there is greater likelihood of shared cultural values and familiarity with social systems between the people of neighbouring countries. There is no doubt that there is a case for attracting more visitors in order to increase the economic impact. At the same time we must understand that this strategy will only assist in poverty reduction if the additional tourists can be encouraged to spend in ways that benefit the poor and if it results in overall sustainability.

The World Bank's World Development Report recognized that economic growth does not necessarily result in swift poverty reduction. This requires an explicitly pro-poor strategy. This means that there should be constant growth, which favours poor in a disproportionate way.

Some of the key components of broad-based growth which assist in benefiting the poor include:

- Government commitment and responsiveness to the needs of the poor
- The expansion of employment opportunities for the poor
- Improved productivity for the poor,
- Improved access for the poor to credit, knowledge and infrastructure,
- Investment in the human capital of the poor.

Increasing Tourists' Length of Stay

The economic returns can be increased with the same number of tourist arrivals if efforts can be made to extend their stay for a longer period. This results in the development of the product by increasing the numbers of bed nights and the expenditure of tourists on boarding and lodging.

There will be a poverty reduction impact, if the additional bed nights can create extra employment or create greater opportunities for the poor to sell goods and services to the tourists or to the tourism industry.

Increasing Visitor Expenditure

Now-a-days there is a market trend towards more experiential holidays. Tourists want to learn more about the countries they are visiting: the people, their cultures, traditions, cuisine, etc. It is much more than mere holidaymaking. The trend is towards more active holidays, greater personal involvement and active participation instead of passive relaxation.

This again has potential for the diversification and enrichment of the tourism product. There is scope to develop more activities and attractions, with increased demand for interpreters and services of guides and transport necessary for their enjoyment. This increases both expenditure and length of stay.

Making more extensive use of natural and cultural heritage, at the same time carefully managing the tourism impacts so as to ensue the conservation of resources, can make an important contribution both to economic development and conservation. This leads to growth in "Special interest tourists" who tend to spend more money on and during their holidays and to stay longer, whether those interests are based on natural, archaeological, historical or cultural heritage, or based on adventure and physical challenge.

Developing Complementary Products

Providing a greater variety and richness of attractions and activities at destination can increase tourists' expenditure. This will increase the propensity of travellers to visit various attractions at the destination and may extend their length of stay and increase their expenditure. This translates into creating more promising opportunities for the development of complementary products that enable the poor to engage in the industry and to profit from it. The growth in established industry results in stimulating interest in the development of complementary products: tourism services and goods.

This complements the core tourism facilities of transport, excursions and accommodation. The list of complementary effects goes on increasing. These complementary tourism products often provide experiences that are not provided by the tour operators but which enrich their product. Hoteliers and tour operators can encourage local people to develop tourism products and services and to support them in doing so with training and marketing. This will increase the attractiveness of the destination and increase tourist expenditure in the local economy and will also develop the complementary products.

Local communities can often engage in the provision of complementary products because it requires less capital investment and is therefore less risky. Tourism is often best considered as an additional diversification option for the poor, rather than a substitute for their core means of livelihood. As an additional source of income it can play an important part in improving living standards and raising people above the poverty threshold. The poor can maximize their returns by choosing forms of participation, which complement their existing livelihood strategies. It also helps them earn from their cultural and social assets.

Tourists are interested in the "everyday lives" of local communities and there are a host of smallenterprise opportunities for local people. Local guides and cyclerickshaw driver/guides in India's Keoladeo National Park, and guides and charter-boat operators in Indonesia's Komodo National Park are examples of local people diversifying their livelihood strategies. The boat operators also earn their living from fishing and many of the cycle-rickshaw drivers work in town when the tourist season is low.

Spreading the Benefits of Tourism Geographically

Tourism destinations are geographically diverse in nature. There are different geographical sites like beaches, mountains and urban attractions and holidaymakers can be encouraged to travel further, beyond established destinations, which can enhance and diversify their experience of particular environmental, cultural or natural heritage attractions. Heritage Trails and other similar products have been developed to extend length of stay and to spread the advantages of tourism development to new areas and communities.

They can be used as initiatives, which may benefit the poor. National Parks, cultural sites and World heritage sites are often the major attractions, the primary "tourism magnets" in significant parts of the developing world and they often attract people to marginal rural areas. It can be argued that natural and cultural heritage sites as the major attractions should be taking a wider view of their potential to contribute to tourism development and the well-being of local communities. These areas otherwise are of no interest to tourists.

Changing the way in which tourism is organized in and around attractions can increase the economic development impact. For example, at Kamodo National Park in Indonesia, non-local carriers and package tour operators take away a big slice of tourism trip expenditure, *i.e.*, about 85%, which could have otherwise gone to local economy. Estimates for average local expenditure at Komodo per visitor demonstrate the importance of minimizing enclave tourism.

Cruise ship tourists spent on average US $0, 03 in the local economy, package tourists spent US $52.5 and independent travellers US $97.4. The Parks and other major tourism attractions in rural areas can be developed to assist the development of small-scale, locally owned attractions and tourism services. Nature-based tourism and cultural heritage tourism in rural areas can provide significant local markets and economic development opportunities. It contributes to integrated rural development and offers local employment and supplementary income-generating opportunities for poor people. The development of tourism in such areas can significantly improve incomes for local communities and the poor. For this these flagship attractions can be planned and managed so as to maximize the opportunities for local economic development and poverty reduction.

Infrastructure and Planning Gain

The development of infrastructure and tourism development are interrelated. Tourism can contribute to overall socio-economic development through the provision of roads, telephones, and electricity, piped and treated water supplies, waste disposal and recycling and sewage treatment. Roads developed for tourism provide opportunities for trade and new roads opened to improve trade also bring tourism opportunities if they open access to tourism resources. New economic corridor development projects often create tourism development opportunities for local communities in addition to improving trade linkages.

These facilities enhance opportunities for other forms of local economic development, but more could be done at the local and national level to maximize those benefits, particularly when new projects are licensed. It is possible to maximize the planning gains through appropriate policies by government and tourism planners. The right policy in the right direction will encourage local economic development and benefit the poor.

Local Management of Tourism and Partnerships

Local communities and the poor amongst them are more likely to benefit from planning gain where they are involved in discussions and decisions about tourism developments. Benefits can be maximized where the complementarities between different forms of tourism development and their livelihood strategies are given due consideration. Appropriate planning structures can facilitate effective community participation in the tourism development process and provide a mechanism for capturing planning gain through infrastructure, employment and economic linkages. A planning process should define carrying capacity and set limits of acceptable change. This will influence local communities' active participation in tourism development and help in achieving anti-poverty goals. It is through participation by these local community people whose traditional and local knowledge can be utilized for empowering them. This will also help in maintaining the environmental, social and cultural integrity of destinations.

Small and Medium Enterprises Development

The increased interest in local tourism experience results in increased opportunities for the development of new locally owned enterprises. This helps in providing competitive and complementary goods and services. This trend is found in developed country destinations. This can be supported by government policy and SME development strategies. The tourism industry offers viable opportunities for the development of a wide range of SME's. Even in the developed countries they contribute to the largest part of local tourism supply.

In Europe small and medium-sized firms meet 70% of tourist accommodation demand. Some estimates for the developing world put the comparable figure as high as 85% In well-established developing country destinations, like Goa, increasing numbers of international tourists are staying in locally owned accommodation. SME's are very important in the provision of restaurants and bars, handicrafts, the supply of furnishings and other consumables to hotels, the provision of transport, local tour operating, guiding and attractions. All this requires access to capital resources and training in business management for SME's. This requirement is critical in the field of marketing. Providing information, advice and mentoring to small and micro enterprises and emerging entrepreneurs can make a significant contribution to their success.

Reducing Seasonality

Seasonality in tourist arrivals is the major cause of seasonal and casual unemployment. There are a number of strategies that can be employed to extend the tourism season. During festivals arranging melas generates curiosity and helps the development of special interest products. Other strategies include developing places for seminars and conventions, and such pricing policies, which specially address senior citizens who have more flexibility to travel in the low season.

These strategies have an overall impact on the local economy. Strategies that reduce seasonality and successfully attract tourists in significant numbers for a larger part of the year, benefit the hotels and tour operators, their employees and those in the destination who earn all or part of their livelihood by direct or indirect sales to tourists or the tourism industry. Those who benefit from this are most often poor.

EMPLOYMENT LINKAGES

The employment impact of tourism is felt by both direct employment in tourism enterprises and indirect employment in those enterprises and micro-enterprises that supply raw material, goods and services to the tourism industry. The demand of direct employment in tourism is dependent upon the scale and level of tourism development and the extent of tourists' engagement in the local economy and with SME's. This helps in maximizing the employment of locals and nationals in tourism, including managerial grades.

Income is also held within the local and national economies and reduces wage and salary leakages. When wages and salaries are remitted or spent outside the local boundaries, it amounts to leakages from the local economy. However, the success of the tourism enterprise will depend upon the delivery of the appropriate level of service, and in this global industry maintaining high levels of training is an important consideration in the economic sustainability of businesses. One of the ways in which the industry can contribute to poverty reduction is by committing to recruit more local poor people and imparting appropriate training and staff development programmes with the belief that those commitments can be met. Tourism can contribute to poverty alleviation through the creation of employment. Certain changes in existing employment practices can bring desirable developments. Pro-poor employment strategies can be pursued, for example prioritizing the employment of women and youth. Tourism is a relatively labour intensive industry providing direct employment in hotels and tour companies, and indirect employment in taxis, bars, restaurants and other indirect service suppliers, where a proportion of employee time serves the tourism industry and tourists.

Tourism can create jobs, which benefit the poor where specific measures are taken to recruit and train workers from amongst the poor. Where tourism enterprises make these efforts, proper estimates should be made; records should be maintained of its effects on employment to determine to what extent local people, and particularly the poor, benefit and to ensure that their efforts are acknowledged. Beyond the hotels, particular efforts should be made to train and employ local guides, artists, performers and craft workers who are able to interpret their heritage and in the process empower youth and women who have considerable control over it. Entrepreneurship development programmes for tourism SME's do complement these efforts.

These programmes typically include developing business opportunity awareness, business planning including project feasibility analysis and training in management skills. Provision of business advisors and mentoring services may be strengthened for emerging entrepreneurs over several years. Many countries already have small business development and credit programmes and tourism SME development can sometimes be attached to these existing programmes.

MOVING BEYOND "TRICKLEDOWN" EFFECT

It has long been established that tourism development projects, if successful, would attract foreign investment, contribute foreign exchange earnings to the national accounts and generate economic development. Through the process of trickledown, the magnitude of benefits would be amplified. Local communities would benefit through employment and local economic development generated by the additional spending and the new entrepreneurial opportunities which this would create. It must be understood that tourism operations need to be profitable in a competitive world market if they are to survive. There are a number of things, which can benefit the local economy in tourist destinations.

The benefits can arise in the following ways:

- Building and complementing existing livelihood strategies through employment and small enterprise development
- Controlling negative social impacts
- Ensuring the maintenance of natural and cultural assets
- Evaluating tourism projects for their contribution to local economic development not just for their national revenue generation and the increase in international arrivals
- Facilitating local community access to the tourism market
- Maximizing the linkages into the local economy and minimizing leakages

ECONOMIC IMPACT OF TOURISM

EARNER OF FOREIGN EXCHANGE

Tourism has major economic significance for a country. The receipts from international tourism are a valuable source of earning for all countries, particularly, the developing. Visitor-spending generates income for both public and private sectors, besides affecting wages and employment opportunities. Although tourism is sensitive to the level of economic activity in the tourist-generating countries, it provides more fixed earnings than primary products. The income from tourism has increased at a higher rate than primary products. The income from tourism has tended to increase at a higher rate than merchandise export in a number of countries especially in countries having a low industrial base. Now there is practically an assured channel for financial flows from the developed countries to the developing countries raising the latter's export earnings and rate of economic growth. Tourism, therefore, provides a very important source of income for a number of countries, both developed and developing. The figures from World Tourism Organization indicate that, among the world's top 40 tourism earners about 18 were developing countries including India, in the year 1995. Regarding the number of visitor arrivals, in some countries there were more visitor arrivals than the population.

France with a population of 57 million received 74.5 million visitors in the year 2000. Similarly Spain with a population of 37 million received 48.5 million visitors during the same year. Several island countries, like the Caribbean Islands, depend greatly on tourist income resulting from visitor arrivals. These earnings form a major part of the gross domestic product. Even developed countries like Canada which derived over 13 per cent of its gross domestic product from international visitors in the year 1999, rely heavily on income from tourism.

Tourism forms a very important source of foreign exchange, for several countries. Although the quantum contributed in foreign currency per visitor varies from destination to destination, the importance of receipts from tourism in the balance of payment accounts and of tourist activities in the national revenue has become considerable for a number of countries. The major economic benefit in promoting the tourism industry is in the form of earning foreign exchange.

Income from these foreign-exchange earnings adds to the national income and, as an invisible export, may offset a loss of the visible trading account and be of critical importance in the overall financial reckoning. This is truer in the case of developing countries particularly the small countries, which depend heavily upon primary products such as a few basic cash crops where tourism often offers a more reliable form of income. In the case of some European countries, namely Spain, Portugal, Austria, France and Greece, the invisible earnings from tourism are of a major significance and have a very strong positive effect on the balance of payments. Tourism is therefore a very useful means of earning the much-needed foreign currency.

It is almost without a rival as an earning source for many developed as well as developing countries. These earnings assume a great significance in the balance of payment position of many countries. The balance of payments shows the relationship between a country's total payments to all other countries and its total receipts from them. In other words, it may be defined as a statement of income and expenditure on international account.

Payments and receipts on international account are of three kinds:

- The visible balance of trade relating to the import and export of goods
- Invisible items
- Capital transfers.

The receipts from foreign tourism form an 'invisible export', just like other invisibles which come from transportation and shipping, banking and insurance, income on investments, etc. Because most countries at times have serious problems with their international payments, much attention comes to be focused on tourism because of its potentially important contribution to, and also effect upon, the balance of payments. The receipts from international tourism, however, are not always net. Sometimes expenditures are involved which must be set against them.

Net foreign exchange receipts from tourism are reduced principally by the import cost of goods and services used by visitors, foreign exchange costs of capital investment in tourist amenities and promotion and publicity expenditure abroad. Peters, "Certain imports associated with tourist expenditures must be deduced... the importation of material and equipment for constructing hotels and other amenities, and necessary supplies to run them; foreign currency costs of imports for consumption by international tourists; remittances of interests and profits on overseas investment in tourism enterprises, mainly hotel construction; foreign currency costs of conducting a tourism development programme, including marketing expenditure overseas". Reliance on imports to meet the tourist's needs does not, in any way deny developing countries the opportunity of earning foreign exchange in supplying such goods and services. Imports are, to a large extent, essential to the operation of the tourist sector as to that of other sectors.

The important question is whether the value added domestically on an item or service in is maximized? Maximization of import substitution without due regard to the effect on overall tourism receipts may be counter-productive.

Also, differences in the pattern and level of reliance on imported goods and services, capital equipment and manpower are very wide, depending upon the level of development of a country. In some cases, this reliance is simply due to a lack of resources that transform into items which are to be sold by the industry.

In others, the industry has not yet drawn on such supply potential, for which it may be an important stimulus. There is a general need for careful programmes of positive import substitution.

MULTIPLIER EFFECT

The discussion in earlier paragraphs clearly indicates that earnings from tourism occupy an important place in the national income of any country. Without taking into account receipts from domestic tourism, international tourism receipts alone contribute to a great extent. The flow of money generated by tourist spending multiplies as it passes through various parts of the economy.

In addition to an important source of income, tourism provides a number of other economic benefits, which vary in importance from one country to another; depending upon the nature and scale of tourism. The benefits from infrastructure investments, justified primarily for tourism such as airports, roads, water supply and other public utilities, may be widely shared by the other sectors of the economy. This enables us to understand how tourism impacts development in the economy. Tourist facilities such as hotels, restaurants, museums, clubs, sports complexes, public transport, and national parks are also used by domestic tourists and visitors, businessmen and residents, but still a significant portion of the costs are sometimes borne by international tourists. Tourists also contribute to tax revenue both directly through sales tax and indirectly through property, profits and income taxes.

Tourism provides employment, develops infrastructural facilities and may also help regional development. Each of these economic aspects can be dealt with separately, but they are all closely related and are many times considered together. Let us first look at the income aspect of tourism. Income from tourism cannot be easily measured with accuracy and precision. This is because of the multiplier effect. The flow of money generated by tourist spending multiplies as it passes through various parts of the economy through the operation of the multiplier effect. The multiplier is an income concept. The Concept: The 'multiplier' measures the impact of extra expenditure introduced into an economy by a person. It is, therefore, concerned with the marginal rather than average changes.

In the case of tourism, this extra expenditure in a particular area can take the following forms:

- Spending on goods and services by tourists visiting the areas
- Investment of external sources in tourism infrastructure or services;
- Government spending
- Exports of goods stimulated by tourism

The expenditure can be analysed as follows:

- *Direct Expenditure*: In the case of tourism, this expenditure is made by tourists on goods and services in hotels and other supplementary accommodation units, restaurants, other tourist facilities like buses, taxis coaches, railways, domestic airlines, and for tourism-generated exports, or by tourism related investment in the area.
- *Indirect Expenditure*: This covers a sum total of inter-business

transactions which result from the direct expenditure, such as purchase of goods by hoteliers from local suppliers and purchases by local suppliers from wholesalers.

- *Included Expenditure*: This is the increased consumer spending resulting from the additional personal income generated by the direct expenditure, *e.g.*, hotel workers using their wages for the purchase of goods and services. Indirect and induced expenditure together are called secondary expenditure.

There are several different concepts of the multiplier. Most multipliers in common use incorporate the general principle of the Keynesian model.

The four types of multipliers are intrinsically linked as follows:

- *Sales Multiplier*: This measures the extra business turnover created by an extra unit of tourist expenditure. Output Multiplier: This is similar to the sales multiplier but it also takes into account inventory changes, such as the increase in stock levels by hotels, restaurants and shops because of increased trading activity.
- *Income Multiplier*: This measures the income generated by an extra unit of tourist expenditure. The problem arises over the definition of income. Many researchers define income as disposable income accruing to households within the area, which is available to them to spend. However, although salaries paid to overseas residents are often excluded, a proportion of these salaries may be spent in the local area and should therefore be included.

  Income Multipliers can be expressed in two ways:
  - The ratio method which expresses the direct and indirect incomes generated per unit of direct income;
  - Normal method, which expresses total income generated in the study area per unit increase in final demand created within a particular sector.

Ratio multipliers indicate the internal linkages which exist between various sectors of the economy, but do not relate income generated to extra sales. Hence, on their own, ratio multipliers are valueless as a planning tool. Employment Multiplier:

The employment multiplier can be expressed in one of the two ways:

- As a ratio of the combination of direct and secondary employment generated per additional unit of tourist expenditure;
- Direct employment created by tourism per unit of tourist expenditure. Multipliers can be further categorized by the geographical area which is covered by the research, such as local community, a region within a country or the country as a whole.

The multiplier mechanism has also been applied to tourism and, in particular, to tourist expenditure. The nature of the tourism multiplier and its effect may be described in the example: "The money paid by a tourist in paying his hotel bill will be used by the management of the hotel to provide for the costs which the hotel had incurred in meeting the demands of the visitor, *e.g.*, such goods and services as food, drink, furnishing, laundering, electricity, and entertainment. The recipients, in turn, use the money they have thus received to meet their financial commitments and so on.

Therefore, tourist expenditure not only supports the tourist industry directly but also helps indirectly to support many other industries which supply goods and services to the tourist industry. In this way money spent by tourists is actually used several times and spreads into various sectors of the economy. In sum, the money paid by the tourist, after a long series of transfers over a given period of time, passes through all sectors of the national economy, stimulating each in turn throughout the process".

On each occasion when the money changes hands, it provides 'new' income and these continuing series of exchanges of the money spent by the tourists form what economists term the multiplier effect. The more often the conversion occurs, the greater its beneficial effect on the economy of the recipient country.

However, this transfer of money is not absolute as there are 'leakages' which occur. Such leakages may occur as a result of importing foreign goods, paying interest on foreign investments, etc.

The following are some examples of such leakages:

- Payment for goods and services produced outside, and imported into, the area;
- remittance of incomes outside the area, for example, by foreign workers;
- indirect and direct taxation where the tax proceeds are not re-spent in the area;
- savings out of income received by workers in the area.

Any leakages of these kinds will reduce the stream of expenditure which, in consequence, will limit and reduce the multiplier effect. Income generated by foreign tourist expenditure in countries possessing more advanced economies, which generally are more self-sufficient and less in need of foreign imports which are less self-sufficient and need to support their tourist industries by substantial import. If the developing countries are desirous of gaining maximum economic benefits from tourism, they should strictly control the imported items for tourist consumption and keep foreign investment expenditure at a reasonable level. If the leakages are not controlled then the benefits arising from tourism will be greatly reduced or even cancelled.

The most important leakage would arise from expenditure on import of agricultural products like food and drink. In a primary macro-economic approach to the prospects opened up by tourism establishment in a developing country, it is regarded as advantageous that a good portion of tourist consumption should consist of food products. It is estimated that the major part of these products can be found in those countries, whose economic structure is largely agricultural in character. In this sense tourist consumption, derived from international flow, can offer an assured outlet to a production which is already active within the domestic economy, without raising problems connected with export of such products and could thus be substituted for imported foodstuffs and a significant saving effected thereafter.

The host country derives maximum economic benefits from the tourism industry as these savings help in increasing the benefits from the tourism multiplier. This aspect of the question is all the more important as the multiplier effect maintains its efficacy and effectiveness as long as no importation takes place.

It follows that if the national economy is to derive the maximum benefit from the impact of international and national tourism, there is an elementary obligation to find all those products needed for tourist consumption. The dynamics of agricultural production in recent years confirms the ability of developing countries to produce the major part of their agricultural products required for tourist consumption without resorting to massive imports. The tourist economy of any country, if it is to remain healthy, must rely upon local agricultural production and this condition seems today to be on its way to realization in most of the developing countries.

Multiplier of Tourism Income

To sum up, Multipliers are a means of estimating how much extra income is produced in an economy as a result of initial spending or after cash is injected. Every time the money changes hands it provides new income and the continuing series of conversion of money spent by the tourists form the multiplier effect. The more often the conversion occurs, the greater its beneficial effect on the economy of the recipient country.

GROWTH OF INFRASTRUCTURE

A significant benefit of tourism is development and improvement of infrastructure. The benefits from infrastructure investments, justified primarily for tourism–airports, roads, water supply and other public utilities–may be widely shared by the other sectors of the economy. In addition to development of new infrastructure, the improvements in the existing infrastructure which are undertaken in order to attract tourists are also of great importance. These improvements may benefit the resident population by providing them with amenities which they desire. Furthermore, the provision of infrastructure may provide the basis or serve as an encouragement for greater economic diversification. A variety of secondary industries may be promoted which may not directly serve the needs of tourism.

Therefore, it is evident that tourist expenditure is responsible for stimulating other economic activities. One of the characteristics of under development is that of deficiencies in the basic infrastructures, which lie at the root of a series of problems related to the development of tourism. Development of infrastructure requires a certain size of investment. Tourism provides the size of demand which justifies the development of infrastructure. On the basis of this minimum demand for such facilities and for such social capital, the size of such infrastructural services evolves. Construction of primary infrastructures represents the foundation of any future economic growth, even though they are not directly productive. The tourism industry shows the elementary need for basic infrastructure.

It has today the important benefit of being able to profit from the existing infrastructures and thus to make a decisive contribution to the growth of the national economy. The international and national tourist traffic, moreover, represents a reward for the capital invested and can now contribute to the financial efforts required for maintenance. The satisfactory degree of development achieved in this specific sector now permits major tourist progress, while also giving further proof of the complementary character of tourism in relation to other economic sectors. Creation of basic infrastructures for tourist usage will also be of service to the other sectors of the economy such as industry and agriculture. This results in better equilibrium of general economic growth.

TOURISM AND TAXATION

Tourism also results in tax revenues both at national and local levels. Taxes can provide the financial resources for the development of infrastructure, enhancing and maintenance of some types of attractions and other public facilities and services, tourism marketing and training required for developing tourism, as well as to help finance poverty alleviation programmes by governments both at local and national levels.

In addition, tourism-related tax revenues help finance general community improvements and services used by all residents. WTO's 1998 report on tourism taxation emphasizes that taxation policies in a country must be carefully evaluated in an integrated manner to ensure that tourism-related taxes are giving the necessary substantial revenues. However, taxes should not be so high for the country's international competitive position to be counter productive and produce a loss of tourist traffic.

The aim should be to strike a balance between, a level of taxation that maintains a competitive position for the country and reasonable profits for the industry, and, receiving adequate revenues to support investment in and maintenance of the tourism sector, and to contribute towards general community welfare.

BALANCED REGIONAL DEVELOPMENT

Another important domestic effect relates to the regional aspects of tourist expenditure. Such expenditure is of special significance in marginal areas, which are relatively isolated, economically underdeveloped, and have unemployment problems. The United Nations Conference on International Travel and Tourism held in Rome in 1963 stated that tourism was important not only as a source of earning foreign exchange, but also as a factor determining the location of industry and in the development of underdeveloped regions. It further stated that in some cases the development of tourism may be the only means of promoting the economic advancement of less-developed areas lacking in other resources. In fact underdeveloped regions of the country usually greatly benefit from tourism development. Many of the economically backward regions contain areas of high scenic beauty and of cultural attractions. These areas, if developed for use by tourists, can bring in a lot of prosperity to the local people.

Tourism development in these regions accordingly becomes a significant factor in redressing regional imbalances in employment and income. Tourist expenditure at a particular tourist area helps the development of the many areas around it. Many countries both developed as well as developing have realised this aspect of tourism development and are contemplating developing tourist facilities in underdeveloped regions with a view to bringing prosperity there. Khajuraho in India, which is now an internationally famous tourist spot, is an example of one such region.

To show, Khajuraho, a remote and unknown small village about forty years ago, is now on the world tourist map which attracts thousands of tourists, both domestic as well as international. Today, Indian Airlines flies a jet plane between the capital city of New Delhi and Khajuraho and seats are not easy to come by.

Thousands of tourists visit the place by air, rail and road transport every month to see the architectural beauty of temples and erotic sculptures whose creators were the Chandela kings, who ruled in North India from the 9th to the 13th centuries. Today 22 glorious temples remind us of the classic Indian architecture and culture of those times and represent the finest expression of the art of medieval India. The area around Khajuraho is well developed and full of life. The place has provided employment to hundreds of local people in hotels and shops.

There is a thriving clay-model industry devoted to making replicas of the famous temple sculptures and a number of shops dealing with items of presentation, handlooms and handicrafts, have created jobs for many. Tourists love to purchase various souvenirs to take home.

Thus local people are recipients of additional income which has increased the prosperity of the region. Subsequently areas around Khajuraho have also prospered and reaped the benefits from the tourist multiplier. There is no dearth of areas which could, after they are developed for tourism, become great assets

great encouragement to economic development and, especially, employment. However at this point it is, necessary to consider the seasonal nature of the tourism industry. Where general diversification alternatives are scarce, a combination of heavy dependence on tourism and highly marked seasonality calls for measures to develop off -season traffic. Employment multiplier: This multiplier is similar to the Income Multiplier except that in this case a multiplier impact on employment is observed.

Employment Multiplier can be expressed in the following two ways:

- As a ratio of the combination of direct employment. At the destination, the jobs are directly created in the industry there.
- As a ratio of secondary employment generated per additional unit of tourist expenditure to direct employment. The workers and their families require their own goods and services giving rise to further indirectly created employment in shops, schools, health care institutions, etc.

OTHER DIMENSIONS

The World Tourism conference which was held at Manila, Philippines in October 1980, considered the nature of tourism phenomenon in all its aspects. The role tourism is bound to play in a dynamic and vastly changing world was also identified. Convened by the World Tourism Organization the conference also considered the responsibility of various states for the development and enhancement as more than a purely economic activity of nations and peoples.

The significance of tourism was discussed in during the conference. The participants in the World Tourism Conference attached particular importance to its effects on the developing countries. It stated its conviction "that the world tourism can contribute to the establishment of a new international economic order that will help to eliminate the widening economic gap between developed and developing countries and ensure the steady acceleration of economic and social development and progress in particular of the developing countries."

3

Travel Law

COUPONS AND CREDITS

In the United States both state and federal courts have procedures permitting the aggregation of similar claims into a class action where the named plaintiff prosecutes a claim on behalf of hundreds or thousands of absent class members. Australia and the Canadian Provinces of Quebec, Ontario and British Columbia have class action procedures similar to those in the United States.

BROAD SPECTRUM OF CLAIMS

Travel class actions have been brought against:

- Airlines for physical injuries 60,000 flight attendants injured from second hand smoke in passenger cabins, flight delays 8,000 passengers delayed and many stranded for 8 hours in aircraft waiting on runways during snowstorm, cancellations 2,000 passengers stranded when tour operator goes out of business, overbooking, discrimination, misrepresented cargo rates, misrepresenting an air carrier's liability for lost jewelry, price fixing nine domestic airlines fix prices for air transportation between city pairs by signaling price changes on CRS, three airlines conspire to fix and stabilize prices on North Atlantic routes, price overcharges consumers challenge airline's 25% cancellation fee, improper collection of taxes airline collects federal excise tax from passengers during period when taxes were not authorized by Congress, imposing unreasonable penalties for replacing lost tickets, mismanaging consumer funds for the payment of charter tours, and failing to deliver advertised itineraries and hotel accommodations.
- Cruiseships for physical injuries contaminated food and water, vomiting and diarrhea, Legionnaires' disease, respiratory attacks, delays, port-skipping and itinerary changes, discomfort aboard ship QEII sailed before major refitting work on cabins and other facilities was completed, malfunctioning toilet flushing systems, breakdown of air conditioning

system and lack of fresh water, misrepresentations capability of ship to meet scheduled itinerary, availability of promised services, facilities and activities aboard ship, deceptive port charges " The gravamen of plaintiff's complaint is that...each passenger is required to pay an amount referred to as a` port and handling charge`...often exceeds $150 per passenger...Cunard intentionally misleads passengers into believing that these port charges are paid to port authorities Cunard does not disclose that only a small percentage of the separate port charge is actually turned over to port authorities...the substantial balance is pocketed by Cunard ", lost, damaged or stolen baggage loss resulting from fire on board ship and bumping some passengers " bumped" from QEI.

- Railroads, Buses and Rental Car Companies for
  - Physical injuries,
  - Misrepresenting the nature, sponsorship and licensing of interstate ski tour services, price overcharges rental car company imposed $1.00 surcharge on customers' bills, taxi company uses " fast metres ", unconscionable replacement gasoline charges,
  - Age discrimination rental car companies refused to rent cars to persons under the age of 2539,
  - Price fixing insurance tie-in and fleet purchase price fixing conspiracy,
  - Failure to deliver insurance coverage, rental cars as part of package tour.
- Hotels, Resorts and Time Shares for
  - Physical injuries failing skywalks, food poisoning, gastrointestinal disorders, " crater lake crud ",
  - Overbooking hotels on tours to England and Germany overbooked and consumers sent to inferior hotels, misrepresentations of major renovations at hotel and the availability of Glatt Kosher food, of the quality of the services, of the availability of accommodations in Munich, Germany, of the availability of numerous free sports activities and proximity to the beach,
  - Price overcharging and price fixing [overcharges for telephone calls, room rate overcharges, overcharges for out of state residents,
  - Time share " bait and switch "schemes and other frauds.
- Entertainment Suppliers and Vacation Clubs for fraud and misrepresentation season ticket holders sue football team that relocates, season ticket holders sue hockey team that goes out of business, season ticket holders sue basketball team when star player is traded, campground facilities and services inadequate.
- Tour Operators for

- Physical injuries bus accident, gastrointestinal disorders,
- Flight delays and cancellations,
- Hotel "bait and switch "schemes,
- Misrepresentations available hotels and itineraries, Glatt kosher food, services, facilities and proximity to the beach
- Mismanagement and theft of consumer deposits.

How To Settle Travel Class Actions

At some point after the class action is commenced the parties will, typically, begin settlement discussions.

Ideally, the class members should receive compensation of:

- Travel services not delivered,
- Out of pocket expenses incurred
- The discomfort endured, discounted by the difficulty of proving the case and the ability of plaintiffs and defendants to finance continued litigation.

Cash Settlements are the Best

When possible travel class actions should be settled with a cash payment to each class member. For example, in Neilan v. Value Vacations, Inc in excess of $1.5 million was tendered by the defendants for distribution to class members who filed claims and the payment of attorneys' fees and costs. The distribution formula provided for various payments depending upon each class members' circumstances.

In Charleston-Coad v. Cunard Line Limited cruise passengers were offered cash and credits towards the purchase of a future cruise. And in Irving Trust Company v. Nationwide Leisure Corporation class members were offered specific sums of money for being accommodated at an inferior hotel in London, England or Munich, Germany [$50.00] or having suffered through a flight delay during a snowstorm $35.00.

Issuing Coupons for the Purchase of Travel Services

There are occasions when it may be appropriate for the court to approve a non-cash settlement which provides for the distribution of coupons or credits for the purchase of travel services from the defendants. For example, In Re Domestic Air Transportation Antitrust Litigation, In re North Atlantic Air Travel Antitrust Litigation, Pickett v. Holland America Line-Westours, Charleston-Coad v. Cunard Line Limited and Geelan v. Pan American World Airways, Inc. class claims were resolved, in whole or in part, with the issuance of coupons or credits for the purchase of future travel services from the defendants. The reasons for allowing these types of settlements include recovery of de minimus damages which would make the cost of distribution of each individual's cash award higher than that individual's claims, and the inability to identify class members. Another reason that may be acceptable to a court is the defendant's inability to afford to pay a cash recovery to the class. In this instance, as a threshold issue, the court should require that the defendant affirmatively establish its financial inability to pay cash. Without such a showing, a non-cash settlement on the grounds of "poverty " should not be approved. In all cases, non-cash settlements must be carefully examined by the court for adequacy since such settlements are generally worth less to consumers than cash and may benefit the defendant and class attorneys more than they benefit class members. Yet these settlements are justified because they solve manageability problems and require a defendant to disgorge improperly obtained monies.

Transferability

Typically, non-cash settlements such as coupons will require the class member to make a purchase of specific travel services which the consumer may not want. As a result, a settlement that relies on the distribution of coupons should provide that the distributed paper be convertible to cash either by redemption of or allowing them to be transferable to others. In one instance, to assist class members to convert their certificates to cash, the defendants agreed to "establish a clearinghouse for the purpose of helping those certificate holders desiring to find buyers ". The court approved the settlement stating "that there will be a lively market for certificates ".

A non-cash settlement may be acceptable if the coupons are convertible into cash albeit at a discount. In any event, without a feature allowing the conversion of coupons into cash by making them transferable or otherwise, the court should reject a non-cash settlement.

Redemption Rate

The most attractive feature for defendants of a non-cash coupon settlement is that, for a variety of reasons, not all of the issued coupons will be redeemed and used by class members. In fact, the average redemption rates on food and beverage coupons, have consistently been between 2% and 6%77. In evaluating the merit of a non-cash settlement, the only proper means of measuring true value is by estimating the actual redemption rate of the offered coupon. Unfortunately, in approving non-cash settlements most courts have neglected to require post settlement tracking of how many class members actually redeem the coupons.

In one of the few cases for which this data was available, the claim rate was only 0.54%79, and the subsequent coupon redemption rate was even lower. Such a low redemption rate makes a mockery of the concept that class members should receive value for settling their claims. This is especially true when class attorneys are paid in cash while the class receives coupons of dubious value.

To prevent this emasculation of the settlement concept the court should require that be 100% redemption of the offered coupons. This means not only that the coupons must be transferable and cash convertible, but the defendant must continue to issue coupons until the agreed upon cash face value of the settlement is reached.

Time of Redemption

The time of redemption is an important factor in measuring the actual value of coupons. If the retailer is aware that the consumer intends to use a coupon he may increase the sale price to compensate for the reduced payment. This potential problem was circumvented in Branch v. Crabtree, a consumer class action alleging misrepresentations in the sale of Hyundai motor vehicles. A proposed settlement provided for the issuance of $1,000 certificates towards the purchase of a new or used car. The certificates could be withheld by the consumer until he or she had negotiated the best price. At that point the certificate could be produced for a further reduction in the vehicle price.

The Problem of Attorneys Fees

Non-cash settlements must be carefully reviewed by the courts, not the least reason being that there is an opportunity for substantial self-dealing on the part of class counsel. Considering the low redemption rate of coupon settlements, defendants may be willing to pay inordinately high cash fees to class counsel in return for support in promoting a non-cash settlement in which the class receives near worthless coupons. Certainly, fee awards should not be based on a percentage of an estimated settlement value which itself is based upon an estimated redemption rate.

To prevent this opportunity for abuse, the court should require that class counsel accept all or a substantial portion of his fee in the same non-cash consideration being offered in settlement or fees should be based upon the actual recovery to the class. The rationale for requiring class counsel to share and share alike with class members is that this ensures value for the non-cash component on the theory that class counsel would not accept as a fee something that is relatively worthless. The settlement of travel class actions with the issuance of coupons or credits for the purchase of travel services from the defendants can be good for business and good for the consumer. Such settlements, however, must be carefully designed so that consumers actually receive something of value in return for releasing their claims against defendants.

Having regard to the Treaty establishing the European Community, and in particular Article 80(2) thereof, Having regard to the proposal from the Commission, Having regard to the opinion of the European Economic and Social Committee, After consulting the Committee of the Regions, Acting in accordance with the procedure laid down in Article 251 of the Treaty, in the light of the joint text approved by the

Conciliation Committee on 1 December 2003, Whereas:

- Action by the Community in the field of air transport should aim, among other things, at ensuring a high level of protection for passengers. Moreover, full account should be taken of the requirements of consumer protection in general.
- Denied boarding and cancellation or long delay of flights cause serious trouble and inconvenience to passengers.
- While Council Regulation (EEC) No 295/91 of 4 February 1991 establishing common rules for a denied boarding compensation system in scheduled air transport created basic protection for passengers, the number of passengers denied boarding against their will remains too high, as does that affected by cancellations without prior warning and that affected by long delays.
- The Community should therefore raise the standards of protection set by that Regulation both to strengthen the rights of passengers and to ensure that air carriers operate under harmonised conditions in a liberalised market.
- Since the distinction between scheduled and non-scheduled air services is weakening, such protection should apply to passengers not only on scheduled but also on non-scheduled flights, including those forming part of package tours.
- The protection accorded to passengers departing from an airport located in a Member State should be extended to those leaving an airport located in a third country for one situated in a Member State, when a Community carrier operates the flight.
- In order to ensure the effective application of this Regulation, the obligations that it creates should rest with the operating air carrier who performs or intends to perform a flight, whether with owned aircraft, under dry or wet lease, or on any other basis.
- This Regulation should not restrict the rights of the operating air carrier to seek compensation from any person, including third parties, in accordance with the law applicable.
- The number of passengers denied boarding against their will should be reduced by requiring air carriers to call for volunteers to surrender their reservations, in exchange for benefits, instead of denying passengers boarding, and by fully compensating those finally denied boarding.
- Passengers denied boarding against their will should be able either to cancel their flights, with reimbursement of their tickets, or to continue them under satisfactory conditions, and should be adequately cared for while awaiting a later flight.

- Volunteers should also be able to cancel their flights, with reimbursement of their tickets, or continue them under satisfactory conditions, since they face difficulties of travel similar to those experienced by passengers denied boarding against their will.
- The trouble and inconvenience to passengers caused by cancellation of flights should also be reduced. This should be achieved by inducing carriers to inform passengers of cancellations before the scheduled time of departure and in addition to offer them reasonable rerouting, so that the passengers can make other arrangements. Air carriers should compensate passengers if they fail to do this, except when the cancellation occurs in extraordinary circumstances which could not have been avoided even if all reasonable measures had been taken.
- Passengers whose flights are cancelled should be able either to obtain reimbursement of their tickets or to obtain re-routing under satisfactory conditions, and should be adequately cared for while awaiting a later flight.
- As under the Montreal Convention, obligations on operating air carriers should be limited or excluded in cases where an event has been caused by extraordinary circumstances which could not have been avoided even if all reasonable measures had been taken. Such circumstances may, in particular, occur in cases of political instability, meteorological conditions incompatible with the operation of the flight concerned, security risks, unexpected flight safety shortcomings and strikes that affect the operation of an operating air carrier.
- Extraordinary circumstances should be deemed to exist where the impact of an air traffic management decision in relation to a particular aircraft on a particular day gives rise to a long delay, an overnight delay, or the cancellation of one or more flights by that aircraft, even though all reasonable measures had been taken by the air carrier concerned to avoid the delays or cancellations.
- In cases where a package tour is cancelled for reasons other than the flight being cancelled, this Regulation should not apply.
- Passengers whose flights are delayed for a specified time should be adequately cared for and should be able to cancel their flights with reimbursement of their tickets or to continue them under satisfactory conditions.
- Care for passengers awaiting an alternative or a delayed flight may be limited or declined if the provision of the care would itself cause further delay.
- Operating air carriers should meet the special needs of persons with reduced mobility and any persons accompanying them.
- Passengers should be fully informed of their rights in the event of

denied boarding and of cancellation or long delay of flights, so that they can effectively exercise their rights.

- Member States should lay down rules on sanctions applicable to infringements of the provisions of this Regulation and ensure that these sanctions are applied. The sanctions should be effective, proportionate and dissuasive.
- Member States should ensure and supervise general compliance by their air carriers with this Regulation and designate an appropriate body to carry out such enforcement tasks. The supervision should not affect the rights of passengers and air carriers to seek legal redress from courts under procedures of national law.
- The Commission should analyse the application of this Regulation and should assess in particular the opportunity of extending its scope to all passengers having a contract with a tour operator or with a Community carrier, when departing from a third country airport to an airport in a Member State.
- Arrangements for greater cooperation over the use of Gibraltar airport were agreed in London on 2 December 1987 by the Kingdom of Spain and the United Kingdom in a joint declaration by the Ministers of Foreign Affairs of the two countries. Such arrangements have yet to enter into operation.
- Regulation (EEC) No 295/91 should accordingly be repealed.

Subject

- This Regulation establishes, under the conditions specified herein, minimum rights for passengers when:
  - They are denied boarding against their will;
  - Their flight is cancelled;
  - Their flight is delayed.
- Application of this Regulation to Gibraltar airport is understood to be without prejudice to the respective legal positions of the Kingdom of Spain and the United Kingdom with regard to the dispute over sovereignty over the territory in which the airport is situated.
- Application of this Regulation to Gibraltar airport shall be suspended until the arrangements in the Joint Declaration made by the Foreign Ministers of the Kingdom of Spain and the United Kingdom on 2 December 1987 enter into operation. The Governments of Spain and the United Kingdom will inform the Council of such date of entry into operation.

For the purposes of this Regulation:

- 'Air carrier' means an air transport undertaking with a valid operating licence;

- 'Operating air carrier' means an air carrier that performs or intends to perform a flight under a contract with a passenger or on behalf of another person, legal or natural, having a contract with that passenger;
- 'Community carrier' means an air carrier with a valid operating licence granted by a Member State in accordance with the provisions of Council Regulation (EEC) No 2407/92 of 23 July 1992 on licensing of air carriers;
- 'Tour operator' means, with the exception of an air carrier, an organiser within the meaning of Article 2, point 2, of Council Directive 90/314/EEC of 13 June 1990 on package travel, package holidays and package tours;
- 'Package' means those services defined in Article 2, point 1, of Directive 90/314/EEC;
- 'Ticket' means a valid document giving entitlement to transport, or something equivalent in paperless form, including electronic form, issued or authorised by the air carrier or its authorised agent;
- 'Reservation' means the fact that the passenger has a ticket, or other proof, which indicates that the reservation has been accepted and registered by the air carrier or tour operator;
- 'Final destination' means the destination on the ticket presented at the check-in counter or, in the case of directly connecting flights, the destination of the last flight; alternative connecting flights available shall not be taken into account if the original planned arrival time is respected;
- 'Person with reduced mobility' means any person whose mobility is reduced when using transport because of any physical disability (sensory or locomotory, permanent or temporary), intellectual impairment, age or any other cause of disability, and whose situation needs special attention and adaptation to the person's needs of the services made available to all passengers;
- 'Denied boarding' means a refusal to carry passengers on a flight, although they have presented themselves for boarding under the conditions laid down in Article 3(2), except where there are reasonable grounds to deny them boarding, such as reasons of health, safety or security, or inadequate travel documentation;
- 'Volunteer' means a person who has presented himself for boarding under the conditions laid down in Article 3(2) and responds positively to the air carrier's call for passengers prepared to surrender their reservation in exchange for benefits.
- 'Cancellation' means the non-operation of a flight which was previously planned and on which at least one place was reserved.

to the region in particular and to the country as a whole. The French government has created a series of new resorts particularly to bring prosperity to the areas which traditionally have been underdeveloped. The Italian government is likewise attempting to develop tourism in Southern Italy in order to help redress the economic imbalances which have long existed between the northern and the southern parts of Italy. Tourism is to be regarded not as an area of peripheral investment whose benefits will help in creating employment opportunities and in the regeneration of backward regions. In India a similar approach needs to be adopted to develop areas with great tourism potential.

GENERATION OF EMPLOYMENT

Employment is an important economic effect of tourism. The problems of unemployment and under-employment are more active in the developing countries. Tourism can be looked upon in this light as a major industry which employs manpower on a large scale.

The problems which the industrialized countries face in recruiting manpower for the tourists industry confirm that, in any productive process consisting of services, human labour remains the basic need. If a comparisòn is to be drawn with the productive sector none of the technological progress achieved has succeeded in rendering the human factor less indispensable than in this sector, and this is true to an absolutely indisputable extent.

The high social impact of the tourist industry is well known, for it has repercussions in every other national economic sector through the multiplier effect, which is particularly marked in those services that are complementary to the tourist accommodation industry. The tourist industry is a highly labour-intensive service industry and hence is a valuable source of employment. It employs a large number of people and provides a wide range of jobs which extend from the unskilled to the highly specialized. In addition to those involved in management there are a large number of specialist personnel required to work as accountants, housekeepers, waiters, cooks and entertainers, who in turn need a large number of semi-skilled workers such as porters, chambermaids, kitchen staff, gardeners, etc. Tourism is also responsible for creating employment outside the industry in its more narrowly defined sense and in this respect those who supply goods and services to those directly involved in tourism are beneficiaries from tourism.

Such indirect employment includes, those involved in the furnishing and equipment industries, souvenir industries and farming and food supply. Construction industry is another very big source of employment. The basic infrastructures-roads, airports, water supply and other public utilities and also construction of hotels and other accommodation units create jobs for thousands of workers, both unskilled and skilled. In many of the developing countries, where chronic unemployment often exists, the promotion of tourism can be a

Scope

- *This Regsulation shall apply*:
  - To passengers departing from an airport located in the territory of a Member State to which the Treaty applies;
  - To passengers departing from an airport located in a third country to an airport situated in the territory of a Member State to which the Treaty applies, unless they received benefits or compensation and were given assistance in that third country, if the operating air carrier of the flight concerned is a Community carrier. 2. Paragraph 1 shall apply on the condition that passengers:
  - Have a confirmed reservation on the flight concerned anad, except in the case of cancellation referred to in Article 5, present themselves for check-in,—as stipulated and at the time indicated in advance and in writing (including by electronic means) by the air carrier, the tour operator or an authorised travel agent, or, if no time is indicated,—not later than 45 minutes before the published departure time; or
  - Have been transferred by an air carrier or tour operator from the flight for which they held a reservation to another flight, irrespective of the reason.
- This Regulation shall not apply to passengers travelling free of charge or at a reduced fare not available directly or indirectly to the public. However, it shall apply to passengers having tickets issued under a frequent flyer programme or other commercial programme by an air carrier or tour operator.
- This Regulation shall only apply to passengers transported by motorised fixed wing aircraft.
- This Regulation shall apply to any operating air carrier providing transport to passengers covered by paragraphs 1 and 2. Where an operating air carrier which has no contract with the passenger performs obligations under this Regulation, it shall be regarded as doing so on behalf of the person having a contract with that passenger.
- This Regulation shall not affect the rights of passengers under Directive 90/314/EEC. This Regulation shall not apply in cases where a package tour is cancelled for reasons other than cancellation of the flight.

Denied Boarding

- When an operating air carrier reasonably expects to deny boarding on a flight, it shall first call for volunteers to surrender their reservations in exchange for benefits under conditions to be agreed between the passenger concerned and the operating air carrier.

Volunteers shall be assisted in accordance with Article 8, such assistance being additional to the benefits mentioned in this paragraph.

- If an insufficient number of volunteers comes forward to allow the remaining passengers with reservations to board the flight, the operating air carrier may then deny boarding to passengers against their will.
- If boarding is denied to passengers against their will, the operating air carrier shall immediately compensate them in accordance with Article 7 and assist them in accordance with Articles 8 and 9.

Cancellation

In case of cancellation of a flight, the passengers concerned shall:

a. Be offered assistance by the operating air carrier in accordance with Article 8;
b. Be offered assistance by the operating air carrier in accordance with Article 9(1)(a) and 9(2), as well as, in event of rerouting when the reasonably expected time of departure of the new flight is at least the day after the departure as it was planned for the cancelled flight, the assistance specified in Article 9(1)(b) and 9(1)(c);
c. Have the right to compensation by the operating air carrier in accordance with Article 7, unless:
   i. They are informed of the cancellation at least two weeks before the scheduled time of departure;
   ii. They are informed of the cancellation between two weeks and seven days before the scheduled time of departure and are offered re-routing, allowing them to depart no more than two hours before the scheduled time of departure and to reach their final destination less than four hours after the scheduled time of arrival;
   iii. They are informed of the cancellation less than seven days before the scheduled time of departure and are offered re-routing, allowing them to depart no more than one hour before the scheduled time of departure and to reach their final destination less than two hours after the scheduled time of arrival.

When passengers are informed of the cancellation, an explanation shall be given concerning possible alternative transport. An operating air carrier shall not be obliged to pay compensation in accordance with Article 7, if it can prove that the cancellation is caused by extraordinary circumstances which could not have been avoided even if all reasonable measures had been taken. The burden of proof concerning the questions as to whether and when the passenger has been informed of the cancellation of the flight shall rest with the operating air carrier.

Delay

When an operating air carrier reasonably expects a flight to be delayed beyond its scheduled time of departure:

a. For two hours or more in the case of flights of 1 500 kilometres or less;
b. For three hours or more in the case of all intra-Community flights of more than 1 500 kilometres and of all other flights between 1 500 and 3 500 kilometres;
c. For four hours or more in the case of all flights not falling under (a) or (b), passengers shall be offered by the operating air carrier:
   i. The assistance specified in Article 9(1)(a) and 9(2); and
   ii. When the reasonably expected time of departure is at least the day after the time of departure previously announced, the assistance specified in Article 9(1)(b) and 9(1)(c);
   iii. When the delay is at least five hours, the assistance specified in Article 8(1)(a).

In any event, the assistance shall be offered within the time limits set out above with respect to each distance bracket. L 46/4 EN Official Journal of the European Union 17.2.2004

Right to Compensation

Where reference is made to this Article, passengers shall receive compensation amounting to:

a. EUR 250 for all flights of 1 500 kilometres or less;
b. EUR 400 for all intra-Community flights of more than 1 500 kilometres, and for all other flights between 1 500 and 3 500 kilometres;
c. EUR 600 for all flights not falling under (a) or (b). In determining the distance, the basis shall be the last destination at which the denial of boarding or cancellation will delay the passenger's arrival after the scheduled time.

When passengers are offered re-routing to their final destination on an alternative flight pursuant to Article 8, the arrival time of which does not exceed the scheduled arrival time of the flight originally booked

a. By two hours, in respect of all flights of 1 500 kilometres or less;
b. By three hours, in respect of all intra-Community flights of more than 1 500 kilometres and for all other flights between 1 500 and 3 500 kilometres;
c. By four hours, in respect of all flights not falling under (a) or (b), the operating air carrier may reduce the compensation provided for in paragraph 1 by 50%.

The compensation referred to in paragraph 1 shall be paid in cash, by electronic bank transfer, bank orders or bank cheques or, with the signed agreement of the passenger, in travel vouchers and/or other services. The distances given in paragraphs 1 and 2 shall be measured by the great circle route method.

Right to Reimbursement or Re-routing

Where reference is made to this Article, passengers shall be offered the choice between:

a. Reimbursement within seven days, by the means provided for in Article 7(3), of the full cost of the ticket at the price at which it was bought, for the part or parts of the journey not made, and for the part or parts already made if the flight is no longer serving any purpose in relation to the passenger's original travel plan, together with, when relevant,—a return flight to the first point of departure, at the earliest opportunity;
b. Re-routing, under comparable transport conditions, to their final destination at the earliest opportunity;
c. Re-routing, under comparable transport conditions, to their final destination at a later date at the passenger's convenience, subject to availability of seats.

Paragraph 1(a) shall also apply to passengers whose flights form part of a package, except for the right to reimbursement where such right arises under Directive 90/314/EEC.

When, in the case where a town, city or region is served by several airports, an operating air carrier offers a passenger a flight to an airport alternative to that for which the booking was made, the operating air carrier shall bear the cost of transferring the passenger from that alternative airport either to that for which the booking was made, or to another close-by destination agreed with the passenger.

Right to Care

Where reference is made to this Article, passengers shall be offered free of charge:

- Meals and refreshments in a reasonable relation to the waiting time;
- Hotel accommodation in cases—where a stay of one or more nights becomes necessary, or—where a stay additional to that intended by the passenger becomes necessary;
- Transport between the airport and place of accommodation (hotel or other).

In addition, passengers shall be offered free of charge two telephone calls, telex or fax messages, or e-mails. In applying this Article, the operating air carrier shall pay particular attention to the needs of persons with reduced mobility and any persons accompanying them, as well as to the needs of unaccompanied children.

Upgrading and Downgrading

If an operating air carrier places a passenger in a class higher than that for which the ticket was purchased, it may not request any supplementary payment. If an operating air carrier places a passenger in a class lower than that for which the ticket was purchased, it shall within seven days, by the means provided for in Article 7(3), reimburse,

a. 30% of the price of the ticket for all flights of 1 500 kilometres or less, or 17.2.2004 EN Official Journal of the European Union L 46/5
b. 50% of the price of the ticket for all intra-Community flights of more than 1 500 kilometres, except flights between the European territory of the Member States and the French overseas departments, and for all other flights between 1 500 and 3 500 kilometres,
c. 75% of the price of the ticket for all flights not falling under (a) or (b), including flights between the European territory of the Member States and the French overseas departments.

Persons with Reduced Mobility or Special Needs

Operating air carriers shall give priority to carrying persons with reduced mobility and any persons or certified service dogs accompanying them, as well as unaccompanied children. In cases of denied boarding, cancellation and delays of any length, persons with reduced mobility and any persons accompanying them, as well as unaccompanied children, shall have the right to care in accordance with Article 9 as soon as possible.

Further Compensation

This Regulation shall apply without prejudice to a passenger's rights to further compensation. The compensation granted under this Regulation may be deducted from such compensation. Without prejudice to relevant principles and rules of national law, including case-law, paragraph 1 shall not apply to passengers who have voluntarily surrendered a reservation under Article 4(1).

Right of Redress

In cases where an operating air carrier pays compensation or meets the other obligations incumbent on it under this Regulation, no provision of this Regulation may be interpreted as restricting its right to seek compensation from any person, including third parties, in accordance with the law applicable. In particular, this Regulation shall in no way restrict the operating air carrier's right to seek reimbursement from a tour operator or another person with whom the operating air carrier has a contract.

Similarly, no provision of this Regulation may be interpreted as restricting the right of a tour operator or a third party, other than a passenger, with whom an operating air carrier has a contract, to seek reimbursement or compensation from the operating air carrier in accordance with applicable relevant laws.

Obligation to Inform Passengers of their Rights

The operating air carrier shall ensure that at check-in a clearly legible notice containing the following text is displayed in a manner clearly visible to passengers: 'If you are denied boarding or if your flight is cancelled or delayed for at least two hours, ask at the check-in counter or boarding gate for the text stating your rights, particularly with regard to compensation and assistance'.

An operating air carrier denying boarding or cancelling a flight shall provide each passenger affected with a written notice setting out the rules for compensation and assistance in line with this Regulation. It shall also provide each passenger affected by a delay of at least two hours with an equivalent notice. The contact details of the national designated body referred to in Article 16 shall also be given to the passenger in written form. In respect of blind and visually impaired persons, the provisions of this Article shall be applied using appropriate alternative means.

Exclusion of Waiver

Obligations vis-à-vis passengers pursuant to this Regulation may not be limited or waived, notably by a derogation or restrictive clause in the contract of carriage. If, nevertheless, such a derogation or restrictive clause is applied in respect of a passenger, or if the passenger is not correctly informed of his rights and for that reason has accepted compensation which is inferior to that provided for in this Regulation, the passenger shall still be entitled to take the necessary proceedings before the competent courts or bodies in order to obtain additional compensation.

Infringements

Each Member State shall designate a body responsible for the enforcement of this Regulation as regards flights from airports situated on its territory and flights from a third country to such airports. Where appropriate, this body shall take the measures necessary to ensure that the rights of passengers are respected.

The Member States shall inform the Commission of the body that has been designated in accordance with this paragraph. L 46/6 EN Official Journal of the European Union 17.2.2004 Without prejudice to Article 12, each passenger may complain to any body designated under paragraph 1, or to any other competent body designated by a Member State, about an alleged infringement of this Regulation at any airport situated on the territory of a Member State or concerning any flight from a third country to an airport situated on that territory. The sanctions laid down by Member States for infringements of this Regulation shall be effective, proportionate and dissuasive.

The Commission shall report to the European Parliament and the Council by 1 January 2007 on the operation and the results of this Regulation, in particular regarding:—the incidence of denied boarding and of cancellation of flights,—the possible extension of the scope of this Regulation to passengers having a contract with a Community carrier or holding a flight reservation which forms part of a 'package tour' to which Directive 90/314/EEC applies and who depart from a third-country airport to an airport in a Member State, on flights not operated by Community air carriers,—the possible revision of the amounts of compensation referred to in Article 7(1). The report shall be accompanied where necessary by legislative proposals.

Selecting a Good Travel Agent

Selecting a good travel agent is a risky business. Very few States require travel agents to be licensed, tested annually for competence and proficiency or financially responsible, *e.g.*, maintaining insurance and surety bonds for the benefit of consumers, escrowing consumer deposits and funding consumer compensation funds.

Nonetheless, there are certain things to look for when selecting a reliable travel agent. "There are good travel agents and there are bad travel agents. The good ones find airfares and cruises priced below advertised rates, negotiate free upgrades, find rooms in ` full ` hotels, understand and tell you about travel insurance, and, when things go wrong, either fight for you or try to make it up to you. The bad ones don't do any of this...Word of mouth is a good way to find a reliable agent.

But if you're looking for one on your own, consider the following:

- How experienced is the agent?,
- How knowledgeable is the agent about your destination? How often has he or she traveled to a place or sent other clients there?
- Does the agent ask about your needs, desires and travel habits?
- Is the agent certified by the Institute of Certified Travel Agents?
- Is the agent skilled at using the computer reservations systems?
- Does the agency belong to a consortium? Small, independent agencies join consortiums in order to offer competitive rates on travel opportunities.
- Does the agency use a consolidator who sells discounted airline tickets, usually at rates below those advertised to the public?
- Does the agency have a 24-hour phone line?
- Does the agency protect client's deposits? Does it put them in an escrow account or post a bond? "

The Legal Status of Travel Agents

Travel agents are agents of the consumer and have been declared to be fiduciaries with a high standard of care in several States including Arizona Maurer v. Cervenik-Anderson Travel, Inc. (teenager on student tour is crushed by steel wheels of tour operator's Party Train traveling to Mazatlan, Mexico), California McCollum v. Friendly Hills Travel Centre (tourist injured while water skiing at resort), District of Columbia, Illinois. McCoy v. MTI Vacations, Inc. (travel agent failed to notify consumer of flight changes); Louisiana Philippe v. Lloyd's Aero Boliviano (tourist suffers cerebral hemorrhage on chartered aircraft in Bolivia); New Jersey Rodriquez v. Cardona Travel Bureau (charter air carrier goes bust and defaults in delivery of flight); New York Pelegrini v. Landmark Travel Group (consumer misinformed by travel agent that tour vouchers refundable); Ohio Grigsby v. O.K. Travel (tour operator defaults in delivery of tour); Oklahoma Douglas v. Steele (tour operator defaults in delivery of tour); and Pennsylvania Touhey v. Trans National Travel (accomm-odations and facilities at hotel misrepresented.

The virtue of being a fiduciary is that the travel agent's duties and obligations to the consumer are independent from the travel agent's relationship with airlines, cruise lines, hotels or tour operators. What should consumers reasonably expect from their travel agents?

Duty to Make and Confirm Reservations

After selecting specific travel services the consumer expects the travel agent to contact the supplier or tour operator and make reservations. This function may be accomplished by computer, telephone or in writing. A failure to make the agreed upon reservations renders the travel agent liable for the consumer's damages Slade v. Cheung and Risser Enterprises (travel agent liable for consumer's lost deposit for failing to contact insolvent cruise company and establish availability of cruise); Reservations Desk v. ALIA (failure to confirm airline reservations); Carro v. Parente World Travel Centre (travel agent responsible for making airline reservations); Lathigra v. British Airways (passengers stranded in Nairobi for five days because airline reconfirmed reservations on discontinued flight); Rosen v. DePorter-Butterworth Tours (failure to inform consumer of itinerary change); Van Rossem v. Penney Travel Service (failure to confirm hotel accommodations); Zobler v. Windward Travel Centre (failure to deliver tickets for honeymoon trip); Fuller v. Healey Transportation (failure to send consumers to proper airport for flight).

Independent Duty to Verify Reservations

Travel agents may find it convenient to rely upon various sources of information in confirming reservations. For example, the travel agent may rely upon wholesalers or tour operators Bucholtz v. Sirotkin Travel Service (travel agent relied upon wholesaler to make reservations at selected Las Vegas hotel) or computers Bhattal v. Grand Hyatt-New York (computer error results in guest's baggage being sent to Saudi Arabia) to verify that reservations have been made. Such reliance may be insufficient, however, since travel agents should be prepared to contact suppliers such as air carriers, cruise lines and hotels, directly, and independently verify that the purchased travel services will, in fact, be delivered [Prechtl v. Travel House of Garden City (travel agent should have contacted air carrier instead of relying on computer to make reservations on a flight which air carrier had discontinued); Trip Tours, Ltd. v. Zamani (travel agent should have contacted air carrier instead of relying on an irresponsible tour operator to make airline reservations that never materialized); Touhey v. Trans National Travel (travel agent failed to independently verify conditions at half finished hotel; $25,000 in special damages awarded against travel agent).

Failure to Disclose Identity of Supplier

In recommending specific travel services the travel agent must disclose the identity of the supplier or tour operator responsible for delivering the services. If the travel agent fails to make such a disclosure then the travel agent may be held responsible for the supplier's or tour operator's default Spiro v. Delmar Travel Bureau (travel agent will be held liable for defaults of tour operator if it fails to disclose tour operator's identity); Van Rossem v. Penney Travel Service (inferior hotel accommodations substituted during honeymoon vacation in Jamaica; travel agent liable for failing to disclose identity of tour operator).

Vouching for the Reliability of Suppliers

In recommending suppliers and tour operators the travel agent may vouch for or warranty the performance of a specific airline, cruise line, hotel or tour operator. In doing so the travel agent may be held liable for the supplier's or tour operator's default under a variety of legal theories including

- Assumed duty [Hernandez v. Rapid Bus Company (passenger rapes passenger; bus company liable for assuming duty to provide safe transportation); Cohen v. Heritage Motor Tours (tourist slips and falls on slippery rocks crossing stream during tour of Canadian Rockies; tour operator and tour guide may have assumed duty to determine whether stones were safe to use as a path),
- Breach of warranty Glenview Park District v. Melhus (canoeist who drowned during trip down river was promised that canoeing would " be perfectly safe "); Pau v. Yosemite Park and Curry Company (bicycle accident; express warranty of safety claim based on promises of safe trails and " safe and enjoyable cycling areas "); Chan v. Society

Expeditions (tourists being transported from cruise ship to shore excursion drown when Zodiac raft overturns; brochures " advertised the Zodiac's versatility and safety in the hands of (tour operator's) `highly skilled boatman');

- Negligent or fraudulent misrepresentation Maurer v. Cerkvenik-Anderson Travel, Inc. (student on tour falls to death under steel wheels of Party Train to Mazatlan, Mexico; negligent failure to reveal three prior deaths of students on same train); Pelegrini v. Landmark Travel Group (travel agent misrepresents refundability of tour vouchers as being refundable); Marcus v. Zenith Travel (tourists stranded in Japan when tour operator defaults; travel agent negligently misrepresented that tour operator was financial stable); Gelfand v. Action Travel Centre (travel agent negligently misrepresented cruise ship's ability to deal with tourist's physical condition);
- Breach of implied warranty of habitability Touhey v. Trans National Travel (tourists vacation ruined because hotel under construction; travel agent contract carries with it an implied warranty of habitability of hotel accommodations; travel agent failed to make independent investigation of condition of hotel; $25,000 in special damages against travel agent); and
- Promissory estoppel Chow v. Trans World Airlines (passenger relies upon air carrier's false promises of priority seating on connecting foreign carrier and misses flight to Singapore); Keefe v. Bahama Cruise Line (reliance upon false promises resulted in delay in filing claim); Fogel v. Hertz International (rental car accident in Italy; liability of U.S. Hertz corporation may be based upon agency by estoppel).

Duty to Investigate Avtailability of Travel Services

Travel agents have ongoing duties to investigate the availability of the contracted for travel services, *e.g.*,

- Hotel closed, Barton v. Wonderful World of Travel (hotel closed; travel agent liable for failing to investigate conditions),
- Hotel under construction Josephs v. Fuller (hotel substandard; travel agent liable for failing to investigate conditions),
- Canceled charter flight, Rodriquez v. Cardona Travel Bureau (charter air carrier defaults; travel agent liable for failing to warn of risks of charters),
- Canceled scheduled flight Fix v. Travel Help (airline goes bankrupt; travel agent liable for failing to investigate);
- Tour package not delivered Marcus v. Zenith Travel (travel agent liable for failing to reveal trade reports about financial instability of tour operator);

- Cruise ship impounded by a local sheriff Slade v. Cheung and Risser Enterprises (travel agent failed to contact cruise ship company directly and verify cruise availability),
- Tour operator changed the itinerary, Rosen v. DePorter-Butterworth Tours (travel agent failed to advise tourist of change in tour itinerary), and
- Hotel overbooking, Bucholtz v. Sirotkin Travel Service (Las Vegas hotel overbooks and walks customers; travel agent liable for failing to investigate reliability of tour wholesaler). The travel agent's duty to investigate continues even after the initial deposit is made Barton v. Wonderful World of Travel (travel agent required to keep in contact with hotel up to thirty days before departure).

Duty to Convey Needed Information

The most open ended duty of modern travel agents is to disclose any negative information which could have an adverse impact on the consumer's vacation or business trip. This duty is limited only by the actual availability of the information to the travel agent and to the consumer Stafford v. Intrav (travel agent has duty to disclose information unless " obvious and apparent " to the traveller)]; Markland v. Travel Travel Southfield (both travel agent and consumer knew of financial instability of Eastern Airlines prior to default)] and was the accident foreseeable and would the information have prevented the accident [Harvey v. American Airlines (vacation ruined because of inclement weather; no duty to warn of rainy weather); McCollum v. Friendly Hills Travel Centre (waterskiing accident at resort; no duty to warn of danger in the absence of information of prior accidents); Tucker v. Whitaker Travel, Ltd. (no duty to warn of risks of horseback riding); Connolly v. Samuelson (no duty to warn of dangers of walking on safari)].

- *Financial Instability:* Travel agents should investigate the financial stability of suppliers and tour operators and convey this information to the consumer [Marcus v. Zenith Travel (travel agent liable for failing to reveal reports in travel trade press about financial instability of tour operator); Spiro v. Delmar Travel Bureau (travel agent liable for defaults of bankrupt tour operator); Fix v. Travel Help (travel agent negligently misrepresents financial stability of bankrupt airline); Douglas v. Steele (travel agent liable for failing to reveal information regarding financial instability of tour operator)].
- *Inability:* To Deliver Services: Travel agents should investigate the willingness and ability of suppliers and tour operators to actually deliver contracted for travel services. Specifically, the travel agent should find out and inform the consumer if the hotel is closed [Barton v. Wonderful World of Travel (travel agent should have discovered

that hotel was closed)] or under construction [Josephs v. Fuller (travel agent should have discovered that hotel was substandard)], or the cruise vessel has been impounded by the local sheriff [Slade v. Cheung and Risser Enterprises, Inc.], whether the cruise vessel can accommodate physically handicapped passengers [Gelfand v. Action Travel Centre (travel agent negligently misrepresents that cruise vessel could meet the needs of handicapped passenger)], whether the hotel has a policy of overbooking guests [Bucholtz v. Sirotkin Travel Service (travel agent should have investigated tour operator's track record in selling accomm-odations at hotels that overbooks guests)], or whether a specific flight has been canceled [Trip Tours, Inc. v. Zamani (charter tour operator fails to deliver flight; travel agent liable); Prechtl v. Travel House of Garden City (travel agent liable for failing to investigate availability of flight)]. In addition, the travel agent should continue to investigate the ability of a supplier or tour operator to deliver even after the reservations are made [Marcus v. Zenith Travel (the travel agent learned of the tour operator's financial instability after the consumer's made their reservations but failed to reveal this negative information before full payment thus giving the consumers the opportunity to cancel with minimum losses)].

- *Need For Travel Documentation:* Without proper travel documents the purpose of the consumer's vacation or business trip may be defeated, *e.g.*, the traveller may be imprisoned or denied entry and forced to leave the destination country at great expense. Travel agents should investigate and inform consumers of the need for travel documentation [Compaigne Nationale Air France v. Castano (airline liable for failing to advise consumers of need for a visa to enter Spain); Levin v. Kasmir World Travel (travel agent liable for failing to advise consumer of need for a visa to enter China)].
- *Health And Safety Hazards:* The destination country may be suffering from a typhoid epidemic, have a high crime rate or be a violent environment because of war or revolution. Travel agents should contact the U.S. Centre for Disease Control [CDC] and obtain information about diseases and the need for medication and shots, the U.S. State Department and obtain any Travel Advisories warning of dangers and any other reasonably available source of information of health and safety hazards in the destination country [Glenview Park District v. Melhus (canoeist drowned during trip down river; sponsor should have investigate the water levels and determined imminent flood conditions); Loretti v. Holiday Inns (tourist assaulted and raped on beach in Bahamas; travel agent should investigate crime levels in destination);

Philippe v. Lloyd's Aero Boliviano (tourist suffered severe physical injuries because of a lack of oxygen during a flight in La Paz, Bolivia]; Maurer v. Cerkvenik-Anderson Travel (student falls to death under steel wheels of the Party Train to Mazatlan, Mexico; tour operator failed to reveal prior three deaths of students on the same train)].

- *Need For Travel Insurance:* Travel agents should advise consumers of the need for and availability of appropriate travel insurance [Rodriquez v. Cardona Travel Bureau (charter air carrier defaults; travel agent failed to advise of need for travel insurance); Markland v. Travel Southfield (travel agent not liable for default of tour operator; travel agent advised consumer to buy travel insurance)].
- *Itinerary Changes:* Travel agents should discover and warn consumers of any changes in flight schedules [McCoy v. MTI Vacations, Inc. (travel agent failed to notify consumers of flight changes); Vick v. National Airlines (failure to warn of schedule changes)] or tour itineraries [Rosen v. DePorter-Butterworth Tours, Inc. (failure to advise consumer of change in tour starting point)].
- *Restrictions:* On Tickets and Vouchers: Travel agents should discover and advise consumers of any restrictions on the use of tickets and vouchers [Das v. Royal Jordanian Airlines (travel agent failed to inform consumer that flight was wait listed); Burnap v. Tribeca Travel (travel agent failed to inform consumer of ticket restrictions); Pelegrini v. Landmark Travel Group (travel agent misrepresents refundability of tour vouchers)].

Recoverable Damages

The damages which a consumer may recover from a travel agent for breach of contract, negligence, fraud or violation of a Consumer Protection Statute will depend upon the nature of the injuries sustained. In non-physical injury cases recoverable should include the value of the components of the vacation not delivered, compensation for discomfort, annoyance and harassment and special damages for " loss of what was to have been a pleasant week " [Touhey v. Trans National Travel ($25,000 in special damages awarded)], or loss of " a refreshing, memorable vacation " [Vick v. National Airlines ($2,500 each for couple who suffered from missed flight)] or the " intangible pleasure of a 24 hour vacation day " [Semrod v. Mexicana Airlines88 ($3,000 awarded for loss of one vacation day)] or the loss of a planned vacation [Pelegrini v. Landmark Travel Group ($250 awarded for loss of planned vacation)].

CRUISE PASSENGER'S RIGHT AND REMEDIES

Modern cruise vessels are best viewed as floating hotels that transport their guests from exotic port to exotic port where the passengers stay a few hours for shopping, snorkeling, scuba diving, parasailing and touring. The cruise industry is growing rapidly with 6 million cruise passengers world wide in 1998, a 7.8% increase from the year before. The advertising for cruise vacations is seductive, indeed, with ships now being built that exceed 100,000 tons and accommodate over 3,000 passengers. The commitment of the cruise industry to the future is extraordinary with $10.5 billion invested in the construction of 35 new " mega " ships for delivery by 20023.

Common travel problems experienced by cruise passengers include physical injuries caused by:

- Slips, trips and falls [Bergonzine v. Maui Classic Cruises (350 lb. passenger on honeymoon cruise falls on gangplank); Rainey v. Paquet Cruises(fall on disco dance floor); Lee v. Regal Cruises (fall on melting ice cubes on stairway); Kunken v. Celebrity Cruises (ankle broken entering cabin);
- Drownings and other pool accidents [Carron v. Holland America Line (passenger in pool " propelled into a sharp statute...causing injury "); Brown v. New Commodore Cruise Line (passenger fractures ankle recklessly jumping into pool from one deck above)];
- Flying coconuts [McDonough v. Celebrity Cruises (passenger struck in head with rum filled coconut [a speciality drink called the " Coco Loco "] dropped from a deck above];stray golf balls [Catalan v. Carnival Cruise Lines (passenger driving golf balls into sea strikes another passenger); discharging shot gun shells [Fay v. Oceanic Sun Line (skeet shooting passenger discharges shot gun shell into another passenger); and defective exercise equipment [Berman v. Royal Cruise Lines (passenger injured exercising on treadmill)];
- Legionnaires' disease [Freeman v. Celebrity Cruises, Inc. (exposure to bacteria causing Legionnaires' disease)] and other viruses [Mullen v. Treasure Chest Casino (respiratory disorder caused by improperly maintained air- conditioning and ventilating system)];
- Rapes [Morton v. De Oliveira (rape); Johnson v. Commodore Cruise Lines (rape of passenger and cover up on cruise); York v. Commodore Cruise Line (sexual assault); Travel Weekly, August 16, 1999 (" Cruising Holds Steady Despite Assault Reports...As reported, 108 allegations of sexual misconduct were included in a lawsuit filed in July by a former Carnival employee, who said she was raped by a Carnival officer...")] and assaults by crew members [Corna v. American Hawaii Cruises (crewman assaults passenger) and assaults by passengers [Colavito v. Carnival Cruise Lines, Inc. (assault by intoxicated passenger);];
- Malpractice by ship's doctor [Johnson v. Commodore Cruise Lines (passenger raped by crew member and misdiagnosed as having had

heart attack; removed from ship and abandoned on shore); Gillmore v. Caribbean Cruise Line (ship not liable for medical malpractice)].

- Smoke inhalation [Travel Weekly, Sept. 27, 1999 (" Controversy surrounded Carnival Cruise Lines' Tropicale in the aftermath of a fire that left the ship drifting without power for almost 24 hours as a tropical storm threatened "; Travel Weekly, March 1, 1999 (" Ecstasy Fire Prompts Closer Look At Safety On The Seas ")];
- Collisions [Travel Weekly, Aug. 30, 1999 (" Norwegian cancels sailings in wake of ship collision ")];
- Gastrointestinal disorders [Hernandez v. The Motor Vessel Skyward (contaminated food and water); Barbachym v. Costa Line (food poisoning); Williams v. Carnival Cruise Lines (seasickness; fear of seasickness)];
- Heart attacks [Bailey v. Carnival Cruise Lines, Inc. 27; Warren v. Ajax Navigation Corp. (passenger claimed malpractice by ship's doctor in treatment after heart attack)];
- Malfunctioning toilets [Kornberg v. Carnival Cruise Lines].

ACCIDENTS DURING SHORE EXCURSIONS

Prior to arriving at a port of call the cruise ship's staff will give lectures about the shopping to be expected and the availability of tours to include snorkeling and scuba dive areas, archaeological sites, catamaran rides, para-sailing, helicopter rides and so forth.

Cruise ships may generate substantial income from these tours, which are typically delivered by independent contractors not subject to the jurisdiction of U.S. courts and which may be uninsured, unlicenced and irresponsible [Winter v. I.C. Holidays, Inc.(tourists insured in bus accident; foreign bus company insolvent, uninsured and irresponsible; tour operator has duty to select responsible independent contractors)].

THREE ZONES OF DANGER

There are three zones in which accidents occur beyond the safety of the ship. First, accidents may occur while passengers are being transported from ship to shore [Chan v. Society Expeditions (inflatable raft ferrying passengers to shore capsizes); Favorito v. Pannell (engineer drives inflatable tender with 15 passengers into other vessels). Second, accidents may occur on the pier or areas immediately adjacent thereto [Gillmore v. Caribbean Cruise Line (passengers stabbed and robbed on pier); Sullivan v. Ajax Navigation Corp. (passenger injured on Mexican pier)]. Third, accidents may occur

- In the town [Petro v. Jada Yacht Charters (two passengers have fight in bar in town)];
- On local transportation [Dubret v. Holland America Line (bus accident during shore excursion); Paredes v. Princess Cruises (tour bus

accident during ground tour in Egypt); DeRoche v. Commodore Cruise Line (motor scooter accident during shore excursion)];

- On a private beach [Berg v. Royal Caribbean Cruise (accident at private beach); Carlisle v. Ulysses Line (passengers ambushed, raped and robbed at private beach)];
- At a hotel owned by the cruise line [Rams v. Intrav, Inc. (passenger fell at hotel owned by cruise line during shore excursion)];
- Or while being transported to local ruins [Varey v. Canadian Helicopters Limited (cruise passengers drown when helicopter crashes on return to Cozumel, Mexico from tour of ruins in Chichen Itza) or touring a local site [Metzger v. Italian Line (accident during shore excursion)]. Accidents during shore excursions may involve
- Assaults, rapes, robberies and shootings [Gillmore v. Caribbean Cruise Line; Carlisle v. Ulysses Line; Travel Weekly, Jan. 9, 1997 (" A dozen passengers sailing on Holland America Line's Noordam were robbed at gunpoint at the Prospect Plantation In Ocho Rios, Jamaica ");
- Horseback riding [Colby v. Norwegian Cruise Lines (horse riding accident during shore excursion);
- Jet skis [In re Complaint of Royal Caribbean Cruises (passengers on jet skis collide)];
- Scuba diving [Tancredi v. Dive Makai Charters (scuba accident during shore excursion); Courtney v. Pacific Adventures (scuba diver's leg becomes entangled in boat propeller)];
- Boat tours [United Shipping Co. v. Witmer (cruise passengers drown during boat tour in the Bahamas)];
- Traffic accidents [Young v. Players Lake Charles (intoxicated gamblers leave casino boat and have traffic accident)].
- Medical malpractice [DeRoche v. Commodore Cruise Line (passenger suffered injuries from motor scooter accident in Cozumel, Mexico and subsequent malpractice of Mexican doctors)].

OTHER COMMON COMPLAINTS

Besides physical injuries cruise passengers may have claims arising from:

- Cancellations [Slade v. Cheung and Risser Enterprises (Great Lakes cruise line absconded with passenger payment; travel agent liable for failing to investigate financial responsibility); Ocean Cruise Lines, Inc. v. Abeta Travel Service],
- Flight delays [Harden v. American Airlines (passengers miss two days of cruise because of delayed air transportation)],
- Baggage loss [Mainzer v. Royal Olympic Cruises (cruise vessel losses one peace of passenger's baggage for four days)],
- Port skipping and unannounced itinerary changes [Casper v. Cunard

Line (mechanical breakdown and scheduled itinerary changed); Bloom v. Cunard Line (two ports of call, Puerto Rico and Nassau, canceled)],

- Misrepresentations about
  - The existence of specific facilities [Boyles v. Cunard Line (cruise line misrepresented availability of " Spa at Sea " programme)],
  - The quality of the facilities [Vallery v. Bermuda Star Line ("The drapes were partly dirty and dingy...the headboards of the beds were broken and the mattresses of the beds were concave...The stateroom...did not meet the quality as described in the brochure as being special, luxurious and beautiful nor was it exquisite..."); Gelfand v. Action Travel Centre (cruise vessel misrepresented as being new when only refurbished)], handicapped accessability [Bergonzine v. Maui Classic Charters (cruise line misrepresented that cruise was suitable for handicapped); Deck v. American Hawaii Cruises (passenger charges cruise line with violating American With Disabilities Act)],
- Discomfort [Charleston-Coad v. Cunard Line (QEII sailed before major refitting work on cabins and other facilities was complete; asbestos removal); Simon v. Cunard Line (lack of fresh water and malfunctioning air conditioning system)],
- Deceptive port charges [Cronin v. Cunard Line ("The gravamen of plaintiff's complaint is that in addition to Cunard's advertised all-inclusive fare, each passenger is required to pay an amount referred to as a ` port and handling charge `...but often exceeds $150 per passenger. Plaintiffs allege that Cunard intentionally misleads passengers into believing that these port charges are paid to port authorities and governmental agencies and that Cunard is a mere conduit for the collection of these fees.

In reality...Cunard does not disclose that only a small percentage of the separate port charge is actually turned over to port authorities or government agencies and the substantial balance is pocketed by Cunard. Plaintiffs claim that Cunard's promotional materials deceptively portray the port charges as being a separate fee, beyond the control of Cunard, but are really designed to enhance Cunard's revenue while keeping the price of the fare competitive with other cruise lines"); Travel Weekly, April 12, 1999 ("Royal Caribbean International and Celebrity Cruises each notified hundreds of thousands of their past passengers that they may be eligible for benefits as part of voluntary agreements to settle class-action suits involving port charges")].

21ST CENTURY CRUISING, 19TH CENTURY RIGHTS

" The unpleasant reality is that the cruise vessel's responsibilities and your rights as an injured passenger are governed not by modern, consumer oriented common and statutory law, but by 19th century legal principals, the purpose of which is to insulate the maritime industry from the legitimate claims of passengers. The policy enunciated by the Second Circuit Court of Appeals 35 years ago in Schwartz v. S.S. Nassau, a case involving a passenger's physical injuries, applies equally today, " The purpose of [46 U.S.C. 183c]...' was to encourage shipbuilding and (its provisions)...should be liberally construed in the shipowner's favour `". Although recent years have seen the expansion of travel consumers' rights and remedies in actions against airlines, domestic hotels, international hotels, tour operators, travel agents, informal travel promoters and depository banks, there has been little, if any, change in the passengers' rights and remedies in actions against cruise lines." Cruise passengers are at a distinct disadvantage in prosecuting their claims.

TICKET PRINT SIZE AND LANGUAGE

A cruise passenger's rights are, to a large extent, defined by the terms and conditions set forth in the passenger ticket. Modern consumers expect the size of the print in consumer contracts to be large enough to be visible and readable. New York State, for example, requires consumer transaction contracts to be " printed...clear and legible [in print] eight points in depth or five and one-half points in depth for upper case type [to be admissible] in evidence in any trial ". Cruise passenger tickets, however, may be in any size type [Lerner v. Karageorgis Lines, Inc. (four-point type)]. The microscopic terms and conditions in passenger tickets are, clearly, meant to be unreadable and invisible. In fact, maritime law, which governs the rights and remedies of cruise passengers, preempts all State laws requiring consumer contracts to be in a given type size [Lerner v. Karageorgis Lines, Inc. (enforcement of time limitation provision in four-point type; maritime law preempts New York's statute requiring consumer contracts to be in ten-point type)]. In addition, the terms and conditions in passenger tickets are enforceable even though the passenger can neither read nor understand the language in which the tickets are printed [Paredes v. Princess Cruises (time limitations in passenger ticket in English language enforced even though passenger was unable to read English)].

TIME LIMITATIONS

Most States allow injured consumers, at least, 2½ years in which to commence physical injury lawsuits and up to 6 years for breach of contract and fraud claims. Maritime law, however, allows cruise lines to impose very short time limitations for the filing of claims and the commencement of lawsuits. For physical injuries occurring on cruise vessels that touch U.S. ports [Lerner v. Karageorgis Lines (46 U.S.C. 183b time limitations apply only to cruise vessels touching U.S. shores)] passengers may be required to file a claim within six months and commence a lawsuit within one year [Buriss v. Regency Maritime Corp (passenger's bunk crashed to floor; one year time limitation enforced)]. On occasion the Courts may decide not to enforce the one year time limitation [Dillon v. Admiral Cruises (trip and fall in ship's lounge; cruise line may be stopped from relying on one year time limitation); Rams v. Royal Caribbean Cruise Lines (one year time limitation does not apply to accidents during shore excursions); Berg v. Royal Caribbean Cruises (passenger mislead into not filing lawsuit within one year)].

For non-physical injury claims cruise lines may impose even shorter time limitation periods [Boyles v. Cunard Line (cruise vessel misrepresented availability of exercise facilities in "Spa at Sea "; six months time limitation to file lawsuit enforced); Cronin v. Cunard Line (deceptive port charges; six months' time limitation in which to commence lawsuit enforced)]. On occasion the Courts may decide not to enforce these particularly short time limitations [Johnson v. Commodore Cruise Line (passenger raped by crew member; claim for negligent infliction of emotional distress governed by Mississippi's 3 year statute of limitations; passenger ticket time limitations of 15 days to file claim and 6 months to sue for non-physical claims void)].

JURISDICTION

Most consumers purchase cruise vacations from their local retail travel agent. The cruise will depart from one of several domestic ports of call, *e.g.*, New York or Port of Miami, typically, where the cruise line is headquartered. Modern consumers expect to be able to file a complaint or commence a lawsuit over a defective good or service in their local courts. Such is not the rule, however, when it comes to complaints against cruise lines. To be able to sue a cruise company locally the consumer's court must have jurisdiction. Even though cruise companies may distribute brochures through and take orders from retail travel agents, such marketing activities are insufficient to serve as a basis for jurisdiction [Kaufman v. Ocean Spirit Shipping (dissemination of cruise brochures through travel agents and advertising in scuba magazine insufficient to support long arm jurisdiction)].

The "solicitation-plus doctrine" doctrine governs jurisdiction in travel cases with the "plus" equivalent to contract formation in the local forum [Afflerbach v. Cunard Line, Ltd (national advertising of cruise vacations and sales through travel agents insufficient for jurisdiction)]. With the possible exception of Internet sales through interactive web sites [Dickerson, The Internet, The " Solicitation Plus " Doctrine, And Jurisdiction Over Foreign Hotels and Other Travel Suppliers)] the Courts have, generally, held that contract formation does not take place at the consumer's location [Thompson v. Handa-Lopez (California corporation doing sufficient business in Texas through interactive web site allowing Texans to enter into contracts to play casino games)]. Some courts, however, have been willing to assume jurisdiction on little more than local advertising [Nowak v. Tak How Inv. (guest drowns in Hong Kong hotel pool; being available for litigation in local forum is reasonable cost of doing business in the forum)].

FORUM SELECTION CLAUSES

The passenger ticket may contain a forum selection clause and a choice of law clause, both of which can have a negative impact upon the passenger's ability to prosecute his claim. A forum selection clause will require that all passenger lawsuits be brought in the local court where the cruise line is headquartered [Carnival Cruise Lines, Inc. v. Shute (a clause in the ticket provided that " It is agreed...that all disputes...shall be litigated...before a Court located in the State of Florida, U.S.A., to the exclusion of the Courts of any other state or country ")].

Forum selection clauses are, generally, enforceable if notice is adequate [Osborn v. Princess Tours (passenger must have " ample opportunity to examine... contents " of passenger ticket); Schaff v. Sun Line Cruises (forum selection clause (Athens, Greece) not enforced; ticket delivered too late to allow consumer to seek refund of $1,770 ticket price)] and they are reasonable and fair [Carnival Cruise Lines, Inc. v. Shute (forum selection clauses subject to judicial scrutiny for fundamental reasonableness)].

Stated, simply, it is less expensive and more convenient for injured passengers to be able hire an attorney and sue in a local court than being forced to travel to and prosecute their claim in Greece [Effron v. Sun Line Cruises], Peru [Affram Carriers, Inc. V. Moeykens], Naples, Italy [Hodes v. SNC Achille Lauro], the State of Washington [Carron v. Holland America Line-Westours, Inc.] and even Miami, Florida [Hicks v. Carnival Cruise Lines]. When faced with prosecuting a claim in a distant forum most passengers will be discouraged from doing so. This purpose of forum selection clauses and explains why cruise lines favour their use in passenger tickets.

CHOICE OF LAW CLAUSES

In addition to forum selection clauses, passenger tickets may also designate the law to be applied in resolving any dispute which may arise. The law selected may be that of the Bahamas [Kirman v. Compagnie Francaise (choice of Bahamian law clause enforced; cruise between Singapore and Australia)] or China [Jewel Seafoods Ltd. v. M/V Peace River (choice of Chinese law clause enforced)].

In determining whether choice of law clauses should be enforced, the courts may consider several factors including:

- The place of the wrongful act,
- The law of the flag,

- The allegiance of domicile of the injured passenger,
- The allegiance of the ship owner,
- The place of the contract,
- The inaccessibility of the foreign forum
- The law of the forum [Klinghoffer v. S.N.C. Achille Lauro].

Choice of law clauses are, generally, enforceable unless the passenger can demonstrate that " enforcement would be unreasonable and unjust ", " the clause was invalid for such reasons as fraud or overreaching " or " enforcement would contravene a strong public policy of the forum in which the suit is brought " [Milanovich v. Costa Crociere, SPA].

The law to be applied to an injured traveller's claim can have a dramatic impact on the likelihood of recovering proper damages. For example, in a wrongful death case involving a crash in China in which two Americans were killed, the court, relying on New York choice of law rules, decided to apply Chinese law which limited the maximum recoverable damages to $20,000 [Barkanic v. General Administration of Civil Aviation].

In another case, the traveller was seriously injured when she was thrown from a horse during a vacation in the Bahamas. She sued several Bahamian entities most responsible for her injuries. However, the application of the Foreign Sovereign Immunities Act meant that the foreign entities would be insulated from any liability [Tucker v. Whitaker Travel, Ltd]. In yet another instance, the traveller slipped and fell on an unlighted path while vacationing in Mexico. At issue was whether the court should apply Arizona or Mexican law to the issue of recoverable damages. The difference was dramatic. Mexico allowed no more than twenty-five pesos per day in lost wage claims, while Arizona had no such limits. The court applied the more generous law of Arizona [Wendelken v. Superior Court]. Just the opposite happened in a case involving an accident on a water slide at a Mexican hotel in which the court applied Mexican damages law resulting in a severe limit on the plaintiff's pain and suffering damages[Feldman v. Acapulco Princess Hotel].

DISCLAIMERS OF LIABILITY

As a general rule, cruise vessels are common carriers and held to a relatively high standard of care [Kermarec v. Compagnie Generale Transatlantique]. The passenger ticket will contain a host of invisible clauses many of which seek to disclaim liability for a variety of problems that may arise during the cruise. As with consumer contracts on dry land instances of gross negligence and intentional misconduct can not be disclaimed by common carriers [Royal Ins. Co. v. Southwest Marine].

In addition, some Courts have held that disclaimers of simple negligence, particularly, regarding the health and safety of the passengers can not be disclaimed as well [Kornberg v. Carnival Cruise Lines (malfunctioning toilets)].

The Courts have been willing to enforce disclaimers of liability regarding accidents that occur during shore excursions [Dubret v. Holland America Line Westours (bus accident during shore excursion; disclaimer of liability enforced)]. Such a disclaimer may not be enforceable if the injured passenger relied upon representations, or warranties regarding safety [Bergonzine v. Maui Classic Charters (350 lb. handicapped passenger broke ankle because of inattention and lack of assistance by crew; misrepresentations in brochure that cruises were " suitable for handicapped individuals "; $42,500 in special damages awarded)], competence and reliability of on-shore suppliers of travel services.

LIMITATIONS ON RECOVERABLE DAMAGES

Cruise vessels that touch U.S. shores may not disclaim liability for loss, death, damage or delay caused or contributed to by the vessel's negligence [46 U.S.C. 183c; Kornberg v. Carnival Cruise Lines (malfunctioning toilets; disclaimers not enforced)]. However, in 1996 the cruise industry was able to convince Congress to enact a provision permitting " provisions or limitations in contracts, agreements or ticket conditions of carriage with passengers which relieve...operator of a vessel from liability for infliction of emotional distress, mental suffering or psychological injury " [46 U.S.C. 183c(b)(1)]. Such a disclaimer does not apply to physical injuries, or those arising from being "at actual risk of physical injury "caused by the negligence or intentional misconduct of the cruise vessel or crew. Nor does such a disclaimer limit liability arising from "sexual harassment, sexual assault or rape ". In addition, a cruise vessel may invoke the Limitation of Vessel Owner's Liability Act which allows it to limit liability to the value of the vessel. In one case involving a passenger injured in a jet ski accident the Court would have allowed the cruise vessel to limit its liability for the collision to the value of the jet ski [Mashburn v. Royal Caribbean Cruises].

MEDICAL TREATMENT AND MALPRACTICE

The most disturbing aspect of cruise vacations is what happens when a passenger is sick or injured and needs the care of on board medical professionals. First, there are no uniform standards for medical care professionals or for the nature and quality of the medical equipment in the clinic and operating room. As noted in Consumer Reports Travel Letter "Many passengers would be surprised to discover that there are no international standards for medical care on passenger cruise ships—not even one requiring that a physician be on board.

Although most cruise ships generally do carry doctors, many of them are not US-trained or licensed to practice medicine in the States...No international agency regulates the infirmary facilities or equipment, or requires a standard of training for cruise-ship doctors...Bradley Feuer, DO, surveyed the medical facilities and staff qualifications of 11 cruise lines in 1996...Among the findings:

27% of nurses and doctors were not certified in advanced cardiac life support; 54% of doctors and 72% of nurses were not certified in advanced trauma life support. Nearly half the doctors—45%—weren't board certified in their areas of practice “.

Second, and even more worrisome, is the fact that cruise lines are, typically, not held liable for the medical malpractice committed by their on board doctors and nurses [Gillmore v. Caribbean Cruise Line (ship not liable for medical malpractice); Bonaventure v. Home Lines, Inc. (malpractice by ship's doctor; no jurisdiction; no liability)]. Some Courts, however, have been willing to find a cruise vessel liable for the medical malpractice of a ship's doctors [Fairley v.Royal Cruise Line (rejecting policy that cruise lines not liable for medical malpractice)]. “Such a policy encourages cruise lines to hire less than the best medical personnel and does a great disservice to passengers who mistakenly may believe that new, modern cruise ships have the best medical personnel and equipment available.”

Cruise vacations can be wonderful experiences. However, potential cruise passengers are well advised to think carefully about their legal rights should they be injured and otherwise be dissatisfied with a cruise vacation.

THE AIRLINES PASSENGER'S RIGHT AND REMEDIES

While domestic airline “have a good product that is selling well” and this year the airline industry “will record more than 600 million domestic passenger ` enplanements” the quality and timeliness of domestic air transportation has decreased dramatically in recent years. “ Virtually every independent measure of customer satisfaction has declined...The unfortunate truth is that flying on an airplane today...is as unpleasant for many passengers as it has ever been. “. Between 1998 and 1999 passenger complaints to the U.S. Department of Transportation rose from 9,608 to a staggering 20,4955. Last month 8,590 flights were canceled out of 307,116 scheduled.

A year ago it was 6,487 out of 299,132...weather, air traffic, mechanical difficulties, rules governing crew hours and hundreds of other causes, including human error, can upset schedules “ And regarding flight delays “ Only about three-quarters of planes arrive within 15 minutes of the scheduled time, and in bad months, about one flight in 40 is canceled altogether “ What are your rights and remedies when your flight, domestic or international, is delayed or canceled?

TYPES OF FLIGHT DELAYS

A flight delay is any change from the promised time and date of departure or arrival. Flight delays include, of course,

- Cancellations [Obuzor v. Sabena Belgian World Airlines (canceled flight due to fog causes a 5 day delay in arrival in Lagos, Nigeria);

Pakistan Arts v. Pakistan International Airlines (2 day delay in Karachi, Pakistan forces entertainers to cancel concert in New York City); In Re Arrow Air, Inc. (8,000 consumers stranded when tour operator and air carrier default; settlement of claims);] as well as flight delays caused by

- Mechanical malfunctions (flight diverted because of mechanical malfunction; passengers involuntarily held on tarmac for one hour and fifteen minutes and later confined to transit lounge for one hour and ten minutes without access to telephones); Arkin v. Trans International Airlines (tire blow out during takeoff); Burke v. Air France (engine trouble during flight; mental anguish damages recoverable); In re Eastern Airlines, Inc. Engine Failure (all three jet engines fail during flight; one engine restarted);
- Acts of God [De Vera v. Japan Airlines (flight delay caused by typhoon and volcanic eruption which forced closing of Manila airport); Johnson v. Northwest Orient Airlines (flight canceled because of bad weather); Klakis v. Nationwide Leisure Corp. (charter tour delayed 2 ½ days because of snowstorm)];
- Schedule Changes [(Robinson v. American Airlines (passenger misses flight because airline advances departure time by ten minutes); Prechtl v. Travel House of Garden City (flight from Seattle to Hawaii canceled by airline which never informed travel agent who relied upon information in computer reservations system; passengers waited sleepless in Seattle for two days for flight to Hawaii)];
- Hijackings and bombings [Shah v. Pan American World Services, Inc. (hijacking in Karachi, Pakistan); In re Air Disaster at Lockerbie (bomb explodes on aircraft over Scotland); In re Flight Explosion on TQA Aircraft (bomb explodes on aircraft)];
- Noxious body odors [Mohideen v. American Airlines, Inc. (passenger and children removed from aircraft because of noxious body odors)];
- False imprisonment [Bayne v. Adventure Tours USA (passenger detained and baggage searched; claims of false imprisonment); Curley v. American Airlines, Inc. (passenger claims false imprisonment after being detained by authorities who were informed that passenger was smoking marihuana in lavatory); Rombom v. United Air Lines (rude and unprofessional conduct by stewards who spitefully had passenger falsely arrested)];
- Wrongful detention [Uwagbai v. Alitalia Airlines (passenger detained in airport lounge for 3 days because of forged travel documents); Singh v. Tarom Romanian Air Transport (passenger removed from aircraft and detained for 6 days); Donkor v. British Airways, Corp. (passenger detained and deported from England); Macintosh v. Interface Group

(passenger removed from aircraft, arrested, jailed and charged with breach of the peace)];

- Violation of Air Carrier's Access Act [Newman v. American Airlines, Inc. (blind passenger with a heart condition claims violation of Air Carrier Access Act (ACAA) after airline refused transportation in the absence of a medical certificate indicating she could safely fly); Brandt v. American Airlines (passenger's ACAA claim for airline's failure to offer food service dismissed); Rivera v. Delta Air Lines, Inc. (failure to offer wheelchair assistance)];
- Wrongful refusal to board [Chukwu v. British Airways (airline refuses to board passenger's brother); Glavey v. Aer Lingus (passenger not allowed to board unless she wrote a written apology to airline for filing a lost baggage claim 10 days earlier)];
- Failure to confirm or reconfirm reservations [Lathigra v. British Airways (negligent failure to reconfirm flight strands passenger in Nairobi); El-Menshawy v. Egypt Air (failure to confirm flight from Cairo); Burnap v. Tribeca Travel (travel agent fails to confirm reservations and note changes)];
- Discrimination [Mohideen v. American Airlines, Inc. (passenger and children removed from aircraft because of noxious body odour claim religious discrimination); Owolabi v. Air France (blind passenger in wheelchair denied assistance and left unattended in airport for seven hours during which time she urinated on herself; claims discrimination based upon race, age and disabilities); Quinn v. National Railroad Passenger Corp (African-American passengers ejected from train; discrimination based on race and violating ejectment rules); Pearson v. Lake Forest Country Day School (emotional distress and defamation action arising from failure to seat 13 year old boy)];
- Airline overbooking [Minhas v. Biman Bangladesh Airlines (passenger delayed 45 days after being overbooked in New Delhi, India); Lopez v. Eastern Airlines, Inc. (compensatory damages awarded to passenger overbooked on domestic flight); Guerrero v. American Airlines, Inc. (airline not liable for breach of contract for overbooked flight)],
- Wrongful ejection [Hermano v. United Airlines (passenger suspected of having a gun is removed from aircraft); Huggar v. Northwest Airlines, Inc. (dispute over storage of carry-on baggage in overhead bin leads to removal of passenger from aircraft); Schaeffer v. Cavallero (passenger removed from flight after vociferously demanding a receipt for a piece of carry-on baggage); Rombom v. United Air Lines, Inc. (disruptive passenger removed from aircraft)];
- Failure to assist disabled passenger [Owolabi v. Air France (blind passenger in wheelchair denied assistance and left unattended in

airport for seven hours during which time she urinated on herself); Shupe v. American Airlines (failure to meet and assist passenger making connecting flight)];

- Misinformation [Lewis v. Continental Airlines, Inc. (passenger missed connection after being misinformed about flight departure time); Siben v. American Airlines, Inc. (airline misrepresented location and arrival time of lost baggage); Carro v. Parente World Travel Centre (travel agent failed to include tickets as part of package tour)];
- Civil disorder [Jamil v. Kuwait Corp. (four day flight delay because of coup in Pakistan)];
- Shortage of fuel [Daniel v. Virgin Atlantic Airways Limited (25 hour flight delay caused by mechanical malfunctions and shortage of fuel)];
- Misplaced tickets [Ragonese v. Rosenfeld (airline ticket agent fails to locate ticket at airport; passenger forced to buy a second ticket at a higher price)];
- Collapsing ticket counters [Romero v. American Airlines, Inc. (passenger delayed and injured when airport check-in counter sign collapsed on her)]; and
- Altered tickets [Peralta v. Continental Airlines, Inc. (passenger removed from aircraft because of altered ticket lost business deal in Costa Rica and claims lost profits of $30,000)].

RIGHTS AND REMEDIES

The passenger's rights and remedies for a cancellation or a flight delay will depend upon several factors. Was the flight international or domestic? If it was international then the Warsaw Convention or its progeny may apply. If not then the law of the country having the greatest contacts to the incident may apply [Barkanic v. General Administration of Civil Aviation (air disaster; China not a signatory to Warsaw Convention; Chinese law applied on issue of recoverable damages; $20,000 maximum allowable); Glavey v. Aer Lingus (passenger refused boarding; statute of limitations for asserting claim for intentional infliction of emotional distress determined by law of New York and not that of Ireland); Macintosh v. Interface Group (unruly passenger removed from aircraft; Connecticut law applies to claims)]. If the flight was domestic then the passenger's rights and remedies will depend upon the application of the common law as modified or preempted by the regulations of the DOT. Such regulations give domestic airline passengers greater or lesser rights than would otherwise be available at common law.

These regulations raise the following additional issues:

- If the flight was regularly scheduled domestic air transportation then the passenger ticket may contain disclaimers which limit the airline's liability for flight delays. Under what circumstances are these disclaimers enforceable?

- Was the flight part of a Public Charter Tour?
- Was the delay caused by airline overbooking or discrimination?
- Was the passenger detained because he was unruly or otherwise a threat to the safety and well being of the other passengers on the aircraft?

INTERNATIONAL FLIGHT DELAYS

If the delayed flight was international, *i.e.*, between signatories to the Warsaw Convention, then the obligations of the air carrier are set forth in Article 19 of the Warsaw Convention [" The carrier shall be liable for damage occasioned by delay in the transportation by air of passengers, baggage, or goods "]. To establish liability the passenger must show that

- The air carrier accepted the passenger on the flight [Malik v. Gulf Air (international bumping causes delay; Article 19 of the Warsaw Convention applies)],
- The delay was material [Tasar v. Pakistan International Airlines]
- The delay caused the injury being alleged [Jamil v. Kuwait Airways Corp. (four day delay; damages from loss of business opportunity not foreseeable)].

INTERNATIONAL FLIGHT DELAY DAMAGES

The Warsaw Convention permits the recovery of:

- Compensatory damages which are reasonable and foreseeable,
- Damages for inconvenience but
- Bars the recovery of punitive damages [Daniel v. Virgin Atlantic Airways (25 hour flight delay; damages for inconvenience are recoverable); Harplani v. Air-India (6 day delay in India; compensatory but not punitive damages are recoverable); Pakistan Arts v. Pakistan International Airlines (2 day delay in Pakistan causes cancellation of concert in New York City; all contemplated and foreseeable damages recoverable); Saiyed v. Transmediterranean Airways (delayed shipment of goods; all consequential damages recoverable up to limits provided in the Warsaw Convention); Kupferman v. Pakistan International Airlines (baggage delayed 15 days during tour of South America; passengers were entitled to " fair and just compensation for physical discomfort, inconvenience, humiliation, embarrassment and loss of a refreshing memorable vacation ")].

ALL NECESSARY MEASURES

However, the air carrier may be able to escape liability if it can show that it took " all necessary measures to avoid the damage or...it was impossible...to take such measures "[Duff v. Trans World Airlines, Inc.(flight delay; all necessary measures taken); Peralta v Continental Airlines, Inc (passenger removed from aircraft because ticket appeared altered; airline took all necessary measures to get passenger to Costa Rica after establishing that ticket was valid); Obuzor v. Sabena Belgian World Airlines)(5 day flight delay; airline took all necessary measures to avoid delay)].

WILFUL MISCONDUCT

The Warsaw Convention provides in Article 25 that the air carrier may not "exclude or limit "its liability if the delay is caused by its wilful misconduct. Proving wilful misconduct is difficult but it has been done in cases involving flight delays [Tasar v. Pakistan International Airlines (delay in the delivery of a casket for a funeral; wilful misconduct proven)], baggage loss or delay in delivery [Bank of Nova Scotia v. Pan American World Airways, Inc. (failure to follow internal procedures regarding loss of gold is wilful misconduct); Cohen v. Varig Airlines, Inc.(failure to deliver baggage during extended tour of South America is wilful misconduct); Kupferman v. Pakistan International Airlines (wilful misconduct in the handling of baggage)] and physical injuries and death [Shah v. Pan American World Services, Inc (hijacking in Karachi, Pakistan; fraudulent misrepresentation of adequacy of security system is wilful misconduct); In re Air Disaster at Lockerbie (bomb explodes on aircraft; failure to comply with FAA regulations in screening baggage is wilful misconduct)].

DOMESTIC FLIGHT DELAYS

Air transportation is sold to the general public with the promise that it will depart and arrive at specific times on specific dates. Applying the common law some courts have held that a failure to deliver air transportation "on time" is a breach of contract [Farmilant v. Singapore Airlines, Ltd. (flight delay was a " tortious breach of contract ")]. The breach must be material and may be 2 hours and 16 minutes [Liechtung v. Tower Air, Inc. (flight misrepresented as " non-stop " stops over in Paris causing a delay in arriving in Tel Aviv); 3 hours [Sporn v. Metro International (3 hour delay when airline loans aircraft to film company for background to a movie)], 8 ½ hours [Koczara v. Wayne County (snowstorm at airport results in the stranding of hundreds of passengers on aircraft queued on taxiways for up to 8 ½ hours without food service and toilets overflowing)]; 10 hours[Freedman v. Northwest Airlines Inc. (exculpatory clause in tariff not enforced in breach of contract claim arising from a 10 hour flight delay)]; 2 days [Prechtl v. Travel House of Garden City (flight from Seattle to Hawaii canceled by airline which never informed travel agent who relied upon information in computer reservations system; passengers waited sleepless in Seattle for two days for flight to Hawaii)] and 2 ½ days [(Klakis v. Nationwide Leisure Corp. (charter tour participants stranded for 2 ½ days at airport during snowstorm)]. Such a breach may also constitute negligence [Reservation Desk v. A.L.I.A. (air carrier liable in negligence for failure to advise travel agency that reservations could not be confirmed); Sporn v. Metro International Airways (3 hour flight delay may be the result of negligence] and fraud [Jawal v. British Airways (passenger detained because of stolen tickets)].

Some Courts, however, have refused to find a breach of the contract of carriage stating that timetables do not constitute a " warranty of punctuality " [Chendrimada v. Air-India (passengers forced to stay on aircraft for 11 ½ hours; flight schedules are not guarantees); Padua v. Eastern Air Lines, Inc. (ticket clause stating that timetables not guaranteed enforced; no liability for flight delay and missed connection); Robinson v. American Airlines]. The contract of carriage applies to point-to-point air transportation. There is no continuing common law contractual duty to the passenger once he or she disembarks the aircraft [Martinez v. American Airlines (passenger suffered medical difficulties after arrival at initial destination; airline has no obligation to assist him or transport him to his final destination after becoming ill)].

DISCLAIMERS IN PASSENGER TICKETS

Domestic air carriers are permitted by the DOT to file tariffs limiting their liability and damages for flight delays and other travel problems and to incorporate those terms by reference in the passenger ticket [Wolst v. American Airlines, Inc., (discussion of the incorporation by reference system)]. Although the passenger may never be aware of such disclaimers some Courts have enforced them [Padua v. Eastern Air Lines, Inc. (ticket clause stating that timetables not guaranteed enforced; no liability for flight delay and missed connection); Macintosh v. Interface Group (unruly passenger removed from aircraft; air carrier tariff " Carrier will refuse to carry, cancel the reserved space of, or remove en route any passenger (a) When such action is necessary for reasons of safety " enforced); Robinson v. American Airlines (passenger missed flight because airline advanced departure time by ten minutes; ticket disclaimer " Carrier shall not be liable for failing to operate any flight according to schedule " enforced); Sethi v. KLM Royal Dutch Airlines (passenger denied boarding because of improper visas; tariff disclaiming liability for misinformation enforced); Madia v. Austin Travel Agency (passengers denied entry because of improper visas; tariffs absolving airline of liability enforced)] while others have not [Coughlin v. Trans World Airlines, Inc. (violation of tariff voids liability limit); Freedman v. Northwest Airlines, Inc. (exculpatory clause in ticket not enforced in breach of contract claim arising from 10 hour flight delay); Klakis v. Nationwide Leisure Corp. (2 ½ day flight delay; disclaimer which strikes at heart of the bargain unenforceable); Larken v. Tourlite International, Inc. (tour operator liable for failing to deliver return air transportation; disclaimers unenforceable)].

PRIVITY OF CONTRACT DEFENCE

An air carrier hired by a tour operator may claim that the passenger has no standing to assert a flight delay claim [Carro v. Parente World Travel Centre (travel agent failed to deliver air tickets; summary judgment for air carrier and tour operator; lack of privity of contract)]. It has been held, however, that passengers are third party beneficiaries of the contracts between air carriers and tour operators and have standing to assert a cause of action against the air carrier [Neal v. Republic Airlines; Harris v. Waikane Corp.; Agosto v. Leisure World Travel, Inc. (tour operator of Rose Bowl package tours fails to deliver rental cars; participants third party beneficiaries of contract between tour operator and rental car company)].

ACT OF GOD DEFENCE

The airline may claim that it was prevented from delivering timely air transportation because of an Act of God [The Majestic (" the act of God is limited...to causes in which no man has any agency whatever; because it was never intended to arise ")] such as a snowstorm [Klakis v. Nationwide Leisure Corp. (charter tour passengers stuck at airport for 2 ½ days during snowstorm)], a typhoon or volcanic eruption [De Vera v. Japan Airlines (Manila Airport closed because of volcano and typhoon)] or a revolution or civil disorder [Jamil v. Kuwait Corp. (flight delayed 4 days due to coup in Pakistan)]. To prevail, however, the air carrier must establish a causal connection between the Act Of God and its failure to deliver timely air transportation. In addition, the air carrier must prove that it acted reasonably to reinstitute the flight once the snowstorm or unexpected event ceased and the airport completed clean-up operations [Bernstein v. Cunard Line, Ltd.].

MECHANICAL MALFUNCTION DEFENCE

The air carrier may assert that the delay was caused by a mechanical malfunction. Such a defence is unlikely to be accepted by the Courts unless the air carrier can prove that the malfunction was truly unforeseeable [Feuer v. Value Vacations, Inc. (48 hour delay due to engine malfunction; disclaimer void)].

PUBLIC CHARTER TOURS

If the air transportation is part of a Public Charter Tour then the duties of both the air carrier and tour operator are governed by DOT regulations. The air carrier is, for example, obligated to return passengers stranded abroad after a tour operator becomes insolvent. Some Courts have held the Public Charter Tour Operator liable for the flight delays caused by a cooperating charter air carrier and other travel suppliers [Irving Trust Company v. Nationwide Leisure Corp. (tour operator strictly liable as principal for defaults of hotels and air carriers in failing to deliver travel services)]. Some Courts, however, have enforced disclaimers in the tour participant contract absolving tour operators for flight delays [Accomando v. Trans National Travel (tour operator not liable for 36 hour flight delay; disclaimer enforced)]. Both Public Charter Tour Operators and cooperating air carriers are required to place consumer deposits into escrow accounts [Neilan v. Value Vacations, Inc. (8,000 passengers stranded; escrow bank liable for failing to properly handle escrowed monies)] and/or to have surety bonds to protect consumer deposits [Irving Trust Company v. Nationwide Leisure Corp. (surety bonds cover all types of claims against tour operator)].

AIRLINE OVERBOOKING

On occasion passengers with confirmed reservations may be "bumped" because the airline has oversold the flight. Domestic air carriers are permitted to deliberately breach the contract of carriage on the theory that it is more efficient to oversell a flight than to fly an aircraft half-empty. If they overbook a specific flight the air carrier must comply with DOT " Part 250- Oversales " regulations which require an " auction " procedure whereby " bumped " passengers may obtain a seat if seated passengers can be induced to give up their position. Otherwise the air carrier must compensate the bumped passenger " at the rate of 200 per cent of the sum of the values of the passenger's remaining flight coupons up to the passenger's next stopover, or if none, to the passenger's final destination, with a maximum of $400 ". If the bumped passenger does not wish to accept the denied boarding compensation then he or she may sue at common law for breach of contract or negligence.

While bumped passengers may not sue for fraud and punitive damages [West v. Northwest Airlines, Inc. (" Federal regulations contemplate overbooking as an acceptable practice so long as passengers received compensation ")] they may sue for compensatory damages alleging a breach of the contract of carriage [Semrod v. Compania Mexicana De Aviacion (overbooking; beach of contract damages include $3000 for loss of one vacation day; food allowance of $300 and a room allowance of $250 per day); Lopez v. Eastern Airlines, Inc. (actual compensatory damages awarded to passenger bumped from flight due to overbooking)].

UNRULY PASSENGERS

Passengers may be removed from airplanes because their actions may endanger the safety of the other passengers. Such grounds may serve as a defence in a passenger's action seeking damages for flight delays [Schaeffer v. Cavallero (passenger removed from aircraft after dispute over carry-on luggage); Macintosh v. Interface Group (unruly passenger removed from aircraft; air carrier tariff allowing removal for safety of passengers enforced);

Huggar v. Northwest Airlines, Inc. (passenger removed from aircraft after threatening another passenger over the use of overhead bin)].

DAMAGES FOR FLIGHT DELAYS

Damages arising from a canceled flight may consist of the cost of alternate air transportation which is more expensive than the original flight[McMurray v. Capital International Airways, Inc.]. Consequential damages for cancellations and fight delays that are reasonably foreseeable are recoverable [Reservation Desk v. ALIA (air carrier liable for all consequential damages for failure to deliver air transportation); Smith v. Piedmont Aviation, Inc. (delay due to bad weather; air carrier liable for consequential damages)] including $3,000 for the loss of one vacation day [Semrod v. Compania Mexicana De Aviacion], $2,500 for the loss of " a refreshing memorable vacation " [Vick v. National Airlines, Inc.,] and $240 for " waiting time " [Das v. Royal Jordanian Airlines].

TRAVEL CLASS ACTIONS

Class actions allow many similar claims to be aggregated into one lawsuit for discovery, trial and/or settlement. Passengers victimized by the same canceled flight [Neilan v. Value Vacations (2,000 stranded passengers)] or delayed flight have been certified as a class and allowed to assert class wide claims for breach of contract, negligence and fraud [Irving Trust Company v. Nationwide Leisure Corp.(charter passengers delayed 2 ½ days because of snowstorm)]. Class actions arising from a failure to deliver a " non-stop " flight have also been certified [Liechtung v. Tower Air, Inc. (unexpected stop over caused a delay of 2 hours and 16 minutes) and the standing passengers for 8 ½ hours in aircraft on runaways during a snowstorm in Michigan [Koczara v. Wayne County].

4

International Trade Theory, Practice and Policy

The choice of free trade versus protection policy that has dominated issues of trade policy over the last few decades has been debated with even greater intensity in developing countries than in developed countries. In order to assess the policies of developing countries toward trade, it is useful to return to "first principles" and examine trade theories, with the objective of understanding the implications of theory for trade policy. Since in both developing and developed countries there are typically various perspectives on the extent to which the country should engage in trade, it is appropriate to begin any discussion of trade with the fundamental question, "Why do countries trade with each other?" The answer to this question lies in the analyses of the eighteenth and nineteenth-century classical economists, the "neoclassical" theories developed more recently by twentieth-century economists, and newer classes of trade theories introduced by economists and business scholars only during the last few decades.

ABSOLUTE ADVANTAGE

It is well known that the first important classical trade theorist was Adam Smith. In his 1776 treatise, The Wealth of Nations, Smith suggested that countries would gain from trade, both exporting and importing, as long as each country had an absolute advantage in the production of a particular good. Such an advantage would be recognized in that country's ability to produce the good more cheaply than every other country. This conclusion was interesting at the time because it disagreed with the prevailing notion of mercantilism in which each country emphasized the advantages of exporting over importing.

Since countries received gold as payment for their exports during the period of mercantilist philosophy (circa 1500-1800), this trade strategy allowed countries to expand their holdings of wealth in the form of gold. Smith's theory of absolute advantage, on the other hand, disagreed with the mercantilist philosophy of national wealth. Instead, he suggested that a country's wealth was reflected in the living standards of its residents. Consequently, importing was not only necessary but also beneficial to a country if it imported goods that other countries could produce more efficiently.

Using an illustration that corresponds to the reality and imagery of the era in which Smith developed his theory, let us assume, that England and France had equal quantities of productive resources and that England could produce with all its productive resources either 100 units of machinery or 40 units of wine, and France using all of its productive resources could produce either 30 units of machinery or 120 units of wine.

Under these conditions, with England having an absolute advantage in the production of machinery and France an absolute advantage in the production of wine, England should specialize in machinery, France in wine, and both countries should export their surplus production and import the wine or machinery that their residents demand.

In this example, note that the potential welfare of both countries clearly improves after trade. If there were no trade between these countries and they each decided to split their productive resources equally between machinery and wine, their combined production would be 65 units of machinery and 80 units of wine. If, on the other hand, both countries specialize in the area of their absolute advantage, recognizing that they can export their surplus production and import the good that they desire but do not produce, their combined production increases to 100 units of machinery and 120 units of wine. Joint production has increased by 35 units of machinery and 40 units of wine, and both countries can increase their consumption of machinery and wine. Thus, the case for specialization and trade is clear in the context of the theory of absolute advantage.

COMPARATIVE ADVANTAGE

Implicit in Adam Smith's theory of absolute advantage is the suggestion that a country that can produce all goods more efficiently than any other country should never import. Of course, were this to be the case in a world of two countries, no trade would ever take place. This seems like a very reasonable conclusion: Why should a country import a good that it can produce more efficiently than can the country from which it would be imported? The Principles of Political Economy and Taxation, and indicated that the apparently reasonable conclusion was wrong. In so doing, Ricardo developed the theory of comparative advantage.

In his theory of comparative advantage, Ricardo argued that trade between any two countries was beneficial as long as these countries produced goods with different relative efficiency. In the Ricardian framework, differences in relative efficiency were based on differences in the productivity of labour across countries. The concept of producing goods with different relative efficiencies is best explained by an example. Suppose that the world comprised two countries— Bolivia and the United States—and that both countries could produce two products: computer software and shoes. Suppose further that the United States used four units of resources to produce a unit of software, and ten units of resources to produce a unit of shoes, while Bolivia used twelve and fifteen units of resources, respectively. According to absolute advantage, since the United States produces both goods more efficiently (with fewer resources) than does Bolivia, the United States should import neither product from Bolivia. According to comparative advantage, however, this example meets the test of a situation where two countries can benefit from trade.

The United States and Bolivia produce two goods with different relative efficiency. The United States has a comparative advantage over Bolivia in the production of computer software relative to shoes because it produces computer software three times as efficiently (with one-third—4 units/12 units—of the resources) as Bolivia, while it produces shoes only 1.5 times as efficiently (with two thirds—10 units/15 units—of the resources) as Bolivia. It is important to note that—based upon these figures—although Bolivia has an absolute disadvantage in the production of both products, it has a comparative advantage over the United States in the production of shoes relative to computer software.

To see the implication of these relative differences in efficiency, think of what happens if the United States gives up shoe production (its area of relative inefficiency) in favour of computer software production (its area of relative efficiency). If the United States produces one fewer unit of shoes, it releases ten units of productive resources that can be used to produce 2.5 units of computer programmes. Since Bolivia would use thirty units of productive resources to produce those 2.5 units of computer programmes, the same as it would use to produce two units of shoes, it would be willing to give up two units of shoes in exchange for the computer programmes.

Consequently, the result of the United States releasing shoe resources in favour of producing computer software is to increase the supply of shoes that both countries produce by one unit while holding constant the supply of computer software. Theoretically, this process of shifting resources should continue until the world's output can no longer be increased by an internal shift of resources in either the United States or Bolivia.

Since "world" production has increased, both countries have the potential to benefit from this specialization and trade. Both countries might not benefit. The United States might be able to negotiate with Bolivia so that it receives all of the extra unit of shoes. The important point to note, however, is that, in the context of the assumptions of comparative advantage theory, the world cannot lose from trade and that both countries have the potential to gain from trade.

Note also that the possibility of gains from trade does not require one to assume that the countries have equivalent quantities of productive resources.

The basis for trade lies in differences in the ratios of productive efficiency not in the quantity of resources a country has available. If, for example, Bolivia had 300 units of productive resources available, while the United States had 3 million, this would reduce neither the desirability of trade nor the direction of trade.

It would only reduce the amount of trade. Although Bolivia would continue to specialize in shoe production, the United States may be unable to completely specialize in computer software production because Bolivia, with its limited resources, might be unable to supply all of the U.S. shoe requirements or consume all of the U.S. excess computer software production. Thus, in this two-country world, the United States might continue to produce shoes but only after it has imported all of Bolivia's excess shoe production, which, in this two-product world, is equivalent to the exporting of all of its excess computer software production.

Not only is trade not dependent upon countries having similar quantities of productive resources; it is also not dependent upon them offering similar payments to the factors of production, including wages to workers. In fact, differences in real payments to the factors of production, land, labour, capital, and enterprise can be expected when there are differences in the productivity of the countries' factors of production or in the relative availability of, and demand for, those resources.

In the previous example, the greater productivity of factors of production in the United States relative to Bolivia would suggest that these factors of production would generate higher incomes in the United States compared with Bolivia. These differences in payments to factors of production, including wages paid to workers, do not reduce the potential gains from trade.

One of the important neoclassical advances to comparative advantage theory was developed by two Swedish economists, Eli Heckscher and Bertil Ohlin, writing in the twentieth century. Together, they developed the factor endowments base for international trade. Using simplifying assumptions, they developed what has come to be known as the Heckscher-Ohlin theory, which suggests that a country has a comparative advantage in the good that uses intensively the factor of production of which it has an abundant supply.

The theory is based upon the proposition that different products require productive factors in different proportions and that countries have different endowments of these productive factors. Thus, the theory suggests that a country with a large pool of capital will find that capital is cheap relative to other factors of production and, therefore, such a country should have a comparative advantage in capital-intensive products. Similarly, a country with abundant supplies of labour will find that labour is relatively cheaper, providing that country with a comparative advantage in labour-intensive products.

Classical trade theories and, to a lesser extent, neoclassical theories rely upon assumptions that diverge from reality. At issue is whether this divergence affects the generalizability of the theories.

ASSUMPTIONS OF COMPARATIVE ADVANTAGE THEORY THAT DIVERGE FROM REALITY

There are certain assumptions of the simple Ricardian model of comparative advantage theory that do not correspond to reality. Some of these assumptions are easily incorporated into neoclassical versions of the theory and may be viewed as weakly realistic; others are unrealistic and are not easily incorporated into classical or neoclassical trade theory.

Multiple Countries, Multiple Products

The assumptions most easily dispensed with are those of a two-country world in which there are only two tradeable goods. The Ricardian model easily expands to take into account multiple countries producing multiple goods without any loss of generality.

Mobility of Factors of Production

The Ricardian model also assumes that factors of production are completely mobile within a country and completely immobile across countries. Of course, neither assumption is correct; and both inaccuracies reduce the power of the model. Since resources are not freely mobile within countries, it is more difficult for countries to specialize by switching from the production of one good to the production of another. In the foregoing thought experiment using the United States and Bolivia, some of the labourers used in the production of computer software in Bolivia might find it difficult to switch to shoe production. Alternately, factors of production move more easily across countries than the theory suggests. Thus, some of the highly productive computer software experts in the United States might be willing to take their professional skills, their capital, and their entrepreneurial abilities and relocate to Bolivia.

Although both assumptions about factor mobility are inaccurate, however, they are also closer to reality than their extreme opposite assumptions. Thus, factors of production within a country are more mobile than immobile, especially over the long term. Further, factors of production, especially land and labour, find it relatively difficult to move among countries. Thus, these assumptions reduce the doctrinaire prescriptions of the theory without reducing its underlying explanatory and prescriptive power.

In some cases, these reality checks can be incorporated formally. Thus, the reduced mobility of factors of production within a country is incorporated into neoclassical trade models by assuming that each productive resource that is transferred from one use to another will be transferred at increasing cost.

(In the jargon of the economist, the production possibility curve becomes concave from the origin in contrast to the use of a straight-line production-possibility curve.)

Transport Costs

The simple Ricardian model ignores transport costs, but these are also easily incorporated into the theory. The result, however, is that for certain types of goods with high transport costs, the benefits of specialization are negated by the costs of transporting goods across countries. Other unrealistic assumptions of comparative advantage theory present much greater threats to the explanatory power of the theory.

Demand Factors and Consumer Tastes

Classical and neoclassical comparative advantage theory is concerned principally with production and supply issues. There are two important assumptions with respect to demand. The first is that there is assumed to be sufficient demand for goods that are produced. Second, it is assumed that consumers in different countries have similar tastes in goods. Of course, neither of these assumptions reflect reality. Consumer demand constrains the extent of specialization, although it does not affect the direction. The United States may have a comparative advantage in the production of commercial aircraft. The resources it places into commercial aircraft production, however, are likely to be constrained by the demand for this product, even worldwide demand.

The other significant demand-related assumption is that of monolithic consumer tastes. Clearly, consumers around the world do not have the same tastes in goods despite apparent trends to create global products and markets. These differences in taste may provide an opportunity for production and sale of a good to be based on an ability to identify the particular tastes of consumers rather than be based only on least-cost production, as is true of export production according to classical and neoclassical trade theories.

Constant Returns to Scale

If firms produced according to constant returns to scale and did not benefit from a learning curve, then the early identification of a market segment interested in a different type of product would not represent a competitive advantage. Once this market was identified, other firms could seek to serve it, thus forcing competition to return to least-cost considerations.

Because these assumptions do not hold, there are advantages to being the first company to move into new markets. Firms do not produce according to constant returns to scale; that is, as the firm increases production, the cost per unit of output does not remain the same. On the contrary, in most industries, firms benefit from increasing returns to scale or economies of scale; that is, as output increases, there is a decline in the unit cost of producing that output.

Experience-Learning Curve

A concept that is related to increasing returns to scale is the learning curve, or its first cousin, the experience curve. Both curves convey the notion that as a firm learns more about a production process because of its experience producing the product, it will be able to reduce the costs of producing the product. In contrast to the message of these curves, comparative advantage theory assumes that there are no cost-reduction benefits associated with experience and learning in the same way that there are none associated with volume.

Each of these three unrealistic assumptions significantly reduces the explanatory and prescriptive power of comparative advantage theory. The prescriptions that have built upon the intellectual underpinning of comparative advantage theory include the notion that rational governments should specialize in the goods they produce most competitively based on their natural endowment of factors of production.

Further, it is said that they should maintain open borders that allow the export of their surplus production and the importing of the other goods their residents demand. Implicit in comparative advantage theory with its traditional factor-endowment focus is a pattern of trade in which most of the trade flowing across national borders would be in dissimilar products and between dissimilar countries, that is, countries with different factor endowments.

TRADE PRACTICE AND NEW TRADE THEORIES

In fact, the practice of trade is quite different from the prescriptions implicit in comparative advantage theory. Most countries restrict trade using a plethora of techniques. In using these techniques, countries seek to "create" comparative advantage instead of relying on nature's endowments. Where trade does take place, a significant proportion takes place among countries with similar factor endowments (e.g., some 80 percent of world trade takes place among industrialized countries). Further, instead of the interindustry trade that is implied by comparative advantage theory, much of worldwide trade is of the intraindustry variety. For some products, the degree of intraindustry trade is particularly high. In the mid-1980s, for example, Yoffie reports that some 70 percent of worldwide exports of antifriction bearings, a critical component in most manufactured products, went to countries that also exported antifriction bearings.

New Theories of Trade

While classical and neoclassical comparative advantage theories do not explain these worldwide trading patterns, they are explained by new theories of trade that have attempted to build trade models that incorporate more real istic assumptions than those of comparative advantage theory. These models, developed by economists and business scholars such as Paul Krugman, Ray Vernon, and Michael Porter, suggest that increasing returns to scale and product differentiation furnish a basis for trade independent of comparative advantage. Increasing returns to scale and the learning curve phenomenon suggest, unlike comparative advantage, that a country's pattern of trade may be determined by acquired expertise rather than naturally endowed factors of production.

The Product Cycle theory, for example, places special consideration on the impact of demand factors in determining trade patterns. It argues that products tend to be developed to meet the needs of a market close to the home of the producer. The idea is that firms do not have perfect information on all markets around the world and that they are most likely to respond to the opportunities close to home. Further, not all countries are likely to spawn innovating firms. Rather, they are likely to emerge in countries with plentiful supplies of skilled labour that can be employed to produce the product and high-income consumers that are likely to purchase the innovative good. It is usually the developed countries that meet these criteria.

Thus, innovations will be spawned in a developed country; and during the new product stage of the product cycle, these products will principally be sold in that home market with exports beginning to other developed countries. As the product matures, exports will increase and will include exports to developing countries. Over time, the product becomes standardized and competition becomes driven by cost. In many such cases, the product may be produced in developing countries to take advantage of lower costs and be exported back to the original innovating country.

This view of trade patterns suggests that comparative advantage is driven by demand as well as supply and that it is not static. A country's relative ability to produce a product can change over time and is as dependent upon acquired skills as it is on natural endowments. This theory—with its recognition of the probability of product differentiation—also explains the reality of intra industry trade.

Generally, product differentiation furnishes a basis for trade independent of comparative advantage, and this trade may well be intra industry trade. Station wagons, for example, are more popular in the United States than they are in most other countries. Demand factors within the United States are particularly conducive to this type of automobile. Americans have access to a very well-developed interstate highway system, the country is large, and Americans travel extensively by automobile. While there are individuals in other countries that purchase station wagons, the largest concentration of consumers of these automobiles resides in the United States. Consequently, the Japanese automobile company, Honda, builds station wagons in the United States, close to its most demanding customers, and exports these to Japan. At the same time, Honda builds sedans in Japan and exports them to the United States.

Increasing returns to scale and learning also furnish a basis for trade independent of comparative advantage. A country could become competitive in a particular product because of a historical accident or because the product appealed to its consumers. Once the firms in this country begin producing the product, the country's "first-mover" advantages become quite significant because of increasing returns to scale and the ability of these firms to climb a learning curve. These firms will be able to lower their unit production costs because of their ever-expanding operations and their continuous learning about how best to produce the product.

These cost advantages will allow firms in this country to out compete their rivals elsewhere. One should note that in trade theories that rely on increasing returns to scale the direction of trade is indeterminate; that is, it is not possible to predict based on any characteristics of any two countries which country will eventually export or which will import. That is entirely dependent upon which country happens to be the "first mover."

A final set of new theories surrounds the role of multinational corporations. These corporations dominate several industries in which there is a significant level of international trade. In fact, trade among affiliates of multinational corporations amounts to some 40 percent of worldwide trade flows. In such cases, contrary to the assumptions of comparative advantage theory, trade cannot be assumed to be a series of discrete arm's-length transactions.

Rather, international trade, in these cases, results more from the competitive strategies of these companies and the strategic actions of governments in these countries than it does from the inherent characteristics of a nation, whether these are supply characteristics or demand characteristics. This leads Yoffie to suggest that "when industries become globally concentrated, visible hands rather than anonymous market forces emerge to guide trade."

For example, Wells points out that bauxite is mined in Ghana and that Ghana is the site of a world-class aluminum smelter built and operated by Kaiser. Ghana imports alumina from Jamaica to feed its aluminum smelter, and it exports bauxite to North America and Europe for conversion and smelting in facilities that are owned by the same companies that own mines in Ghana—this, despite the fact that each step in the conversion process cuts the weight to be shipped by one-half.

These trade effects that would not be predicted by traditional trade theory are explained by the actions of companies operating in oligopolistic industry settings. Much of the world's bauxite is mined and processed by a few vertically integrated firms. These firms, argues Wells, opted to separate their mining and smelting facilities as a hedge against nationalization. It is this set of corporate strategies that explains some components of trade patterns in this industry. These are the new theories of trade. Note that these theories do not displace comparative advantage. Rather, they complement comparative advantage; that is, countries specialize and trade with other countries because of differences in factor endowments, but they also trade with other countries because they were or were not able to capture the economies of scale and learning in a particular industry, because their consumers have tastes that differ from those of consumers in other countries, and because of the corporate and governmental strategies pursued by firms in highly concentrated industries.

These new versions of trade theory are captured in the recent work of business scholars. Porter adds to factor endowments the effect of demand patterns, of the competitive structure of industries, and of linkages among industries in explaining patterns of trade competitiveness. Yoffie argues that country based factors, such as factor endowments and demand patterns, are appropriate for explaining trade patterns in competitive and fragmented industries in which government intervention is low.

In oligopolistic industries where scale and learning effects are critical, however, and in industries in which there is a significant amount of government intervention, it is the dynamics of the global oligopoly, the strategies of these global firms, and the strategies of national governments that will determine the nature of trade flows.

The role of national governments is a particularly controversial one with respect to the impact on trade patterns. There are certain industries, such as commercial aircraft, where the late-mover disadvantages were so great because of the significant economies of scale and steep learning curve that it was inconceivable that a firm could challenge the dominance of the U.S. aerospace industry without government support. It was this argument that, of course, led the European governments to establish the Airbus Consortium in an effort to compete with U.S. firms, Boeing and McDonnell Douglas. It is the subject of the government's role in trade policy to which the remainder of the chapter is devoted.

IMPLICATIONS OF TRADE THEORY FOR TRADE POLICY IN DEVELOPING COUNTRIES

Independent governments in developing countries had never felt particularly comfortable with classical and neoclassical theories of trade. They looked around at developed countries and noted that, without exception, all of these countries were also industrial countries; yet it seemed that comparative advantage trade theory would consign them to forever following their "comparative advantage" in minerals; agricultural products; and light, labourintensive manufactured goods. In the 1950s, under the intellectual tutelage of Raul Prebisch, Hans Singer, and other economists that spawned the dependency school of development, many developing countries decided to ignore the dictates of comparative advantage and instead to restrict trade in an effort to develop their industrial base. The theoretical contribution of Prebisch and Singer was the development of the concept of the declining terms of trade.

A country's terms of trade represents the relationship between the price of a typical unit of exports and the price of a typical unit of imports. Trends in the terms of trade over time are identified by comparing export and import price indices calculated using the same base period. Prebisch argued that developing countries exported primarily mineral and agricultural commodities with low income elasticities (i.e., products for which demand, and therefore price, increased less than proportionately to increases in income).

Developed countries, on the other hand, manufactured and exported goods with higher income elasticities, which saw greater price increases over time. Consequently, developing countries faced declines in their terms of trade. Prebisch's policy advice was that developing countries should seek to avoid this situation by moving into the production of manufactured goods.

Prebisch's analysis found a ready audience throughout the developing world. Jamaica's former prime minister Michael Manley writes in his book, The Poverty of Nations, for example, that when Jamaica became independent in 1962, a tractor could be financed with the proceeds of 18 tons of sugar; by 1980, it took 60 tons of sugar to finance the same tractor. Even though evidence is sketchy and this issue is hotly debated along North-South lines especially, it does appear that there has been a long-term decline in the terms of trade for nonfuel commodities.

During the period of Prebisch's original analysis, Prebisch calculated that England experienced a 36-percent increase in its net barter terms of trade, implying that the countries with which England traded—primarily colonies producing agricultural commodities—experienced a decline in their terms of trade. Between the mid-1950s and 1980, there was little change in the terms of trade for non petroleum-exporting developing countries. Between 1980 and 1990, however, there has been a relatively significant deterioration in the terms of trade for non petroleum-exporting developing countries.

Some analysts would explain away any apparent declines in the terms of trade by suggesting that manufactured products have changed over time. Thus, they would argue that it is inappropriate to compare, as Manley did, a ton of sugar—which is essentially the same in 1980 as it was in 1962—with a tractor that may have changed significantly over the same period.

One suspects that Prebisch and his supporters would have said that whatever the cause of the declining terms of trade, the fact that declines are taking place lends support to the idea that developing countries should move away from commodities and move toward goods that are more likely to increase in price over time. This could be accomplished either by further refining, and thereby adding more value, to resource-based products or by shifting from resource-based products to manufactured goods.

Many developing countries did follow the prescriptive advice of Prebisch and the dependency school and engaged in attempts to develop their economies by shifting from an open trading strategy in which they imported manufactured goods and exported raw materials and commodities to an import-substitution development strategy. In a programme of import substitution, countries placed high tariffs on imported goods in an effort to stimulate the production of domestic goods that would substitute for imports. This trade strategy was exactly the opposite of the open trade strategy prescribed by comparative advantage principles.

This strategy tended to occur in phases. The first, known as the easy stage of import substitution, involved the substitution of domestic production for the import of consumer goods. The development strategy of import substitution was accomplished through the trade strategy of protection. Governments throughout the developing world placed tariffs on imported goods. In the heyday of the import-substitution strategy, these nominal tariffs were often as high as 100 percent on consumer goods.

These nominal tariffs, however, actually understated the extent of protection. This is because governments often allowed firms to import the raw materials that would be used for the assembly of the final products at low or, in extreme cases, zero rates of duty. Such a combination had the effect of making the degree of effective protection much higher than the rate of nominal protection.

Effective protection measures the protection afforded to the value that is added in the production or assembly process locally, compared with the value added to this process overseas. Essentially, it identifies to what extent the sum of local labour, materials, and other local costs can exceed the value that would have to prevail if the firm faced open competition from world markets.

Thus, for example, if a product faces a nominal protection rate of 100 percent, if the imported raw materials that are used to produce this product face no import duties, and if the value that is added in the country granting the tariffs is 50 percent, then a nominal duty of 100 percent translates into an effective rate of protection of 200 percent. That is, if e is the effective tariff rate, n is the nominal tariff rate, and v is the amount of value added internationally, then

$$e = n\ (1/1 - v).$$

To take this example further, if a local company was producing a car for \$10,000, in which 50 percent of the production cost represented local costs, then a 100-percent duty on car imports, coupled with duty-free entry of imported raw materials would allow this company to increase its local costs from \$5,000 to \$15,000 and still remain competitive with imported cars.

During the period when import substitution was a popular development strategy, rates of effective protection in developing countries were, in fact, quite high. Average effective rates of protection were at about 200 percent for India and Pakistan during the 1960s. In the early 1980s, the average effective rate of protection in Indonesia was 124 percent for all sectors; but for the manufacturing sector, effective protection was an astounding 305 percent.

Not surprising, in retrospect, the development strategy of import-substitution industrialization had many unintended consequences. Firms producing in domestic markets with the high effective rates of protection that prevailed in most of the developing countries that undertook this strategy had little incentive to operate efficiently. Indeed, many of the firms that benefited from this protection and operated inefficiently behind high tariff walls were foreign firms invited into developing countries by governments following the path of import substitution by invitation.

Further, these firms invariably stayed at the easy stage of import substitution, rarely developing backward linkages to other sectors because of the attractiveness of the consumer goods sector. Consequently, imports of raw materials continued to burden the balance of payments of developing countries. Last, in concert with the import-substitution strategy, many developing country governments maintained overvalued exchange rates that made it less costly to import raw materials; but that hurt those entities seeking to export to world markets.

This was not an automatic consequence of an import substitution industrialization strategy, but most countries that pursued such a strategy maintained overvalued exchange rates.

By the 1980s, most developing-country governments were admitting that import-substitution strategies had not been particularly successful. That is not to say that there were not pockets of success. Particularly in large countries, import-substitution strategies created a rather broad industrial infrastructure.

India, for example, has probably the broadest and deepest industrial infrastructure in the developing world, producing a range of products from pins to satellites. In part, this is because of the intensity with which India pursued an import-substitution strategy, maintaining extremely high nominal and effective rates of protection for decades.

Although India achieved a measure of self-sufficiency through this development strategy, the Indian experience also points to the inadequacies of this strategy. Some forty years after the initiation of an import-substitution strategy, Indian industry continued, in large part, to operate quite inefficiently by world standards. For example, in the late 1980s, most automobiles driven in India were produced within that country, a feat matched by only one other developing country—Korea. In contrast to Korea, however, Indian cars were produced based on 1950s automotive technology.

Other data reported by the World Bank indicate a strong positive correlation between productivity growth and open trade strategies in a sample of developing countries in the periods of 1960 to 1984 and 1977 to 1988.

The mounting evidence pointing to the problems associated with a highly protectionist trade strategy in pursuit of development through import substitution has led many countries to reconsider this strategy and to move, instead, to a strategy of development via export promotion. The principle behind this strategy is to promote exports from the developing country by putting in place certain elements. One important element associated with an export-promo propriate point on the industry learning curve before they are able to penetrate export markets.

Indeed, this is no more than the classic infant-industry argument for protection. The countries of East Asia that are held out as models of export promotion—particularly Japan and South Korea—did, in fact, use protectionist trade be at the loss of another. A significant concern also is that developed countries are restricting their markets at the same time as developing countries are seeking to increase their exports.

5

The Market of Hospitality

A market is a social arrangement that allows buyers and sellers to discover information and carry out a voluntary exchange of goods or services. It is one of the two key institutions that organize trade, along with the right to own property. Allowing markets to arrive at a pareto efficient outcome is one of the key components of capitalism. In everyday usage, the word "market" may refer to the location where goods are traded, sometimes known as a marketplace, or to a street market.

The function of a market requires, at a minimum, that both parties expect to become better off as a result of the transaction. Markets generally rely on price adjustments to provide information to parties engaging in a transaction, so that each may accurately gauge the subsequent change of their welfare. In less sophisticated markets, such as those involving barter, individual buyers and sellers must engage in a more lengthy process of haggling in order to gain the same information. Markets are efficient when the price of a good or service attracts exactly as much demand as the market can currently supply. The chief function of a market, then, is to adjust prices to accommodate fluctuations in supply and demand in order to achieve allocative efficiency. An economic system in which goods and services are exchanged by market functions is called a market economy. An alternative economic system in which non-market forces (often government mandates) determine prices are called planned economies or command economies. The attempt to combine socialist ideals with the incentive system of a market is known as market socialism.

Although many markets exist in the traditional sense—such as a flea market—there are various other types of them and various organizational structures to assist their functions. A market can be organized as an auction, as a shopping center, as a complex institution such as a stock market, and as an informal discussion between two individuals.

In economics, a market that runs under laissez-faire policies is a free market. It is "free" in the sense that the government makes no attempt to intervene through taxes, subsidies, minimum wages, price ceilings, etc. Markets may be distorted by a seller or sellers with monopoly power, or a buyer with monopsony power. Also, the level of organization or negotiation power of buyers, markedly affects the functioning of the market. Markets where price negotiations do not arrive at efficient outcomes for both sides are said to experience market failure.

Most markets are regulated by state wide laws and regulations. While barter markets exist, most markets use currency or some other form of money. Markets of varying types can spontaneously arise whenever a party has interest in a good or service that some other party can provide. Hence there can be a market for cigarettes in correctional facilities, another for chewing gum in a playground, and yet another for contracts for the future delivery of a commodity.

Market failure

If advertising is poor, definitely there will be market failure. Market failure is a term used to describe a situation in which markets do not efficiently allocate goods and services. To economists, the term would normally be applied to situations where the inefficiency is particularly dramatic, or when it is suggested that non-market institutions (such as public policing and firefighting) would be more efficient and wealth-producing than their private alternatives.

On the other hand, the term "market failure" is also often used to describe situations where market forces do not serve the perceived public interest. In this article, however, the focus is on market failure as defined by mainstream economics. Economists use model-like theorems to explain or understand such cases. The two main reasons that markets fail are:

- The inadequate expression of costs or benefits in prices and thus into microeconomic decision-making in markets.
- Sub-optimal market structures.

The existence of a market failure in a certain economic activity is often used as an argument that the activity in question should not be directed by market forces. This generally leads to a debate on the question of what - if anything - should be used to replace markets. The most common response to a market failure in the present day is to use the government to produce certain goods and services. However, government intervention may cause nonmarket failure by the intevention itself causing externalitites.

Types of Market Failures

Imperfect Competition

In economic theory, imperfect competition, is the competitive situation in any market where the conditions necessary for perfect competition are not satisfied.

Forms of imperfect competition include:

- Monopoly, in which there is only one seller of a good.

- Oligopoly, in which there is a small number of sellers.
- Monopolistic competition, in which there are many sellers producing highly differentiated goods.
- Monopsony, in which there is only one buyer of a good.
- Oligopsony, in which there is a small number of buyers.

There may also be imperfect competition in markets due to buyers or sellers lacking information about prices and the goods being traded. There may also be imperfect competition due to a time lag in a market. For example, in the 1990s, there was a shortage of computer programmers, but becoming a skilled programmer requires several years of experience. This drove up salaries. Another example is the "jobless recovery". There are many growth opportunities available after a recession, but it takes time for employers to react, leading to high unemployment. High unemployment decreases wages, which makes hiring more attractive, but it takes time for new jobs to be created.

Market Power

In economics, market power is the ability of a firm to alter the market price of a good or service. A firm with market power can raise price without losing all customers to competitors. When a firm has market power it faces a downward-sloping demand curve. In perfectly competitive markets, market participants have no market power. A firm with market power has the ability to individually affect either the total quantity or the prevailing price in the market. If the demand curve is downward sloping (that is, the most common situation where price increases lead to a lower quantity demanded), then the decrease in supply as a result of the exercise of market power creates an economic deadweight loss in comparison with a situation of perfect competition. This is often viewed as socially undesirable, and as a result, many countries have anti-trust or other legislation with the aim of limiting the ability of firms to accrue market power. Such legislation often regulates mergers and sometimes introduces a judicial power to compel divestiture.

A firm usually has market power by virtue of it controlling a large portion of the market. In extreme cases - monopoly and monopsony - the firm controls the entire market. However, market size alone is not a good indicator of market power. Highly concentrated markets may be contestable if there are no barriers to entry or exit, limiting the incumbent firm's ability to raise its price above competitive levels.

Market power gives firms the ability to engage in unilateral anti-competitive behaviour. Some of the behaviours that firms with market power are accused of engaging in include predatory pricing, product tying, and creation of overcapacity or other barriers to entry. If no individual participant in the market has significant market power, then anti-competitive behaviour can take place only through collusion, or the exercise of a group of participants' collective market power.

When several firms control a significant share of market sales, the resulting market structure is called an oligopoly or oligopsony. An oligopoly may engage in collusion, either tacit or overt, and thereby exercize market power. An explicit agreement in an oligopoly to affect market price or output is called a cartel. The behaviour of firms in perfect competition or monopoly can be treated as a simple optimization, but an oligopoly requires game theoretic analysis.

Monopoly power is an example of market failure which occurs when one or more of the participants has the ability to influence the price or other outcomes in some general or specialized market. The most commonly discussed form of market power is that of a monopoly, but other forms such as monopsony, and more moderate versions of these two extremes, exist. Market participants that have market power are sometimes referred to as "price makers", while those without are sometimes called "price takers".

A well known example of monopolistic market power is Microsoft's market share in PC operating systems. The United States v. Microsoft case concerned the allegation that Microsoft illegally exercised its market power by bundling its web browser with its operating system. Some have suggested that Wal Mart exercises monopsonistic market power; its size allows it to extract extremely low prices from its suppliers.

Monopoly

In economics, is defined as a persistent market situation where there is only one provider of a product or service. Monopolies are characterized by a lack of economic competition for the good or service that they provide and a lack of viable substitute goods. Monopoly should be distinguished from monopsony, in which there is only one buyer of the product or service; it should also, strictly, be distinguished from the (similar) phenomenon of a cartel. In a monopoly a single firm is the sole provider of a product or service; in a cartel a centralized institution is set up to partially coordinate the actions of several independent providers.

STRATEGIES IN MARKETING

Marketing strategy is a powerful process that gives an organization a competitive advantage in the marketplace. While just defining a marketing strategy will not automatically create a competitive advantage, it will allow the organization to concentrate its (always limited) resources on the greatest opportunities to increase sales and achieve a sustainable competitive advantage.

The word strategy comes from the Greek word strategos meaning general. Strategy is what generals use to win battles. Thus properly understood, marketing strategy is a high-level exercise involving the "generals" of the organization in determining how to build on the firm's strengths while (ethically) taking advantage of competitors' weaknesses. Marketing strategy is most effective when it is a vital component of corporate strategy, defining how the organization will engage customers, prospects and the competition in the market arena for consistent success.

A marketing strategy also serves as the foundation of a marketing plan. A marketing plan contains a set of specific actions required to successfully implement a specific marketing strategy. For example: "Use a low cost product to attract consumers. Once our organization, via our low cost product, has established a relationship with consumers, our organization will sell additional, higher-margin products and services that enhance the consumer's interaction with the low-cost product or service."

A strategy is different from a tactic. While it is possible to write a tactical marketing plan without a sound, well-considered strategy, it is not recommended. Without a sound marketing strategy, a marketing plan has no foundation. Marketing strategies serve as the fundamental underpinning of marketing plans designed to reach marketing objectives. It is important that these objectives have measurable results. A good marketing strategy should integrate an organization's marketing goals, policies, and action sequences (tactics) into a cohesive whole. The objective of a marketing strategy is to provide a foundation from which a tactical plan is developed. This allows the organization to carry out its mission effectively and efficiently.

Marketing strategies are partially derived from broader corporate strategies, corporate missions, and corporate goals. They should flow from the firm's mission statement. They are also influenced by a range of microenvironmental factors. Marketing strategies are dynamic and interactive. They are partially planned and partially unplanned.

Commercial Planning

In the modern world of business, it is useless to be a creative original thinker unless you can also sell what you create. Management cannot be expected to recognize a good idea unless it is presented to them by a good salesman. The success of a new product depends not only on the idea behind the product, but also on the marketing of the new product before, during and after the product launch. Commercializing a product is commonly known as Commercial Planning. No concrete methods are currently available for New Product Launching (NPL). However, several articles are published about NPL and the essential activities, to launch a new product. This article describes a set of activities and products, that are essential for launching a new product. New Product Launching is part of the New Product Development method.

Strategic Management

An organization's strategy must be appropriate for its resources, environmental circumstances, and core objectives. The process involves matching the company's internal resources (eg IT) and capabilities (eg quality management) to the external business environment the organization faces.

Strategy formulation involves:

- Doing a situation analysis: both internal and external; both micro-environmental and macro-environmental.
- Concurrent with this assessment, objectives are set. This involves crafting vision statements (long term view of a possible future), mission statements (the role that the organization gives itself in society), overall corporate objectives (both financial and strategic), strategic business unit objectives (both financial and strategic), and tactical objectives.
- These objectives should, in the light of the situation analysis, suggest a strategic plan. The plan provides the details of how to achieve these objectives.

This three-step strategy formulation process is sometimes referred to as determining where you are now, determining where you want to go, and then determining how to get there. These three questions are the essence of strategic planning. SWOT Analysis: I/O Economics for the external factors and RBV for the internal factors.

Strategy implementation involves:

- Allocation of sufficient resources (financial, personnel, time, technology support)
- Establishing a chain of command or some alternative structure (such as cross functional teams)
- Assigning responsibility of specific tasks or processes to specific individuals or groups
- It also involves managing the process. This includes monitoring results, comparing to benchmarks and best practices, evaluating the efficacy and efficiency of the process, controlling for variances, and making adjustments to the process as necessary.
- When implementing specific programs, this involves acquiring the requisite resources, developing the process, training, process testing, documentation, and integration with (and/or conversion from) legacy processes.

Strategy formulation and implementation is an on-going, never-ending, integrated process requiring continuous reassessment and reformation. Strategic management is dynamic. It involves a complex pattern of actions and reactions. It is partially planned and partially unplanned. Strategy is both planned and emergent, dynamic, and interactive. Some people (such as Andy Grove at Intel) feel that there are critical points at which a strategy must take a new direction in order to be in step with a changing business environment. These critical points of change are called strategic inflection points.

Strategic management operates on several time scales. Short term strategies involve planning and managing for the present. Long term strategies involve preparing for and preempting the future. Marketing strategist Derek Abell (1993), has suggested that understanding this dual nature of strategic management is the least understood part of the process. He claims that balancing the temporal aspects of strategic planning requires the use of dual strategies simultaneously.

Strategic Management is actually a solid foundation or a framework within which all the functionning managerial operations are bundled together. This is the highest level corporate activity that sets the terms and goals for a company that it should follow for prosperity.

Strategic management techniques can be viewed as bottom-up, top-down, or collaborative processes. In the bottom-up approach, employees submit proposals to their managers who, in turn, funnel the best ideas further up the organization. This is often accomplished by a capital budgeting process. Proposals are assessed using financial criteria such as return on investment or cost-benefit analysis. The proposals that are approved form the substance of a new strategy, all of which is done without a grand strategic design or a strategic architect. The top-down approach is the most common by far. In it, the CEO, possibly with the assistance of a strategic planning team, decides on the overall direction the company should take. Some organizations are starting to experiment with collaborative strategic planning techniques that recognize the emergent nature of strategic decisions.

In most (large) corporations there are several levels of strategy. Strategic management is the highest in the sense that it is the broadest, applying to all parts of the firm. It gives direction to corporate values, corporate culture, corporate goals, and corporate missions. Under this broad corporate strategy there are often functional or business unit strategies.

Functional strategies include marketing strategies, new product development strategies, human resource strategies, financial strategies, legal strategies, and information technology management strategies. The emphasis is on short and medium term plans and is limited to the domain of each department's functional responsibility. Each functional department attempts to do its part in meeting overall corporate objectives, and hence to some extent their strategies are derived from broader corporate strategies.

Many companies feel that a functional organizational structure is not an efficient way to organize activities so they have reengineered according to processes or strategic business units (called SBUs). A strategic business unit is a semi-autonomous unit within an organization. It is usually responsible for its own budgeting, new product decisions, hiring decisions, and price setting. An SBU is treated as an internal profit centre by corporate headquarters. Each SBU is responsible for developing its business strategies, strategies that must be in tune with broader corporate strategies. The "lowest" level of strategy is operational strategy. It is very narrow in focus and deals with day-to-day operational activities such as scheduling criteria. It must operate within a budget but is not at liberty to adjust or create that budget. Operational level strategy was encouraged by Peter Drucker in his theory of management by objectives (MBO). Operational level strategies are informed by business level strategies which, in turn, are informed by corporate level strategies. Business strategy, which refers to the aggregated operational strategies of single business firm or that of an SBU in a diversified corporation refers to the way in which a firm competes in its chosen arenas.

Corporate strategy, then, refers to the overarching strategy of the diversified firm. Such corporate strategy answers the questions of "in which businesses should we compete?" and "how does being in one business add to the competitive advantage of another portfolio firm, as well as the competitive advantage of the corporation as a whole?"

Since the turn of the millennium, there has been a tendency in some firms to revert to a simpler strategic structure. This is being driven by information technology. It is felt that knowledge management systems should be used to share information and create common goals. Strategic divisions are thought to hamper this process. Most recently, this notion of strategy has been captured under the rubric of dynamic strategy, popularized by the strategic management textbook authored by Carpenter and Sanders. This work builds on that of Brown and Eisenhart as well as Christensen and portrays firm strategy, both business and corporate, as necessarily embracing ongoing strategic change, and the seamless integration of strategy formulation and implementation. Such change and implementation are usually built into the strategy through the staging and pacing facets.

Management by Objectives (MBO) is a process of agreeing upon objectives within an organization so that management and employees buy in to the objectives and understand what they are. Management By Objectives term was first popularized by Peter Drucker in 1954 in his book 'The Practice of Management'.

It is all too easy for managers to fail to outline, and agree with their employees, what it is that everyone is trying to achieve. MBO substitutes for good intentions a process that requires rather precise written description of objectives (for the period ahead) and timelines for their monitoring and achievement. The process requires that the manager and the employee agree to what the employee will attempt to achieve in the period ahead, and (very important) that the employee accept and buy into the objectives (otherwise commitment will be lacking).

For example, whatever else a manager and employee may discuss and agree in their regular discussions, let us suppose that they feel that it will be sensible to introduce a key performance indicator to show the development of sales revenue in a part of the firm. Then the manager and the employee need to discuss what is being planned, what the time-schedule is and what the indicator might or might not be. Thereafter the two of them should liaise to ensure that the objective is being attended to and will be delivered on time.

Organizations have scarce resources and so it is incumbent on the managers to consider the level of resourcing but also to consider whether the objectives that are jointly agreed within the firm are the right ones and represent the best allocation of effort. Also, reliable Management information systems are needed to establish relevant objectives and monitor their "reach ratio" in an objective way.

MBO is often achieved using set targets. MBO introduced the SMART criteria: Objectives for MBO must be SMART (Specific, Measurable, Agreed, Realistic, and Time-Specific). However, it has been reported in recent years that this style of management receives criticism in that it triggers employees' unethical behaviour of distorting the system or financial figures to achieve the targets set by their short-term, narrow bottom-line, and completely self-centered thinking.

Marketing Strategy Tools and Models

Ansoffs Matrix

A common tool used within marketing was developed by Igor Ansoff in 1957. His model gives organisation five strategic business options.

1. Market Penetration: This involves increasing sales of an existing product and penetrating the market further by either promoting the product heavily or reducing prices to increase sales.
2. Product Development: The organisation develops new products to aim within their existing market, in the hope that they will gain more custom and market share. For Example Sony launching the Playstation 2 to replace their existing model.
3. Market Development: The organisation here adopts a strategy of selling existing products to new markets. This can be done either by a better understanding of segmentation, i.e who else can possibly purchase the product or selling the product to new markets overseas.
4. Diversification: Moving away from what you are selling (your core activities) to providing something new eg Moving over from selling foods to selling cars.
5. Consolidation: Where the organisation adopts a strategy of withdrawing from particular markets, scaling back on operations and concentrating on its existing products in existing markets.

Product Life Cycle

The product life cycle concept suggests that a product passes through four stages of evolution. Introduction, growth, maturity and decline. As a product evolves and passes through theses four stages profit is affected, and different strategies have to be employed to ensure that the product is a success within its market. As a new product much time will be spent by the organisation to create awareness of it presence amongst its target market. Profits are negative or low because of this reason.

Growth: If consumer clearly feels that this product will benefit them in some ways and they accept it, the organisation will see a period of rapid sales growth.

Maturity: Rapid sales growth cannot last forever. Sales slow down as the product sales reach peak as it has been accepted by most buyers.

Decline: Sales and profits start to decline, the organisation may try to change their pricing strategy to stimulate growth, however the product will either have to be re-modified, or replaced within the market.

Value Chain Analysis

Michael Porter in 1985 introduced in his book ' The competitive advantage' the concept of the Value Chain. He suggested that activities within the organisation add value to the service and products that the organisation produces, and all these activities should be run at optimum level if the organisation is to gain any real competitive advantage. If they are run efficiently the value obtained should exceed the costs of running them i.e. customers should return to the organisation and transact freely and willingly. Michael Porter suggested that the organisation is split into 'primary activities' and 'support activities'.

Primary Activities

Inbound logistics: Refers to goods being obtained from the organisations suppliers ready to be used for producing the end product.

Operations: The raw materials and goods obtained are manufactured into the final product. Value is added to the product at this stage as it moves through the production line.

Outbound logistics: Once the products have been manufactured they are ready to be distributed to distribution centres, wholesalers, retailers or customers.

Marketing and Sales: Marketing must make sure that the product is targeted towards the correct customer group. The marketing mix is used to establish an effective strategy, any competitive advantage is clearly communicated to the target group by the use of the promotional mix. Services: After the product/service has been sold what support services does the organisation have to offer. This may come in the form of after sales training, guarantees and warranties.

With the above activities, any or a combination of them, maybe essential for the firm to develop the competitive advantage which Porter talks about in his book.

Support Activities

The support activities assist the primary activities in helping the organisation achieve its competitive advantage. They include:

Procurement: This department must source raw materials for the organisation and obtain the best price for doing so. For the price they must obtain the best possible quality

Technology development: The use of technology to obtain a competitive advantage within the organisation. This is very important in today's technological driven environment. Technology can be used in production to reduce cost thus add value, or in research and development to develop new products, or via the use of the internet so customers have access to online facilities.

Human resource management: The organisation will have to recruit, train and develop the correct people for the organisation if they are to succeed in their objectives. Staff will have to be motivated and paid the 'market rate' if they are to stay with the organisation and add value to it over their duration of employment. Within the service sector eg airlines it is the 'staff' who may offer the competitive advantage that is needed within the field.

Firm infrastructure: Every organisations needs to ensure that their finances, legal structure and management structure works efficiently and helps drive the organisation forward.

As you can see the value chain encompasses the whole organisation and looks at how primary and support activities can work together effectively and efficiently to help gain the organisation a superior competitive advantage.

SWOT Analysis

A tool used by organisations to help the firm establish its Strengths, Weaknesses, Opportunities and Threats (SWOT). A SWOT analysis is used as a framework to help the firm develop its overall corporate, marketing, or product strategies. Note:Strengths and Weaknesses are internal factors which are controllable by the organisation. Opportunities & threats are external factors which are uncontrollable by the organisation.

Strength examples could include:

- A strong brand name.
- Market share.
- Good reputation.

- Expertise and skill.
- Weaknesses could include:
- Low or no market share.
- No brand loyalty.
- Lack of experience.
- Opportunities could include:
- A growing market.
- Increased consumer spending.
- Selling internationally.
- Changes in society beneficial to your company.

Threats could include:

- Competitors
- Government policy eg taxation, laws
- Changes in society not beneficial to your company

A SWOT analysis is an excellent tool to use if the organisation wants to take a step back and assess the situation they are in. Issues raised from the analysis are then used to assist the organisation in developing their marketing mix strategy. A SWOT analysis must form the part of any prudent marketing strategy.

Generic Strategies

For an organisation to obtain a sustainable competitive advantage Michael Porter suggested that they should follow either one of three generic strategies.

Strategy one: Cost Leadership

This strategy involves the organisation aiming to be the lowest cost producer within their industry. The orgainisation aims to drive cost down through all the elements of the production of the product from sourcing, to labour costs. The cost leader usually aims at a broad market, so sufficient sales can cover costs. Low cost producers include Easyjet airline, Ryan air, Asda and Walmart. Some organisation may aim to drive costs down but will not pass on these cost savings to their customers aiming for increased profits clearly because their brand can command a premium rate.

Strategy 2: Differentiation

To be different, is what organisations strive for. Having a competitive advantage which allows the company and its products ranges to stand out is crucial for their success. With a differentiation strategy the organisation aims to focus its effort on particular segments and charge for the added differentiated value. If we look at Brompton folding cycles their compact design differentiates them from other folding bike companies. New concepts which allow for differentiation can be patented, however patents have a certain life span and organisation always face the danger that their idea that gives the competitive advantage will be copied in one form or another.

Strategy 3: Niche strategies

Here the organisation focuses its effort on one particular segment and becomes well known for providing products/services within the segment. They form a competitive advantage for this niche market and either succeed by being a low cost producer or differentiator within that particular segment. Examples include Roll Royce and Bentley.

Are you 'Stuck in the Middle'

The danger some organisation face is that they try to do all three and become what is known as stuck in the middle. The have no clear business strategy, be all to all consumers, which adds to their running costs causing a fall in sales and market share. 'Stuck in the middle' companies are usually subject to a takeover or merger.

Industry Analysis Model

Porters fives forces model is an excellent model to use to analyse a particular environment of an industry. So for example, if we were entering the PC industry, we would use porters model to help us find out about:

1) Competitive Rivalry
2) Power of suppliers
3) Power of buyers
4) Threats of substitutes
5) Threat of new entrants.

The above five main factors are key factors that influence industry performance, hence it is common sense and practical to find out about these factors before you enter the industry.

Competitive Rivalry

A starting point to analysing the industry is to look at competitive rivalry. If entry to an industry is easy then competitive rivalry will likely to be high. If it is easy for customers to move to substitute products for example from coke to water then again rivalry will be high. Generally competitive rivalry will be high if:

- There is little differentiation between the products sold between customers.
- Competitors are approximately the same size of each other.
- If the competitors all have similar strategies.
- It is costly to leave the industry hence they fight to just stay in (exit barriers)

Power of Suppliers

Suppliers are also essential for the success of an organisation. Raw materials are needed to complete the finish product of the organisation. Suppliers do have power. This power comes from:

- If they are the only supplier or one of few suppliers who supply that particular raw material.
- If it costly for the organisation to move from one supplier to another (known also as switching cost)
- If there is no other substitute for their product.

Power of Buyers

Buyers or customers can exert influence and control over an industry in certain circumstances. This happens when:

- There is little differentiation over the product and substitutes can be found easily.
- Customers are sensitive to price.
- Switching to another product is not costly.

Threat of Substitutes

Are there alternative products that customers can purchase over your product that offer the same benefit for the same or less price? The threat of substitute is high when:

- Price of that substitute product falls.
- It is easy for consumers to switch from one substitute product to another.
- Buyers are willing to substitute.

Threat of New Entrant

The threat of a new organisation entering the industry is high when it is easy for an organisation to enter the industry i.e. entry barriers are low.

An organisation will look at how loyal customers are to existing products, how quickly they can achieve economy of scales, would they have access to suppliers, would government legislation prevent them or encourage them to enter the industry.

So to summaries porters five forces model is essential to carry to help you understand your industry in depth before you enter it.

Diffusion of Innovation

This extension of the product life cycle was developed by Everett M. Rogers in 1962 and simply looks who adopts products at the different stages of the life cycle.

Rogers identified five types of purchasers as the product moves through its life cycle stage. He suggested:

1. Innovator who make up 2.5% of all purchases of the product, purchase the product at the beginning of the life cycle. They are not afraid of trying new products that suit their lifestyle and will also pay a premium for that benefit.
2. Early Adopters make up 13.5% of purchases, they are usually opinion leaders and naturally adopt products after the innovators. This group of purchasers are crucial because adoption by them means the product becomes acceptable, spurring on later purchasers.
3. Early Majority make up 34% of purchases and have been spurred on by the early adopters. They wait to see if the product will be adopted by society and will purchase only when this has happened. They early majority usually have some status in society.
4. Late Majority make up another 34% of sales and usually purchase the product at the late stages of majority within the life cycle.
5. Laggards make up 16% of total sales and usually purchase the product near the end of its life. They are the 'wait and see' group. They wait to see if the product will get cheaper. Usually when they purchase the product a new version is already on the market. Some may call Laggards, bargain hunters!

Boston Consultancy Group (BCG Matrix)

This product portfolio matrix classifies product lines into four categories. The BCG models suggests that organisations should have a healthy balance of products within their range. The Boston Consultancy Group classified these products as following:

Question Mark/Problem Child

These are products with low market share but operate in high market growth rates. The company puts a lot of resources in this product in the hope that it will eventually increase market share and generate cash returns in the future.

Star

Stars have high market shares that operate in growing markets. The product at this stage should be generating positive returns for the company.

Cash Cow

Cash Cow are products at the mature stage of the lifecycle, they generate high amounts of cash for the company, but growth rate is slowing. There are chances that the product may slip into decline, appropriate marketing mix strategies should be employed to try to prevent this from happening.

Managing income

Accounting (methodology) is the measurement, disclosure or provision of assurance about financial information that helps managers, investors, tax authorities and other decision makers make resource allocation decisions. The names come from the use of financial accounts. Financial accounting is one branch of accounting and historically has involved processes by which financial information about a business is recorded, classified, summarized, interpreted, and communicated. Accounting is also widely referred to as the "language of business".

Auditing, a related but separate discipline, has two sub-disciplines: Internal and External auditing. External auditing is the process whereby an independent auditor examines an organization's financial statements and accounting records in order to express an opinion — that conveys reasonable but not absolute assurance — as to the truth and fairness of the statements and the accountant's adherence to Generally Accepted Accounting Principles (GAAP), in all material respects.

Internal auditing is an examination in which management, and not the external public, is the main beneficiary. It is carried out usually by auditors employed by the company, but sometimes by external service providers. The internal auditor's role is broader, and basically depends on what kind of assurance management wants. It usually certifies the efficiency and effectiveness of processes, departments, projects or internal controls. The Institute of Internal Auditors is generally accepted as the custodian of Internal Auditing best practice.

At the heart of accounting is the measurement of financial transactions which are transfers of legal property rights made under contractual relationships. Non-financial transactions are specifically excluded due to conservatism and materiality principles.

Practitioners of accountancy are known as accountants. There are many professional bodies for accountants throughout the world. Many allow their members to use titles indicating their membership. Examples are Chartered Certified Accountant (ACCA or FCCA), Chartered Accountant (FCA, CA or ACA) and Certified Public Accountant (CPA).

Accountancy attempts to create accurate financial reports that are useful to managers, regulators, and other stakeholders such as shareholders, creditors, or owners. The day-to-day record-keeping involved in this process is known as bookkeeping.

At the heart of modern financial accounting is the double-entry bookkeeping system. This system involves making at least two entries for every transaction: a debit in one account, and a corresponding credit in another account. The sum of all debits should always equal the sum of all credits. This provides an easy way to check for errors. This system was first used in medieval Europe, although claims have been made that the system dates back to Ancient Greece. According to critics of standard accounting practices, it has changed little since. Accounting reform measures of some kind have been taken in each generation to attempt to keep bookkeeping relevant to capital assets or production capacity. However, these have not changed the basic principles, which are supposed to be independent of economics as such. In recent times, the divergence of accounting from economic principles has resulted in controversial reforms to make financial reports more indicative of economic reality.

Accountancy's infancy dates back to the earliest days of human agriculture and civilization (the Sumerians in Mesopotamia), when the need to maintain accurate records of the quantities and relative values of agricultural products first arose. Simple accounting is mentioned in the Christian Bible in the book of Matthew, in the Parable of the Talents (Matt. 25:19). Twelfth century writer Ibn Taymiyyah mentioned in his book Hisba (verification, calculation), detailed accounting systems used by the Muslims as early as in the mid-seventh century. The accounting practices were influenced by the Roman and the Persian civilizations that Muslims interacted with. The most detailed example of a complex governmental accounting system is the Divan of Umar, the second Caliph of Islam in which all revenues and disbursements were recorded. The Divan of Umar has been described in detail by various Islamic historians and was used by Muslim rulers with mofidications and enhancements until the fall of the Ottoman Empire.

Applied Modern Accountancy in Hotel

The first book on accounting was written by a Croatian merchant Benedetto Cotrugli, who is also known as Benedikt Kotruljeviæ, from the city of Dubrovnik. During his life in Italy he met many merchants and decided to write, Della Mercatvra et del Mercante Perfetto (On Trade and the Perfect Merchant) in which he elaborated on the principles of modern, double-entry book-keeping. He finished his lifework in 1458. However, his work was not published until 1573, as a result of which his contributions to the field have been overlooked by the general public.

For this reason, Luca Pacioli, also known as Friar Luca dal Borgo, is credited for the "birth" of accounting. His Summa de arithmetica, geometrica, proportioni et proportionalita (Venice 1494), a synthesis of the mathematical knowledge of his time, includes the first published description of the method of keeping accounts that Venetian merchants used at that time, known as the double-entry accounting system. Although Pacioli codified rather than invented this system, he is widely regarded as the "Father of Accounting". The system he published included most of the accounting cycle as we know it today. He described the use of journals and ledgers, and warned that a person should not go to sleep at night until the debits equalled the credits! His ledger had accounts for assets (including receivables and inventories), liabilities, capital, income, and expenses — the account categories that are reported on an organization's balance sheet and income statement, respectively. He demonstrated year-end closing entries and proposed that a trial balance be used to prove a balanced ledger. His treatise also touches on a wide range of related topics from accounting ethics to cost accounting.

The first known book in the English language on accounting was published in London by John Gouge (or Gough) in 1543. It is described as A Profitable Treatyce called the Instrument or Boke to learn to knowe the good order of the kepyng of the famouse reconynge, called in Latin, Dare and Habere, and, in English, Debitor and Creditor.

A short book of instructions was also published in 1588 by John Mellis of Southwark, in which he says, "I am but the renuer and reviver of an ancient old copie printed here in London the 14 of August 1543: collected, published, made, and set forth by one Hugh Oldcastle, Scholemaster, who, as appeareth by his treatise, then taught Arithmetics, and this booke in Saint Ollaves parish in Marko Lane." John Mellis refers to the fact that the principle of accounts he explains (which is a simple system of double entry) is "after the forme of Venice".

A book described as The Merchants Mirrour, or directions for the perfect ordering and keeping of his accounts formed by way of Debitor and Creditor, after the (so termed) Italian manner, by Richard Dafforne, accountant, published in 1635, contains many references to early books on the science of accountancy. In a chapter in this book, headed "Opinion of Book-keeping's Antiquity," the author states, on the authority of another writer, that the form of book-keeping referred to had then been in use in Italy about two hundred years, "but that the same, or one in many parts very like this, was used in the time of Julius Caesar, and in Rome long before."

An early Dutch writer appears to have suggested that double-entry book-keeping was even in existence among the Greeks, pointing to scientific accountancy having been invented in remote times.

There were several editions of Richard Dafforne's book - the second edition in 1636, the third in 1656, and another in 1684. The book is a very complete treatise on scientific accountancy, beautifully prepared and containing elaborate explanations. The numerous editions tend to prove that the science was highly appreciated in the 17th century. From this time on, there has been a continuous supply of literature on the subject, many of the authors styling themselves accountants and teachers of the art, and thus proving that the professional accountant was then known and employed.

The requirements for entry in the profession of accounting vary from country to country. Accountants may be licensed by a variety of organisations, such as the British qualified accountancy bodies including Association of Chartered Certified Accountants (ACCA) and Institute of Chartered

Accountants, and are recognized by titles such as Chartered Certified Accountant (ACCA or FCCA) and Chartered Accountant (UK, Australia, New Zealand, Canada, India, Pakistan, South Africa), Certified Public Accountant (Ireland, Japan, US, Singapore, Hong Kong, the Philippines), Certified Management Accountant (Canada, U.S.), Certified General Accountant (Canada), or Certified Practising Accountant (Australia). Some Commonwealth countries (Australia and Canada) often recognise both the certified and chartered accounting bodies.

The majority of "public" accountants in New Zealand and Canada are Chartered Accountants; however, Certified General Accountants are also authorized by legislation to practise public accounting and auditing in all Canadian provinces, except Ontario and Quebec, as of 2005. There is, however, no legal requirement for an accountant to be a paid-up member of one of the many Institutes and other bodies which are effectively a form of professional trade union. Unlike the Law Society, which can legally stop a solicitor from practising, accountancy institutes do not have such authority. However, auditors are regulated.

Before the Enron and other accounting scandals, there were five large firms and were called the Big Five. Since Arthur Andersen's assurance practice split (after the firm was found guilty in the Enron scandal), with a plurality joining KPMG in the US and Deloitte & Touche outside of the US, Arthur Andersen left from the group. Previous to this there were also groupings referred to as the "Big Six" (Arthur Andersen, plus Coopers & Lybrand before its merger with Price Waterhouse) and the "Big Eight" (Ernst and Young prior to their merger were Ernst & Whinney and Arthur Young and Deloitte & Touche was formed by the merger of Deloitte, Haskins and Sells with the firm Touche Ross).

Enron turned out to be only the first of a series of accounting scandals that enveloped the accounting industry in 2002. This is likely to have far-reaching consequences for the U.S. accounting industry. Application of International Accounting Standards originating in International Accounting Standards Board headquartered in London and bearing more resemblance to UK than current US practices is often advocated by those who note the relative stability of the UK accounting system (which reformed itself after scandals in the late 1980s and early 1990s). Accounting reform of a far more comprehensive sort is advocated by those who see issues with capitalism or economics, and seek ecological or social accountability.

According to Accountancy Age's 2005 league table, fee income amongst the Top 50 accounting firms in the UK rose from £6.3bn to £7.0bn. This followed two successive years in which fee income had declined, largely a result of the sale by some of the larger firms of their consultancy arms. Fee income in most business areas - audit, tax, corporate finance and consultancy - rose in the 2005 survey, with insolvency and wealth management being the only segments where revenue fell.

PricewaterhouseCoopers remains the largest firm with fee income totalling £1,780m followed by Deloitte (£1,350m), KPMG (£1,066m) and Ernst & Young (£945m). The combined revenue of the Big Four accounted for £5.0bn, 72% of the fee income of the Top 50, down from 78-79% in the years up to the 2002 survey and the third year in succession a decline in their share has occurred (Chart 1). Ernst & Young's fee income is the smallest of the largest four firms, but still over three times that of the next largest firm, Grant Thornton. The amount of fee income tapers off amongst the mid-tier firms so that in total there were only 25 firms that each generated more than £15m of revenue in the 2005 survey. For more details regarding British qualified accountancy professionals, please refer to the page of British qualified accountants.

Management Accounting

Management accounting is concerned with the provisions and use of accounting information to managers within organizations, to provide them with the basis in making informed business decisions that would allow them to be better equipped in their management and control functions. Unlike financial accountancy information (which, for the most part, is public information), management accounting information is used within an organization (typically for decision-making) and is usually confidential and access to which is only available to a select few.

According to CIMA, The Chartered Institute of Management Accountants, Management Accounting is "the process of identification, measurement, accumulation, analysis, preparation, interpretation and communication of information used by management to plan, evaluate and control within an entity and to assure appropriate use of and accountability for its resources. Management accounting also comprises the preparation of financial reports for non management groups such as shareholders, creditors, regulatory agencies and tax authorities".

Aims

1. Formulating strategies;
2. Planning and constructing business activities;
3. Making decisions;
4. Well use of resources;
5. Supporting financial reports preparation; and
6. Safeguarding assets.

In the late 1980s, accounting practitioners and educators were heavily criticized on the grounds that management accounting practices (and, even more so, the curriculum taught to accounting students) had changed little over the preceding 60 years, despite radical changes in the business environment.

Professional accounting institutes, perhaps fearing that management accountants would increasingly be seen as superfluous in business organizations, subsequently devoted considerable resources to the development of a more innovative skills set for management accountants.

The distinction between 'traditional' and 'innovative' management accounting practices can be illustrated by reference to cost control techniques. Traditionally, management accountants' principal technique was variance analysis, which is a systematic approach to the comparison of the actual and budgeted costs of the raw materials and labour used during a production period.

While some form of variance analysis is still used by most manufacturing firms, it nowadays tends to be used in conjunction with innovative techniques such as life cycle cost analysis and activity-based costing, which are designed with specific aspects of the modern business environment in mind. Lifecycle costing recognizes that managers' ability to influence the cost of manufacturing a product is at its greatest when the product is still at the design stage of its product lifecycle (i.e., before the design has been finalised and production commenced), since small changes to the product design may lead to significant savings in the cost of manufacturing the product. Activity-based costing (ABC) recognizes that, in modern factories, most manufacturing costs are determined by the amount of 'activities' (e.g., the number of production runs per month, and the amount of production equipment idle time) and that the key to effective cost control is therefore optimizing the efficiency of these activities. Activity-based accounting is also known as Cause and Effect accounting.

Both lifecycle costing and activity-based costing recognize that, in the typical modern factory, the avoidance of disruptive events (such as machine breakdowns and quality control failures) is of far greater importance than (for example) reducing the costs of raw materials. Activity-based costing also deemphasizes direct labour as a cost driver and concentrates instead on acitivities that drive costs, such as the provision of a service or the production of a product component.

The most significant recent direction in managerial accounting is throughput accounting, which recognizes the interdependencies of modern production processes and provide managers with a tool that will allow them to measure the contribution per unit of constrained resource for any given product, customer or supplier.

A seldom expressed alternative view of management accounting is that it is neither a neutral or benign influence in organizations, rather a mechanism for management control through surveillance. This view locates management accounting specifically in the context of management control theory.

There are several related professional qualifications in the field of accountancy including:

- Management Accountancy Qualifications

  - CIMA— CMA
  - Institute of Cost and Works Accountants of India
  - AAFM
- Other Professional Accountancy Qualifications
  - Chartered Certified Accountant, (ACCA)
  - Chartered Accountant, (CA)
  - Certified Public Accountant, (CPA)

Accounting Management (Business) is the practical application of management techniques to control and report on the financial health of the organization. This involves the analysis, planning, implementation, and control of programs designed to provide financial data reporting for managerial decision making. This includes the maintenance of bank accounts, developing financial statements, cash flow and financial performance analysis. Accounting management is a mandatory knowledge module of any MBA programme.

Accounting is often referred to as billing management. The goal is to gather usage statistics for users.

Using the statistics the users can be billed and usage quota can be enforced.

Examples:

- Disk usage
- Link utilisation
- CPU time

For non-billed networks, 'Administration' replaces 'Accounting'. The goals of Administration is to administer the set of authorized users, by establishing users, passwords and permissions; and to administer the operations of the equipment such as by performing software backup and synchronization.

Activity-based Costing

Activity-based costing (ABC) is a method of allocating costs to products and services. It is generally used as a tool for planning and control. This is a necessary tool for doing value chain analysis.

The concepts of ABC were developed in the manufacturing sector of the U.S. during the 1970s and 80s. During this time, the Consortium for Advanced Manufacturing-International, now known simply as CAM-I, provided a formative role for studying and formalizing the principles that have become more formally known as Activity-Based Costing. Robin Cooper and Robert Kaplan, proponent of the Balanced Scorecard, brought notice to these concepts in a number of articles published in Harvard Business Review beginning in 1988. Cooper and Kaplan described ABC as an approach to solve the problems of traditional cost management systems. These traditional costing systems are often unable to determine accurately the actual costs of production and of the costs of related services. Consequently managers were making decisions based on inaccurate data especially where there are multiple products.

Instead of using broad arbitrary percentages to allocate costs, ABC seeks to identify cause and effect relationships to objectively assign costs. Once costs of the activities have been identified, the cost of each activity is attributed to each product to the extent that the product uses the activity. In this way ABC often identifies areas of high overhead costs per unit and so directs attention to finding ways to reduce the costs or to charge more for costly products.

Activity-based costing was first clearly defined in 1987 by Robert S. Kaplan and W. Bruns as a chapter in their book Accounting and Management. They initially focused on manufacturing industry where increasing technology and productivity improvements have reduced the relative proportion of the direct costs of labour and materials, but have increased relative proportion of indirect costs. For example increased automation has reduced labour, which is a direct cost, but has increased depreciation, which is an indirect cost.

Traditionally cost accountants had arbitrarily added a broad percentage onto the direct costs to allow for the indirect costs. However as the percentages of overhead costs had risen, this technique became increasingly inaccurate because the indirect costs were not caused equally by all the products. For example one product might take more time in one expensive machine than another product, but since the amount of direct labour and materials might be the same, the additional cost for the use of the machine would not be recognised when the same broad 'on-cost' percentage is added to all products. Consequently, when multiple products share common costs, there is a danger of one product subsidising another.

Like manufacturing industries, financial institutions also have diverse products which can cause cross-product subsidies. Since personnel expenses represent the largest single component of non-interest expense in financial institutions, these costs must also be attributed more accurately to products and customers. Activity based costing, even though developed for manufacturing, can therefore be a useful tool for doing this. This extended use of ABC to financial institutions was presented in 1990 in an article appearing in the Journal of Bank Cost and Management Accounting (Volume 3, Number 2) by Richard Sapp, David Crawford and Steven Rebishcke.

Direct labour and materials are relatively easy to trace directly to products, but it is more difficult to directly allocate indirect costs to products. Where products use common resources differently, some sort of weighting is needed in the cost allocation process. The measure of the use of a shared activity by each of the products is known as the cost driver. For example, the cost of the activity of bank tellers can be ascribed to each product by measuring how long each product's transactions takes at the counter and then by measuring the number of each type of transaction.

Even in activity-based costing, some overhead costs are difficult to assign to products and customers, for example the chief executive's salary. These costs are termed 'business sustaining' and are not assigned to products and customers because there is no meaningful method. This lump of unallocated overhead costs must nevertheless be met by contributions from each of the products, but it is not as large as the overhead costs before ABC is employed.

Although some may argue that costs untraceable to activities should be "arbitrarily allocated" to products, it is important to realize that the only purpose of ABC is to provide information to management. Therefore, there is no reason to assign any cost in an arbitrary manner. Management accountants can be creative in finding other ways to represent these costs on internal reporting statements.

managing budget

Budget generally refers to a list of all planned expenses and revenues. A budget is an important concept in microeconomics, which uses a budget line to illustrate the trade-offs between two or more goods. A personal budget is among the most important concepts of personal finance. In a personal or family budget all sources of income (inflows) are identified and expenses (outflows) are planned with the intent of matching outflows to inflows (Making ends meet). There are a wide variety of personal budgeting methods and tools that can be employed to help individuals and families with the budgeting process. Also the level of planned finance available to a person, corporation or government, as set by a certain person.

The budget of a government is a summary or plan of the intended revenues and expenditures of that government. In the United States, the federal budget is prepared by the Office of Management and Budget, and submitted to Congress for consideration. Invariably, Congress makes many and substantial changes. Nearly all American states are required to have balanced budgets, but the federal government is allowed to run deficits. In the UK the budget is prepared by the Chancellor of the Exchequer, the second most important member of the government, and must be passed by Parliament. The Parliament seldom makes changes to the budget.

The budget of a company is compiled annually. A finished budget usually requires considerable effort and can be seen as a financial plan for the new financial year. While traditionally the Finance department compiles the company's budget, modern software allows hundreds or even thousands of people in the various departments (operations, human resources, IT etc) to contribute their expected revenues and expenses to the final budget.

If the actual numbers delivered through the financial year turn out to be close to the budget, this will demonstrate that the company understands their business and has been successfully driving it in the direction they had planned. On the other hand, if the actuals diverge wildly from the budget, this sends out an 'out of control' signal and the share

Cost-plus pricing is a pricing method commonly used by firms. It is used primarily because it is easy to calculate and requires little information. There are several varieties, but the common thread in all of them is that you first calculate the cost of the product, then include an additional amount to represent profit. Cost-plus pricing is often used on government contracts, and has been criticized as promoting wasteful expenditures.

Calculating Price Using the Cost-plus Method

There are several ways of determining cost, and the profit can be added as either a percentage markup or an absolute amount. One example is:

P = (AVC + FC%) * (1 + MK%)

where:

- P = price
- AVC = average variable cost
- FC% = percentage allocation of fixed costs
- MK% = percentage markup

For example: If variable costs are 30 yen, the allocation to cover fixed costs is 10 yen, and you feel you need a 50% markup then you would charge a price of 60 yen:

P = (30 + 10) • (1 + 0.50)

P = 40 • 1.5

P = 60

An alternative way of doing a similar calculation is:

P = (AVC + FC%)/ (1 " MK%)

To make things simpler, some firms, particularly retailers, ignore fixed costs and just use the purchase price paid to their suppliers as the cost term. They indirectly incorporate the fixed cost allocation into the markup percentage. To simplify things even further, sometimes a fixed amount is applied rather than a percentage.

This fixed amount is usually determined by head-office to make it easy for franchisees and store managers. This is sometimes referred to as turnkey pricing.

Another variant of cost plus pricing is activity based pricing. This involves being more careful in determining costs. Instead of using arbitrary expense categories when allocating overhead, every activity is linked to the resources it uses.

Cost will need to be recalculated and the percentage markup will likely need to be adjusted as the product goes through its life cycle. This is sometimes referred to as product life cycle pricing, although it is seldom done deliberately or in a planned and organized manner. Price skimming and penetration pricing are also types of product life cycle pricing but they are demand based pricing methods rather cost based.

Advantages of Cost-plus Pricing

1. Easy to calculate
2. Minimal information requirements
3. Easy to administer
4. Tends to stabilize markets - insulated from demand variations and competitive factors
5. Insures seller against unpredictable, or unexpected later costs
6. Ethical advantages

Disadvantages

1. Tends to ignore the role of consumers
2. Tends to ignore the role of competitors
3. Use of historical accounting costs rather than replacement value
4. Use of "normal" or "standard" output level to allocate fixed costs
5. Inclusion of sunk costs rather than just using incremental costs
6. Ignores opportunity costs
7. Contractors may not focus on performance because the cost is always covered by the client

In microeconomics, Production is simply the conversion of inputs into outputs. It is an economic process that uses resources to create a commodity that is suitable for exchange. This can include manufacturing, storing, shipping, and packaging. Some economists define production broadly as all economic activity other than consumption. They see every commercial activity other than the final purchase as some form of production. Production is a process, and as such it occurs through time and space. Because it is a flow concept, production is measured as a "rate of output per period of time". There are three aspects to production processes:

1. The quantity of the commodity produced,
2. The form of the good produced,
3. The temporal and spatial distribution of the commodity produced.

A production process can be defined as any activity that increases the similarity between the pattern of demand for goods, and the quantity, form, and distribution of these goods available to the market place.

A production process is efficient if a given quantity of outputs cannot be produced with any less inputs. It is said to be inefficient when there exists another feasible process that, for any given output, uses less inputs. Some economists (in particular Leibenstein) use the term X-efficiency to indicate that production processes tend to be inherently inefficient due to satisficing behaviour. The "rate of efficiency" is simply the amount of (or value of) outputs divided by the amount of (or value of) inputs. If a production process uses 50 units of input (or $5000 worth of inputs) to produce one unit of output it is more efficient than a process that uses 55 units of input (or $5500 worth of inputs) to produce the same level of output. It is said to be 10% more efficient

({55-50}/50=1/10=10%). The inputs or resources used in the production process are called factors by economists. The myriad of possible inputs are usually grouped into four or five categories. These factors are:

- Raw materials (natural capital)
- Labour services (human capital)
- Capital goods
- Land

Sometimes a fifth category is added, entrepreneurial and management skills, a subcategory of labour services. Capital goods are those goods that have previously undergone a production process. They are previously produced means of production. Some textbooks use "technology" as a factor of production.

In the "long run" all of these factors of production can be adjusted by management. The "short run" however, is defined as a period in which at least one of the factors of production is fixed. A fixed factor of production is one whose quantity cannot readily be changed. Examples include major pieces of equipment, suitable factory space, and key managerial personnel. A variable factor of production is one whose usage rate can be changed easily. Examples include electrical power consumption, transportation services, and most raw material inputs. In the short run, a firm's "scale of operations" determines the maximum number of outputs that can be produced. In the long run, there are no scale limitations.

The total product (or total physical product) of a variable factor of production identifies what outputs are possible using various levels of the variable input. This can be displayed in either a chart that lists the output level corresponding to various levels of input, or a graph that summarizes the data into a "total product curve". The diagram shows a typical total product curve. In this example, output increases as more inputs are employed up until point A. The maximum output possible with this production process is Qm. If there are other inputs used in the process, they are assumed to be fixed.

The average physical product is the total product divided by the number of units of variable input employed. It is the output of each unit of input. If there are 10 employees working on a production process that manufactures 50 units per day, then the average product of variable labour input is 5 units per day.

The average product typically varies as more of the input is employed, so this relationship can also be expresses as a chart or as a graph. A typical average physical product curve is shown (APP). It can be obtained by drawing a vector from the origin to various points on the total product curve and plotting the slopes of these vectors.

The marginal physical product of a variable input is the change in total output due to a one unit change in the variable input (called the discrete marginal product) or alternatively the rate of change in total output due to an infinitesimally small change in the variable input (called the continuous marginal product). The discrete marginal product of capital is the additional output resulting from the use of an additional unit of capital (assuming all other factors are fixed). The continuous marginal product of a variable input can be calculated as the derivative of quantity produced with respect to variable input employed. The marginal physical product curve is shown (MPP). It can be obtained from the slope of the total product curve.

Because the marginal product drives changes in the average product, we know that when the average physical product is falling, the marginal physical product must be less than the average. Likewise, when the average physical product is rising, it must be due to a marginal physical product greater than the average. For this reason, the marginal physical product curve must intersect the maximum point on the average physical product curve.

MPP keeps increasing till it reaches its maximum. Up until this point every additional unit has been adding more value to the total product than the previous one. From this point onwards, every additional unit adds less to the total product compared to the previous one. But the average product is still increasing till MPP touches APP. At this point, an additional unit is adding the same value as the average product. From this point onwards, MPP starts to reduce and so does APP because every additional unit is adding less to APP than the average product. But the total product is still increasing because every additional unit is still contributing positively. Therefore, during this period, both, the average as well as marginal products, are decreasing, but the total product is still increasing. Finally we reach a point when MPP crosses the x-axis. At this point every additional unit starts to diminish the product of previous units, possibly by getting into their way. Therefore the total product starts to decrease at this point. This is point A on the total product curve.

Diminishing returns can be divided into three categories:

1. Diminishing Total returns, which implies reduction in total product with every additional unit of input. This occurs after point A in the graph.
2. Diminishing Average returns, which refers to the portion of the APP curve after its intersection with MPP curve.
3. Diminishing Marginal returns, refers to the point where the MPP curve starts to slope down and travels all the way down to the x-axis and beyond. Putting it in a chronological order, at first the marginal returns start to diminish, then the average returns, followed finally by the total returns.

These curves illustrate the principle of diminishing marginal returns to a variable input (not to be confused with diseconomies of scale which is a long term phenomenon in which all factors are allowed to change). This states that as you add more and more of a variable input, you will reach a point beyond which the resulting increase in output starts to diminish. This point is illustrated as the maximum point on the marginal physical product curve. It assumes that other factor inputs (if they are used in the process) are held constant. An example is the employment of labour in the use of trucks to transport goods. Assuming the number of available trucks (capital) is fixed, then the amount of the variable input labour could be varied and the resultant efficiency determined. At least one labourer (the driver) is necessary. Additional workers per vehicle could be productive in loading, unloading, navigation, or around the clock continuous driving. But at some point the returns to investment in labour will start to diminish and efficiency will decrease. The most efficient distribution of labour per piece of equipment will likely be one driver plus an additional worker for other tasks (2 workers per truck would be more efficient than 5 per truck).

Resource allocations and distributive efficiencies in the mix of capital and labour investment will vary per industry and according to available technology. Trains are able to transport much more in the way of goods with fewer "drivers" but at the cost of greater investment in infrastructure. With the advent of mass production of motorized vehicles, the economic niche occupied by trains (compared with transport trucks) has become more specialized and limited to long haul delivery.

There is an argument that if the theory is holding everything constant, the production method should not be changed, i.e., division of labour should not be practiced. However, the rise in marginal product means that the workers use other means of production method, such as in loading, unloading, navigation, or around the clock continuous driving. For this reason, some economists think that the "keeping other things constant" should not be used in this theory.

The total, average, and marginal physical product curves mentioned above are just one way of showing production relationships. They express the quantity of output relative to the amount of variable input employed while holding fixed inputs constant. Because they depict a short run relationship, they are sometimes called short run production functions. If all inputs are allowed to be varied, then the diagram would express outputs relative to total inputs, and the function would be a long run production function. If the mix of inputs is held constant, then output would be expressed relative to inputs of a fixed composition, and the function would indicate long run economies of scale.

Rather than comparing inputs to outputs, it is also possible to assess the mix of inputs employed in production. An isoquant relates the quantities of one input to the quantities of another input. It indicates all possible combinations of inputs that are capable of producing a given level of output.

Rather than looking at the inputs used in production, it is possible to look at the mix of outputs that are possible for any given production process. This is done with a production possibilities frontier. It indicates what combinations of outputs are possible given the available factor endowment and the prevailing production technology.

You can use a lot of labour with a minimal amount of capital, or you could invest heavily in capital equipment that requires a minimal amount of labour to operate, or any combination in between. For most goods, there are more than just two inputs. For example in agriculture, the amount of land, water, and fertilizer can all be varied to produce different amounts of a crop. An isoquant, in the two input case, is a curve that shows all the ways of combining two inputs so as to produce a given level of output. In the three input case it will be a surface. Iso is Latin for equal and quant is short for quantity. Movement along an isoquant depicts a constant rate of output, but a changing input ratio. A unique isoquant can be constructed for every level of output, and a family of isoquants can be created to represent various output levels. Isoquants further from the origin represent greater amounts of output. Isoquants are usually considered to be everywhere dense, meaning an infinite number of them could be plotted in any two input space.

A typical isoquant is illustrated in the diagram to the right. At point A in the diagram Ka units of capital are combined with La units of labour to produce 100 units of output. It is downward sloping, convex to the origin, and non-intersecting (additional isoquants, not shown, would be drawn parallel to this one). A complete isoquant is actually a closed curve, but only the "down sloping to the right" portion makes economic sense. The upward sloping parts of isoquants, for example, indicate that that level of output could be produced by less of both inputs so this section is of little interest to decision makers. The economic section of the isoquants is defined by a pair of lines called ridge lines.

The "downward to the right" slope of the economic region of an isoquant is due to the possibility of substituting one input for another in the production process while keeping the level of output constant.

Isoquants are typically convex to the origin reflecting the fact that the two factors are substitutable for each other at varying rates. This rate of substitutability is called the "marginal rate of technical substitution" (MRTS) or occasionally the "marginal rate of substitution in production". It measures the reduction in one input per unit increase in the other input that is just sufficient to maintain a constant level of production. For example, the marginal rate of substitution of labour for capital gives the amount of capital that can be replaced by one unit of labour while keeping output unchanged.

To move from point A to point B in the diagram, the amount of capital is reduced from Ka to Kb while the amount of labour is increased only from La to Lb. To move from point C to point D, the amount of capital is reduced from Kc to Kd while the amount of labour is increased from La to Lb. The marginal rate of technical substitution of labour for capital is equivalent to the absolute slope of the isoquant at that point (change in capital divided by change in labour). It is equal to 0 where the isoquant becomes horizontal, and equal to infinity where it becomes vertical.

The opposite is true when going in the other direction. In this case we are looking at the marginal rate of technical substitution capital for labour (which is the reciprocal of the marginal rate of technical substitution labour for capital). It can also be shown that the marginal rate of substitution labour for capital, is equal to the marginal physical product of labour divided by the marginal physical product of capital. In the unusual case of two inputs that are perfect substitutes for each other in production, the isoquant would be linear (linear, a straight line, with a function $y = a - bx$). If, on the other hand, there is only one production process available, factor proportions would be fixed, and these zero-substitutability isoquants would be shown as horizontal or vertical lines.

Fixed Assets Management

Fixed assets management is an accounting process that seeks to track fixed assets for the purposes of financial accounting, preventive maintenance, and theft deterrence. Many organizations face a significant challenge to track the location, quantity, condition, maintenance and depreciation status of their fixed assets. A popular approach to tracking fixed assets utilizes serial numbered Asset Tags, often with bar codes for easy and accurate reading. Periodically, the owner of the assets can take inventory with a mobile barcode reader and then produce a report. Off-the-shelf software packages for fixed asset management are marketed to businesses small and large. Some Enterprise Resource Planning systems are available with fixed assets modules.

Free cash Flow

Free cash flow measures a firm's net increase in

- Cash from operations (this includes the reduction for interest),
- Less the dividends paid to preferred shareholders, and
- Less expenditures necessary to maintain assets.

Increases in non-cash current assets may, or may not be deducted, depending on whether they are considered to be maintaining the status quo, or to be investments for growth.

Problems with CapX

1. The expenditures for maintenance of assets is only part of the capx reported on the Statement of Cash Flows. It must be separated from the expenditures for growth purposes. This split is not a requirement under GAAP, and is not audited. Management is free to disclose maintenance capx or not. Therefore this input to the calculation of free cash flow is easy to manipulate. Since it is a very large number,

maintenance capx's questionable validity is the basis for some people's dismissal of 'free cash flow'.

2. A second problem with the maintenance capx measurement is its intrinsic 'lumpyness'. By their nature, expenditures for capital assets that will last decades are infrequent, but costly when they occur. 'Free cash flow', in turn, will be very different from year to year. No particular year will be a 'norm' that can be expected to be repeated.

Uses of the Metric

1. Free cash flow measures the ease with which businesses can grow and pay dividends to shareholders. Even profitable businesses may have negative cash flows. Their requirement for increased financing will result in increased financing costs reducing future income. It is easier to grow with organic cash flows than with additional financing.
2. According to the discounted cash flow valuation model, the intrinsic value of a company is the present value of all future free cash flows, plus the cash proceeds from its eventual sale. The presumption is that the cash flows are used to pay dividends to the shareholders. Bear in mind the lumpyness discussed.
3. Some investors prefer using free cash flow instead of net income to measure a company's financial performance, because free cash flow is more difficult to manipulate than net income. The problems with this presumption are itemized at cash flow and return of capital.
4. The payout ratio is a metric used to evaluate the sustainability of distributions from REITs, Oil & Gas Royalty Trusts, and Income Trust. The distributions are divided by the free cash flow. Distributions may include any of income, flowed-through capital gains or return of capital.

This metric is used only by shareholders. Debt holders are not concerned with maintaining the operating capital assets, or with growing the business. Nor are they concerned with taxes paid since their payments come first. The appropriate metric for debt holders is EBITDA.

Change Management

There are several phrases regarding organizational change and development that look and sound a lot alike, but have different meanings. As a result of the prominence of the topic, there seems to be increasingly different interpretations of some of these phrases, while others are used interchangeably. Without at least some sense of the differences between these phrases, communications about organizational change and development can be increasingly vague, confusing and frustrating. There are different overall types of organizational change, including planned versus unplanned, organization-wide versus change primarily to one part of the organization, incremental (slow, gradual change) versus transformational (radical, fundamental), etc.. Knowing which types of change you are doing helps all participants to retain scope and perspective during the many complexities and frequent frustrations during change.

Successful change efforts often include several key roles, including the initiator, champion, change agent, sponsor and leaders. Organization-wide change in corporations should involve the Board of Directors. Whether their members are closely involved in the change or not, they should at least be aware of the change project and monitor if the results are being achieved or not. As the change agent, you might be performing different roles during the project.

Appreciative Inquiry is a recent and powerful breakthrough in organizational change and development. It's based on the philosophy that "problems" are often caused as much by our perception of them as problems as by other influencing factors. The philosophy has spawned a strong movement that, in turn, has generated an increasing number of models, tools and tips, most of which seem to build from the positive perceptions (visions, fantasies, wishes and stories) of those involved in the change effort.

There are numerous well-organized approaches (or models) from which to manage a change effort. Some of the approaches have been around for many years — we just haven't thought of them as such. For example, many organizations undertake strategic planning. The implementation of strategic planning, when done in a systematic, cyclical and explicit approach, is strategic management. Strategic management is also one model for ensuring the success of a change effort. There are numerous, major methods and movements to regularly increase the performance of organizations. Each includes regular recurring activities to establish organizational goals, monitor progress toward the goals, and make adjustments to achieve those goals more effectively and efficiently.

Any or all of the following approaches will improve organizational performance depending on if they are implemented comprehensively and remain focused on organizational results. Some of the following, e.g., organizational learning and knowledge management, might be interpreted more as movements than organization performance strategies because there are wide interpretations of the concepts, not all of which include focusing on achieving top-level organizational results. However, if these two concepts are instilled across the organization and focus on organizational results, they contribute strongly to organizational performance. On the other hand, the Balanced Scorecard, which is deliberately designed to be comprehensive and focused on organizational results, will not improve performance if not implemented from a strong design.

6

Reducing Poverty through Tourism

INTRODUCTION

There is enormous scope for the tourism industry to contribute better to less poverty in the world. This booklet outlines ways to do this on a larger scale than at present. It looks at the issues surrounding the subject, refers to the most recent research and suggests how both the tourism industry and the poor can benefit from an integrated approach to growth and equity.

It is still not widely recognized that travel and tourism is one of the world's biggest industries that creates vast economic growth, especially for poor countries. The wider travel and tourism industry now accounts for more than 10 per cent of global gross domestic product (GDP) and creates more than 230 million jobs. For developing countries, tourism generated foreign earnings of more than US$260 billon in 2007, more than six times higher than in 1990.

Tourism is one of the major export sectors of poor countries and the leading source of foreign exchange in 46 of the 49 least developed countries (LDCs). Yet, to date the link between tourism and poverty reduction has lacked focus in the development plans of many poor countries. Many development plans accept that tourism contributes significantly to economic growth.

However, economic growth does not necessarily lead to less poverty. Equally, while many small-scale projects have been developed to link tourism with poverty reduction, large-scale poverty reduction from tourism depends upon clear strategies consulted, articulated and monitored through national poverty reduction strategy plans.

TARGETED INTERVENTIONS

Economic growth is an essential but not a sufficient condition for poverty reduction. Poverty reduction involves growth with a substantial reorientation in favour of the poor. It includes changes in institutions, laws, regulations and practices that help create and perpetuate poverty. It includes targeted interventions to enable poor people to better integrate into economic processes and take advantage of opportunities to improve their economic and social well-being. It means ending harassment of the poor, and eliminating restrictions on how they make their livelihoods. This especially applies to the tourism sector. Interventions must be made to help poor people become part of the processes that drive the industry.

THE ILO

The ILO has always worked to address poverty. The notion that "poverty anywhere is a threat to prosperity everywhere" is part of its Constitution. This booklet aims to show how the potential of the tourism industry to reduce poverty can be realised through decent work in mainstream tourism and related sectors. It also aims to help developing countries highlight the sector in their national poverty reduction strategy plans and encourages international financial institutions to recognize the impact of travel and tourism in their support strategies. For the ILO and its in-country constituents, this booklet outlines how decent work fits with the United Nations Millennium Development Goals (MDGs) in tourism-related poverty reduction strategies, and shows how pro-poor tourism (PPT) projects can be articulated and supported in the development process.

BACKGROUND

The term "pro-poor tourism" is recent. The United Kingdom's Department for International Development (DFID) coined the phrase in the 1990s and many United Nations agencies adopted it this century. This part deals with some of the structures and concepts that relate to its development.

POVERTY REDUCTION STRATEGY PAPERS

In 1999, the World Bank and the International Monetary Fund (IMF) agreed that nationally owned, participatory poverty reduction strategies should be the basis for all concessional lending and debt relief. This approach is reflected in the Poverty Reduction Strategy Papers (PRSPs), which describe a country's economic, social and political policies and programmes over a three-to-five year period.

PRSPs are comprehensive plans prepared by governments, with support from development partners, which identify who the poor are and develop strategies for overcoming poverty, including policy and expenditure targets. PRSPs are supposed to be locally generated, owned and developed through wide participatory dialogue. PRSPs encourage accountability of governments to their own people rather than to external funding agencies.

In this way, the poor can become active participants in development, not just passive recipients. To date, about 50 countries have full PRSPs in place and a number of others have similar national planning instruments. The key difference between PRSP processes and the Structural Adjustment Programmes

(SAPs) that preceded them is this national ownership based on an inclusive participatory process.

MILLENNIUM DEVELOPMENT GOALS

Consistent with their poverty reduction focus, PRSPs are also an instrument for achieving the United Nations MDGs. The MDGs are eight universal goals with global, regional and national application. The 189 member States of the UN endorsed them at the UN Millennium Summit in September 2000. The MDGs apply to the period 2000–15.

The MDGs are becoming even more significant as the world approaches the 2015 deadline. Increasingly development plans and poverty reduction strategies refer to them and incorporate them in their framework of action. The "One UN" reform initiative, whereby all UN agencies deliver as one in each country, has further increased their practical importance.

DECENT WORK

The ILO's concept of "decent work" cuts across the MDGs. Through decent work, the ILO can contribute significantly to MDG achievement, especially to the major goal of halving the incidence of poverty by 2015. The Decent Work Agenda can also have major effects on the other seven goals. Within the list of MDG targets and indicators, the ILO is specifically responsible for indicator 11, on the share of women in waged employment in the non-agricultural sector, as well as indicator 45 on unemployment of 15–24-year-olds.

Target 16, on youth employment is also directly relevant to ILO activities. Work is central to people's well-being. As well as providing income, work can make for social and economic advancement. Work can strengthen individuals, their families and communities.

This, however, hinges on work that is decent. The ILO defines "decent work" as "opportunities for women and men to obtain productive work in conditions of freedom, equity, security and human dignity".

Decent work involves opportunities for productive work that delivers a fair income; security in the workplace and social protection for workers and their families; better prospects for personal development and social integration; freedom for people to express their concerns, organize and participate in decisions that affect their lives; and equality of opportunity and treatment for all. The Decent Work Agenda is an integrated approach to the objectives of full and productive employment for all at global, regional, national, sectoral (industry) and local levels.

It rests on four pillars:

1. Standards and rights at work
2. Employment creation

3. Social protection
4. Tripartism and social dialogue

THE ILO'S MISSION

The ILO's mission is to promote decent work within the context of poverty reduction strategies. In the tourism industry, the strategically important question for the ILO is how to move these activities from niche to mainstream tourism for development. Part of this is ensuring that developing countries highlight the potential of the sector for employment and poverty reduction in their national PRSPs.

It is also important that the ILO helps international financial institutions recognize the impact of tourism in their support strategies.

While there are links between decent work and the MDGs, the ILO and its constituents need to ensure stronger connections between the two frameworks when developing project proposals and strategies–especially in relation to poverty reduction. In particular, this means that the MDG framework should be used wherever possible in outlining project aims and in measuring project impacts.

The ILO's comparative advantage in the design and implementation of PRSPs lies in the integrated approach of decent work, which embraces rights, employment, social protection and (tripartite) social dialogue. Although the well-being of people depends not only on income, it is obvious that income from work is the most important means of survival for poor people.

SURPRISING

It is therefore surprising how few PRSPs include an analysis of labour markets and employment issues. This may be due to a common view that equates employment with waged employment.

In most PRSP countries, less than 20 per cent of the labour force is in waged employment. It is also consistent with the widespread notion that labour markets are best left to the market. In some cases, this neglect of employment policy probably reflects the relative absence of labour ministries and the social partners from the consultation processes for many PRSPs.

TOURISM JOBS

Travel and tourism is itself human-resource intensive due to the service nature of the industry. Further, one job in the core tourism industry creates about one and a half additional (indirect) jobs in the tourism-related economy. The wider travel and tourism economy creates (both directly and indirectly) more than 230 million jobs, which represents about 8 per cent of the global workforce. Half the workers in the industry are aged 25 or younger. Women make up between 60 and 70 per cent of the labour force in the industry. This gender dimension can be especially important: according to the United Nations Development Programme (UNDP), empirical evidence suggests that developing countries with less gender inequality tend to have lower poverty rates. Paid work by women reduces overall poverty and inequality.

In fact, eliminating barriers to women's participation in paid work (as is typical of the tourism industry) has a much stronger effect on poverty and economic growth than ending wage discrimination. In the hotel segment of the industry, globally there is an average of one employee for each hotel room. Further, there are three workers indirectly dependent on each person working in hotels, such as travel agency staff, guides, taxi and bus drivers, food and beverage suppliers, laundry workers, textile workers, gardeners, shop staff for souvenirs and others, as well as airport employees.

TOURISM AND POOR COUNTRIES

The World Economic Forum (WEF) recently produced a competitiveness study on tourism and travel (T&T). According to the report, the tourism industry creates most new jobs in developing countries. Tourism is also the major services export for many developing countries and has much potential to provide competitive advantage for them.

Tourism in developing countries is also growing rapidly. Developing countries' foreign earnings from tourism leapt from less than US$50 billion in 1990 to more than US$260 billon in 2007. For one third of developing countries, tourism is already the main income source. Tourism is also the main source of foreign exchange in 46 of the 49 LDCs. Further, in more than 50 of the world's poorest countries tourism ranks either first, second or third largest of their economic sectors. Tourism is the only service industry to show a positive balance of trade, with flows from first world countries to developing countries exceeding those in the opposite direction by US$6.6 billion in the year 2000. By way of contrast, tourism accounts for between 3 and 10 per cent of GDP in advanced economies, and up to 40 per cent in developing countries. Yet some aid donors, international funding agencies, segments of the industry and even national governments have only very recently recognized tourism as an appropriate instrument for poverty reduction.

RECENT DEVELOPMENTS

As at 2008, the ILO was taking part in a global discussion and activities about PPT. It is actively involved in rural community tourism projects in 14 countries in Latin America. It has held several global meetings on the tourism industry, has an established web site on tourism issues relating to work and social dialogue and is developing PPT studies and projects in Africa.

The ILO works with the United Nations World Tourism Organization (UNWTO) and the International Hotel and Restaurants Association (IH&RA),

as well as with the global union federation, the International Union of Food, Agricultural, Hotel, Restaurant Catering, Tobacco and Allied Workers' Association (IUF). The UNWTO recently launched a programme called "Sustainable Tourism–Eliminating Poverty" (ST–EP). This initiative focuses on long-term measures to encourage sustainable tourism–social, economic and ecological–and which specifically alleviates poverty, bringing development and jobs to people living on less than a dollar a day. A broader development has been the increasing importance of emerging economies in tourism as both destinations and sources of tourists.

According to The Economist magazine, the rise of emerging economies is the third revolution in the travel industry over the past 50 years. The first was during the 1960s with cheap air travel and package tours. The second was the Internet, which meant that travellers could book flights, hotels, cars and tours without using a travel agent.

Now people from high-growth emerging economies such as Dubai, Brazil, Russian Federation, India, China, Republic of Korea and Viet Nam are changing tourism again: These economies are both destinations and sources of newly affluent travellers. Often they visit similar emerging countries, rather than first-world destinations.

According to the UNWTO, while continued growth from emerging tourism will suffer from the economic downturn, fuel price rises and 'mega crises', the numbers of potential travellers are so huge and the logic of targeting tourism for development so pervasive that long-term growth prospects will remain "substantial by any measure". The Organization stresses the need for public-private partnerships to ensure that emerging states access funds for tourism development.

HOTEL, CATERING AND TOURISM SECTOR

For the ILO, the hotel, restaurant and tourism (HCT) sector includes:

- Hotels, boarding houses, motels, tourist camps and holiday centres;
- Restaurants, bars, cafeterias, snack bars, pubs, night clubs and other similar establishments;
- Institutions that provide meals and refreshments within hospitals, factory and office canteens, schools, aircraft, and ships;
- Travel agencies, tourist guides and tourism information offices;
- Conference and exhibition centres.

Other organizations concerned with tourism, including governments, intergovernmental organizations and non-governmental organizations (NGOs) often use much broader definitions of tourism than that used by the ILO. They include all services and products consumed by tourists, including transport. In the ILO HCT sector, the part referring to tourism only covers travel agencies and tour operators. According to the UNWTO, tourism includes the activities of people (visitors) travelling to and staying in places outside their usual environment for less than a year for leisure, business and other purposes. Tourists are people whose main purpose of visit is not an activity paid from within the destination.

Most organizations consider hotels and catering, including restaurants, to belong to the industries with characteristic of tourism, although in some countries only a small part of their services is for tourists. The fact that the ILO definition of the sector is different from that used by other organizations does not prevent it sharing most concerns about tourism development. One such concern is the sector's potential to provide employment. Nevertheless, the ILO's focus on labour issues is unique as it includes all working and employment conditions in the HCT sector.

VISION

The vision embraced by this booklet is for a tourism industry that is both competitive and much more strongly linked to the well-being of poor people who live at the destination. This is consistent with the World Travel and Tourism Council's (WTTC) 2003 policy statement: Blueprint for New Tourism. The blueprint is a strategic framework for a travel and tourism industry that works for all stakeholders. This new tourism looks beyond the short term and focuses on benefits for travellers, as well as for local communities and their natural, social, and cultural environments.

The blueprint has three key components:

1. Governments recognizing travel and tourism as a top priority;
2. Business balancing economics with people, culture, and environment; and
3. A shared pursuit of long-term growth and prosperity.

The vision encompassed by this booklet is, however, more detailed.

Its key elements Are:

- Upgrades local skills;
- Creates decent local jobs;
- Uses local construction;
- Embraces the local culture;
- Improves local infrastructure;
- Helps sustain the local environment;
- Sources locally as much as possible;
- Plans to be inclusive over the long term;
- Provides a unique experience for tourists;
- Promotes itself as a top economic priority;
- Creates partnerships to improve livelihoods.

While some regard corporate social responsibility as a public relations exercise or simply providing charity to poor people, a genuinely inclusive tourism industry promises much more. The difference between a tourism industry that relies on charity and one that embraces inclusion is the results: Only an inclusive industry can achieve greater benefits and at the same time add to human dignity. And it is human dignity that guarantees the motivation and the security to benefit all those who are included, not least benefits for the industry itself.

ISSUES

There are many issues associated with mainstreaming this complex industry to better benefit the poor. There are disagreements about how much tourism benefits local people. Some issues result from mindsets that are out of touch with current reality. Some concern access, information and analysis. Others are more straightforward, practical issues of recognition, planning and implementation.

DEFINITIONS

Apart from the differing definitions of the tourism industry used by different organizations mentioned in the background part above, even definitions of PPT and poverty itself can be issues.

Pro-poor Tourism

According to the Pro-Poor Tourism Partnership, PPT is "tourism that results in increased net benefits for poor people. PPT is not a specific product or niche sector but an approach to tourism development and management. It enhances the linkages between tourism businesses and poor people so that tourism's contribution to poverty reduction is increased and poor people are able to participate more effectively in product development.

Links with many different types of "the poor" need to be considered: staff, neighbouring communities, land-holders, producers of food, fuel and other suppliers, operators of micro tourism businesses, craft-makers, other users of tourism infrastructure (roads) and resources (water), etc. There are many types of PPT strategies, ranging from increasing local employment to building mechanisms for consultation. Any type of company can be involved in PPT–a small lodge, an urban hotel, a tour operator, an infrastructure developer.

The critical factor is not the type of company or the type of tourism, but that an increase in the net benefits that go to poor people can be demonstrated". Even this detailed definition has its limitations, however. Its weakness is that it remains oriented to single operations, rather than to the wider industry. Because tourism is such a large and growing industry, and so important to poor nations, large-scale strategies should now be emphasized in order to make real inroads into poverty.

Poverty

Who are poor people? The United Nations defines extremely poor people as those who live on less than the equivalent of one US dollar per day. This is measured in purchasing power parity (PPP), which is based on the cost of a similar basket of goods in different countries, expressed in United States dollars. Merely poor people are those who live on less than US$2 per day PPP. There are about 1.3 billion people in the developing world (21 per cent of the world population) in extreme poverty, who live on less than US$1 per day.

More than 2.7 billion live on less than US$2 per day. To go further, who are the poorest of the poor and how they can benefit from PPT? It has been pointed out that often the poorest are not subsistence farmers as is often assumed, but rather landless informal agricultural workers and their families. How to include former itinerant sugar workers from Guyana in the new tourism economy of Saint Kitts in the Caribbean is an example of this issue. However, the real meaning of poverty goes beyond just lack of money and its arbitrary measurement.

NET IMPACT

In world (21 per cent of the world population) in extreme poverty, who live on less than US$1 per day. More than 2.7 billion live on less than US$2 per day. To go further, who are the poorest of the poor and how they can benefit from PPT? It has been pointed out that often the poorest are not subsistence farmers as is often assumed, but rather landless informal agricultural workers and their families. How to include former itinerant sugar workers from Guyana in the new tourism economy of Saint Kitts in the Caribbean is an example of this issue. However, the real meaning of poverty goes beyond just lack of money and its arbitrary measurement.

Tourism can have both positive and negative effects on poor people.

There are three:

- *Main ways that tourism can impact on vulnerable people*: through direct effects on the poor, such as tourism jobs and small tourism enterprises;
- Through secondary effects, such as earnings from supply chain industries (for example, food and construction) as well as from tourism workers who spend their earnings in the local economy; and
- Through dynamic effects on the economy such as entrepreneurship, wages and prices, infrastructure development, other export sectors, skill development and the natural environment.

There is no destination where poverty impact has been assessed in all three of these ways. Assessing tourism poverty effects in future needs to look at all three areas of impact. It is most important to be aware that tourism, like any other activity, can have both positive and negative effects on people, especially the poor. It should not be assumed that PPT strategies will have only positive effects. For example, the introduction of new tourist resorts can benefit the poor through job creation, but may have negative effects through increased prices for land and commodities, or reduced access to beaches and fishing grounds. Strategies that aim to reduce poverty must assess the net impact in order to give a true picture. Future approaches need to consider net effects as well as benefits.

A HOLY COW

There is no unanimity of views on tourism and poverty reduction. For example, according to one critic, most of the effects of tourism on poor people are negative. Anita Pleumarom of the Third World Network says that it is time to stop treating tourism as a "holy cow to be protected and nurtured at all costs".

She observes that:

- The more decision-makers parade tourism policies for poverty elimination, the more the gap widens between the rich and the poor among and within nations, due to aggressive and unfair economic liberalization. While people in rich countries drown in conspicuous consumption thereby destroying their own and others' life bases, communities in less and least developed countries only receive the crumbs from the wealth that capitalist growth produces.

Her paper points to "the financial 'leakage' (due to high import content, repatriation of profits by foreign-owned tourism companies, etc.)" that tourism produces, and "unbalanced and inequitable distribution of income." She writes that "... leakages in the tourism sector total up to 85 per cent in some African least developed countries (LDCs), more than 80 per cent in the Caribbean, 70 per cent in Thailand and 40 per cent in India".

She says that rather than a boon, "... in fact, tourism-related jobs are uncertain, seasonal and part time, with a high turnover of staff". Ms Pleumarom calls for better and well-enforced regulation to tackle these issues. Whether or not one agrees with these views of the tourism industry overall, these are issues that need to be tackled. Donors, governments and the social partners need to address environmental challenges, poor communities do need real benefits from the industry, and financial leakages need to be reduced.

GROWTH VERSUS SHARE

As with broader debates about national and global economies, the issue of absolute growth as against equitable share of that growth is often heard in relation to tourism. The underlying assumption behind this issue is that the two goals are in conflict with each other. However, expanding tourism overall with a bigger share for the poor is achievable. In destinations where tourism is already pro-poor, studies suggest that the poor will benefit from a combined approach: expanding the overall size of the sector, while simultaneously tackling the bottlenecks that prevent the poor from earning a greater share. The relative value of either one varies by destination. In Da Nang, Viet Nam, for example, removing blockages to growth in upmarket coastal accommodation was the main short-term priority.

This was more effective than the traditional pro-poor policy goal of strengthening local linkages. This was due to the inherent pro-poor characteristics of tourism and extensive existing linkages in the destination, and also to government tourism land supply policy which had held back the expansion of the sector. By contrast, in Ethiopia existing supply chains are disconnected from the local economy. Interventions that enable the poor to participate must be integrated into expansion of the sector for tourism growth to reach the poor.

SCALE

Pro-poor action remains focused at the micro level. PPT should be applicable to all forms of tourism including mainstream tourism, not just a niche product such as eco-tourism or community tourism. The principles of maximizing linkages with the poor can be applied to beach resorts, urban hotels, conferences, wilderness tours, new building projects and on a national and regional scale. However, most tourism for poverty reduction initiatives remain confined to community-based tourism projects, campsites or trekking. They cannot deliver impact at a significant scale.

The significance of scale is underlined by recent academic papers from the University of the South Pacific in Fiji, which argue that the concept of PPT has become too closely associated with community-based tourism. They say it should be reintegrated into mainstream studies of tourism and development, and focus more on the role of mass tourism in alleviating poverty and bringing development.

MARKETS

Often too little attention is paid to market linkages in PPT ventures. Initiatives often concentrate on providing training and infrastructure. Yet products fail to find a market demand, domestic or international, and do not deliver livelihood benefits. In some cases, when tourism development is attempted because there is no alternative, communities are encouraged to invest labour, land and borrowings that have little chance of success.

INSTITUTIONAL FACTORS

Institutional factors can cause market linkage failures and reduce the chances of success for PPT ventures. For example, expanding the tourism sector and increasing the benefits reaching the poor are often made separate tasks for different people. Governments allocate PPT responsibilities to a part-time community tourism staffer, or put them under a separate project. Also, development practitioners who work with communities often know little about commercial tourism markets.

They attempt to implement projects without bringing in business expertise and private sector partners. In the private sector, tourism companies often regard local donations as corporate social responsibility. But fewer seek the commercial and local advantage that can come from doing business differently. In the public sector, a destination level approach to PPT needs complementary policies from tourism, agriculture, transport, enterprise, land, finance and labour departments, plus authority and skills at local government level. But neither integrated government nor strong local authorities are common.

MONITORING

There is a lack of systematic and documented monitoring of changes in poor people's livelihoods due to tourism. Neither the full range of impacts of tourism development on poverty levels, nor the before-and-after impacts of specific pro-poor measures have been rigorously assessed. Despite plenty of literature that suggests various pro poor strategies to adopt, there is little that actually quantifies results. For example, the significant income increases measured for poor people in the Gambia due to a market access initiative in 2001–02, are still frequently quoted because there are so few examples of published action research in this field.

TECHNICAL ASSISTANCE

The level of technical assistance available to help develop pro poor tourism is still less than ideal. However, the international community is beginning to recognize the importance of tourism as a potential driving force in the social and economic development of poor countries. This is because tourism development makes for much better trading opportunities.

Accordingly, it is one of the most effective ways of avoiding marginalization from the global economy. Because it can be a catalyst, tourism is one of the few economic sectors able to guide a number of developing countries to higher levels of prosperity and for some, to leave behind their LDC status. The UNWTO's ST–EP programme began in 2002, and is a good example of how technical assistance to the industry can work.

It provides technical assistance to developing countries on sustainable tourism development. Based on the recommendations resulting from missions, the help it offers can include product development, marketing, strategic planning and skill enhancement for business and national and local government relevant to tourism. Its recommendations can result in funding from international development agencies. ST–EP also facilitates research and identifies models of best practice. This includes seven mechanisms for poverty reduction through tourism that were identified by the UNWTO after detailed analytical research. These mechanisms have proved to be useful to parties working on development and poverty reduction, including governments, international organizations and NGOs, and community-based organizations. While ST–EP is still relatively new, it builds on work by the increasing number of agencies that have policies linking tourism with poverty alleviation.

These include the Asian Development Bank, the World Bank, the British DFID–ODI, the Netherlands' SNV, UN technical agencies such as the United Nations Conference on Trade and Development (UNCTAD), the United Nations Environment Programme (UNEP), and the World Commission on Environment and Development (WCED), international tourism organizations such as the Pacific Asia Travel Association (PATA) and some international NGOs.

However, tourism development that includes poverty reduction cannot be left to the private sector alone in many developing countries.

This is due to lack of money and weak institutional capacity of the private sector in such destinations. Design and implementation of an effective strategy usually needs strengthening of partnerships between the private sector and national tourism authorities. Help from international agencies is usually needed to achieve objectives.

COMPETITIVENESS

The World Economic Forum (WEF) published an updated travel and tourism report on competitiveness amongst 130 countries in 2008. The travel and tourism competitiveness index (TTCI) measures "the factors and policies that make it attractive to develop the (travel and tourism) sector in different countries". The TTCI is composed of 14 factors of competitiveness.

These factors are grouped into three broad categories:

1. The travel and tourism regulatory framework;
2. The travel and tourism business environment and infrastructure;
3. Travel and tourism human, cultural and natural resources.

All the top ten are developed countries such as Switzerland and the United States, while all of the bottom ten are LDCs such as Bangladesh and Chad. This competitiveness index has generated considerable debate.

For example, the front page of The Jordan Times newspaper related a story about a high-level meeting in Amman during May 2008, during which tourism industry groups criticized the report because Jordan's position on the rankings had dropped from the previous year.

Factors of competitiveness in the travel and tourism industry:

- Policy rules and regulations
- Environmental sustainability
- Safety and security

- Health and hygiene
- Prioritization of travel and tourism
- Air transport infrastructure
- Ground transport infrastructure
- Tourism infrastructure
- Information and communications technology infrastructure
- Price competitiveness
- Human resources
- Affinity for travel and tourism
- Natural resources
- Cultural resources

The index is a useful reference point for analyzing ways to improve economic growth in the industry and to make it more sustainable. While it lacks a strong focus on associated poverty reduction, much of what it recommends is relevant to a future more responsible tourism sector.

Collaboration

The report stresses that the industry should provide value beyond jobs and shareholder returns, as this is of increasing importance to consumers, governments, civil society and even business itself. It says that the industry is in a unique position to make a positive difference to the quality of life, due to its importance as an economic generator and employment provider, as well as because it brings people together.

This means that industry leaders must go beyond traditional day-to-day business. Leaders must also improve individual lives and freedoms by collaborating with governments and civil society to address national and global issues. The competitiveness report says that today's key challenges, such as poverty, climate change, terrorism, disease and corruption, are not part of any one discipline for study, nor can government, business or society solve them on their own. It calls for cross-sector leadership to solve them.

FOREIGN DIRECT INVESTMENT

Whilst tourism is a highly globalized industry, it is not so in terms of foreign direct investment (FDI). This means there is a lot of potential for FDI in poor countries. Conversely, poor countries can take advantage of FDI to improve the industry and benefit development. A recent UN report on this issue cites a growing support from donor and development communities for PPT.

The report points out that much of tourism's development potential results from its links across multiple goods and services activities, as well as from the diversity of enterprises involved. Tourism accounts for no more than one or two per cent of outward FDI from main source countries, such as the United States, United Kingdom, Spain, France and Canada.

Further, much of this FDI is in developed countries. Recently, however, there has been a noticeable increase in FDI for tourism from other sources such as China, Malaysia, Singapore, United Arab Emirates, Cuba, Poland, South Africa and Mauritius. Most FDI in tourism is in hotels and restaurants.

Local Supply

According to the UNCTAD report, the main advantages of attracting FDI in tourism for poor countries are:

- The attraction of new skills, systems and technologies that international capital can bring;
- Greater product diversity;
- Slightly higher wages than those paid by local enterprises; and, surprisingly,
- Better linkages with local suppliers than local enterprises. In order to take advantage of FDI, UNCTAD advises policies that promote linkages and raise local supply standards.

DECENT WORK

Emphasizing the relationship between decent work and PPT is a significant challenge for the ILO and its constituents. While not specifically focusing on PPT, the ILO has been more closely engaging with the poverty reduction strategy process for several years.

There are three main challenges for the ILO in this:

1. The need for PRSPs to include a more thorough analysis of employment and decent work;
2. The need for labour ministries, employers' and workers' organizations to take greater part in the process; and
3. The need for equity as well as growth to be considered in PRSPs.

The ILO has produced several publications to help in this, including a manual on decent work and poverty reduction strategies. As a result, it has made good progress with 15 PRSP processes, and poverty reduction measures increasingly highlight decent work and equity. But because PRSPs are a "crowded marketplace" for ideas and resources, it needs a sustained effort to make sure that decent work continues to get the attention it deserves. Decent work related to PPT is an even greater challenge.

SOCIAL PARTNERS UNDERVALUED

While the ILO encourages governments to invite trade unions and employers' organizations (the social partners) to be involved in PRSPs, often their views and support are undervalued: According to the ILO, employers' organizations and trade unions often find it hard to get involved in the PRSP process because:

- They normally relate to the labour ministry, which usually has little influence over the PRSP process;

- The process emphasizes the participation of civil society organizations, and unions and employers do not think of themselves as part of such a grouping;
- Established tripartite economic and social councils are often left out of the PRSP process;
- Some governments may fear engaging with the social partners because they are too independent;
- World Bank and IMF staff who advise on the PRSP process are often unfamiliar with the work of the ILO and the social partners;
- Some unions oppose involvement in policies they reject;
- Some employers' organizations decide to concentrate on other aspects of public policy.

Further, in some countries the national law effectively excludes the extremely poor from forming trade unions and therefore they are not represented in PRSP consultations. The ILO and its constituents at the country level will be supported if they campaign more around the central place of decent work in poverty reduction and in relation to the democratic base of their views and expertise. The tourism industry is an ideal sector on which to base this course of action.

AGENDAS

The biggest issue is however, getting PPT and decent work onto development agendas. Whether the PPT becomes part of PRSPs, or other forms of development assistance, it first needs more networking and advocacy in order to be heard and understood.

MAINSTREAMING POVERTY REDUCTION THROUGH TOURISM

This part outlines some of the factors that should be considered when devising measures to advance PPT, particularly through PRSPs and related means. Mainstreaming in this context means that sustainable tourism development should be included in wider poverty elimination programmes. Conversely, mainstreaming means that poverty reduction measures should be part of the sustainable development of tourism. It also implies that PPT should be on a big scale rather than a piecemeal microenterprise approach. All forms of decent work should be considered in assessing value chain benefits to the poor.

PARTICIPATION

A country's poverty reduction strategy paper is the centre of development action, and it is where the ILO and its constituents need to take part. A PRSP should be created through wide participation and the process should encourage governments to answer to their own people, rather than to external donors.

The World Bank sourcebook on PRSPs sets out the process and how it should involve different stakeholders. A stakeholder is any organization or group with an interest in the PRSP process, and may include government ministries, including NGOs, religious bodies and donors. Employers' and union organizations are recognized stakeholders who have a right to be involved.

Opportunities

A PRSP is an evolving document that must be regularly reviewed. How often it is reviewed depends on local conditions, but a PRSP must be implemented, monitored and evaluated. At each stage in the PRSP cycle, there are opportunities for stakeholders, including employer and union bodies, to provide input. It is important to see the PRSP as a long-term, ongoing process. Often one cycle lasts three–five years. Wherever the country is in the cycle, organizations can still be usefully involved. Even if issues do not get picked up in the first cycle, organizations can still push for them in a later cycle by lobbying for their priorities to be included.

Aim

For the ILO and its constituents, getting involved in the PRSP process in relation to PPT means being clear about the aim of their participation. The central aim of an involvement strategy is to get the priorities of the organization in the PRSP action summary. This is the summary table listing what measures are to be taken by whom and by when, usually in the latter part of the document. If this does not happen, then there is little chance of wide-scale coordinated interventions in the industry to benefit the poor.

Coordination

It is important that there is coordination and cooperation within and between the ILO and its constituents to maximize resources and effectiveness. Union and employers' organizations, (the social partners) are partners with the government in the social and economic development of the nation. In many countries, there is more than one union or employers' organization at the national level. There may be more than one national union federation, and more than one union directly involved in tourism. Also, there are often different types of organizations for employers. There may be an employers' federation, a chamber of commerce, foreign investor associations and sector-based organizations, like a chamber of tourism. There needs to be coordination within constituents as well so that advocacy for PPT in development plans is clear and united.

BENEFITS

Aside from benefits to the poor and to the industry, there are also considerable wider benefits for the social partners to get involved in PRSPs.

Direct Effects

A PRSP is the key to many policy and programme decisions in a country. It sets the framework for decision-making for years to come on economic and other government policy, programme and spending priorities. It will cover things like sectoral trade and private sector development, as well as social justice initiatives. These decisions will directly affect employers and workers. This especially applies to tourism, which is usually the main source of economic growth in poor countries.

Best Strategies

Creating decent work is central to reducing poverty. Employers' and union organizations have knowledge and experience in this field, which they can use to help develop the best strategies for the industry and the sectors it links with.

Building Networks

A PRSP process involves many different organizations and people working to combat the problem of poverty. Through their involvement, union and employers' organizations are able to extend their networks to other groups and individuals who share common concerns. Any organization gains from a broader pool of people with whom it can work.

The Bigger Picture

Governments often consult employers' and union organizations on industrial relations, and labour matters, but not on the broader issues. Being part of a PRSP process is a way to uncover the bigger picture and have a say. Where the tourism industry fits in the bigger picture in the future is a central part of this.

Organizational Planning

Employers' and union organizations need to plan for their own future and growth, and it helps to know what the policy and programme environment is likely to be. This makes it easier to predict potential opportunities and threats. Within the tourism industry, advance knowledge of proposed developments and policy measures can help synchronize employer development planning, and help bring about decent working conditions through union recruitment and social dialogue.

New Skills

Getting involved in a PRSP will give new and better skills for union and employers' organizations in areas like advocacy, planning, consultation, policy development, programming, monitoring and evaluation. These are all important skills for the social partners.

ACTION PRINCIPLES

When determining the kinds of measures needed to implement PPT, some guidance is available. Based on significant research on PPT, several action principles have been identified that can be used to guide mainstreaming approaches in tourism and its related sectors. These principles should be borne in mind when designing measures to increase benefits to the poor. They provide for growth as well as for more equitable distribution of economic benefits.

Partnerships

Develop partnerships between international, government, non-government and private sector organizations that have the common aim of reducing poverty through tourism. In developing countries, it is especially unlikely that any one organization will have the capacity to implement programmes alone.

Linkages

Build linkages from the local economy to tourism supply chains. In this way, industries related to tourism can grow, become more competitive and contribute to a more dynamic economy.

Markets

Reduce leakages from supply chains based on genuine market opportunities. Leakages can be identified and measured by assessing supplies and services that are imported to fill market needs.

Integration

Integrate approaches with other sectors so there is not an overdependence on tourism. Other sectors such as agriculture, fishing and construction can also be developed to fit with seasonal patterns of tourism demand.

Equity and Growth

Include both equity and economic growth in tourism development strategies. One need not be at the expense of the other. Rather, if the right policy mix is implemented, they can support each other.

Local

Focus specific action at the destination level. These actions should be supported by national policy, resources and a strong relationship between national and local government.

Remove Barriers

Remove discrimination, exploitation and barriers that may apply to poor people seeking to work in the tourism and related supply-chain industries. Decent jobs that can be accessed by the poor are key to reducing poverty.

Access

Ensure that poor people have access to relevant information, influence and are able to make their own decisions. This requires good government at all levels, as well as access to mobile phones and the Internet.

Measurement

Develop valid indicators and systems to measure before and after impact of tourism on poverty. Impact measurement is one of the most neglected areas of PPT. Measurement helps determine what does not work as well as what does.

OTHER SECTORS

One of the characteristics of tourism is its extensive links with other sectors. The more these linkages can be strengthened through deliberate interventions, the greater the benefit to wider economic development and poverty reduction. At the same time, there should be greater efficiencies and other benefits for the tourism industry itself. The main sectors related to tourism are construction, agriculture, fishing, food processing, furniture manufacturing, transport, utilities and services. The provision of infrastructure can also be significant for poor people as well as for general economic growth. The informal sector, including the manufacture and sale of craftwork, as well as microfinance and entertainment and cultural activities also has potential strong relationships with the industry.

Agriculture

In agriculture, it is still common for major tourist facilities to get food supplies from other countries. They do so due to poor quality, limited variety and unreliable local supply. Yet much poverty is associated with subsistence-level agriculture. Often local farmers may simply lack knowledge of what major hotels require, or they may suffer from equipment, water, seed and transport shortages.

Where programmes have been set up (often with government support) to overcome these issues, the results have benefited the industry, the tourists and the farmers involved. The Sandals resort chain in several Caribbean destinations is one example where this has occurred. This luxury resort chain now engages local farmers to supply much of its fresh food needs. Explaining the standards and nature of supplies required was central to the programme's success. Often ensuring facilities for produce display–such as in markets–can be a significant step in maintaining communication between buyers and suppliers. In 2008, some developing countries began export bans on certain staple food items such as rice due to production downturns and rapidly increasing prices. This is a further factor that points to the need to secure local supplies by the industry, as well as by the wider national economy.

Construction

The construction of tourism facilities and infrastructure can benefit the poor significantly. The destination will usually be able to supply significant quantities of unskilled and semi-skilled labour. Where there is minimum wage legislation, or where workers are paid at decent levels, short-term returns to the poor are maximized. Benefits can be extended by getting materials from sustainable local sources and by helping upgrade skills and methods. Wider and more long-term dynamic benefits are also possible.

There are already many examples where unique local skills have been used to build or restore tourist accommodation that combines local styles with upgraded amenities. The Haciendas project in Mexico is one example where local workers have restored abandoned historic buildings in high poverty areas. This project was financed by the Starwood hotel chain and a Mexican company. It combines economic profit and close integration with the local community.

Another successful example is the construction of a series of several lodges and other facilities in traditional style in the Siwa oasis region of Egypt for tourism. The Canadian International Development Agency (CIDA) partly funded the project, which has won several international awards. Often such projects need to train more people with the necessary skills than are immediately available. This can help to support future construction in other sectors and help provide economic opportunity for those trained.

Fishing

Inclusive tourism businesses more often benefit themselves and local people through sourcing fish and crustacean supplies locally. Local catches are often more highly valued by international tourists than expensive frozen supplies, because of freshness, price and because they are connected with the destination. Industry support for the development of fish farming can enhance reliability of supply and increased value added in this sector. Fish stocks worldwide are under increasing pressure and any support to make the sector more sustainable is a good thing.

The downside is that fishing for supply to tourist ventures can compete with local subsistence supply–either directly or by effecting price increases. On the other hand, the tourist industry can help sustain fish supplies, especially with government support for industry regulation. Such regulation can help prevent overexploitation of particular species, and also ensure that waste is not released untreated into catchment areas.

As with agriculture, it is important for the industry to communicate with suppliers on their needs, such as price, quantity, quality, timing and species. The industry also needs to discuss with suppliers on the issues they face, such as accessibility, competition, seasonality, pollution and poaching. Provision of market facilities can maintain and extend benefits to the wider community.

Food Processing

Food processing will often be very limited in many destination countries. The production of basic international items such as meat products, milk and fruit juices may not even exist or be of poor standard. An inclusive tourism sector can help improve the supply of such products by detailing the standards, quantities and prices they need to supplement or replace imported items. Early discussions between the tourism and potential food industry representatives are needed to begin this. Government and international support may be needed. Implementation plans should include dialogue involving the social partners.

Furniture Manufacturing

As with construction, the supply of furniture and its repair to tourism enterprises can often be undertaken locally. Some countries (such as Kenya and Thailand) have developed export markets that were originally based on supplying furniture to the local tourism industry. Despite this, many international tourism enterprises fail to consider or work towards such sourcing. If orders are sufficient, it is also possible for the industry to help develop local skill training in what can be a highly valuable and diverse industry. Textile manufacturing for furniture finishing, soft furnishing and bed linen also links here.

Infrastructure

Major tourism developments are often in otherwise remote parts of developing countries. Developers base these on natural attractions such as sun and sand, or link them to cultural sites such as ancient monuments. In many cases, the viability of such developments depends on upgrading or creating entirely new infrastructure.

The construction of airports, bridges, power and telecommunication links and the upgrading of roads, waterways and port facilities that the development requires can significantly benefit the local poor. Better public transport infrastructure means that the poor can more easily access markets and jobs. It means they can better deliver supplies and services–to the wider economy as well as to tourist developments. Telecommunication links such as mobile phone facilities and Internet coverage benefit the poor because they give access to information.

Services

The tourism industry supports local services (such as guides, haircuts, laundry, massage, and entertainment) since they are supplied only at the point of consumption. However, larger industry developments can be more pro-poor if they make information available on local services available, make services more accessible, and help ensure higher standards. The Starwood Haciendas project in Mexico trains local people in traditional massage techniques, for example. While there was some cultural reluctance initially in supplying this as a service to tourists, it has become popular amongst guests and with workers for the income it generates.

In Fiji, only one tribe traditionally undertakes fire-walking. This cultural exhibition is now popular with tourists and the families of the fire-walkers benefit significantly from the revenue generated. Generally, the communication of standards required is just as important in the provision of services as it is for supplies. So is skill training which can significantly help economic opportunity and mobility. The downside of tourism in some developing countries is often sex tourism. The industry should disavow links with exploitative sex enterprises. It must also work with governments to enforce local laws aimed at preventing exploitation, particularly of women and children, in what has become a form of modern slavery.

Transport

As well as international and domestic air transport, tourism is also associated with most other modes of travel. This can range from taxi and hire cars, motorized and pedalpowered vehicles, buses, boats, rail, and even hot air ballooning. Integration with local transport modes, rather than offering completely separate and expensive hotel-run modes can work best here. Visitors can benefit from the choice of options available to them.

Tour operators often use minibuses and other local forms of transport for tourists. Both can help support employment directly, as well as by using transport support services such as garages for fuel and maintenance. If the industry supports safe driver training for its staff and local people, it can make a further contribution to the welfare of the poor and at the same time help protect visitors from what is a major hazard of travel in developing countries.

Utilities

The tourism industry–especially hotels and restaurants–requires reliable utilities such as electricity, gas and water. These necessities are often in short supply in developing countries. Yet too often major luxury hotels at night will be ablaze with light often from their own generators while nearby poor settlements make do with battery power and candles. Too often luxury hotels secure fresh water supplies from adjacent catchment areas, fresh water that also supports green lawns and golf courses, while surrounding poor communities make do with communal taps or wells of dubious quality. If major tourism developments also help make reliable electricity and water available to the communities they are associated with, then the poor also benefit, even if no longterm employment is generated directly as a result.

VALUE CHAIN ANALYSIS

If tourism's potential to improve the livelihoods of poor people is to be fulfilled, then we need to understand and measure how much of tourism benefits reach the poor. This can help determine how the poor can better access the tourism value chain–whether from employment or from other means. There have been few studies on this. Conventional tourist analysis focused on tourist arrivals, foreign exchange receipts and investments, with little emphasis on measuring benefits to the poor. Because of this, much PPT analysis used a micro-level approach that looked at the livelihood effects on poor people involved with specific niche tourism enterprises.

A limited geographical scale, descriptive nature and niche focus meant these studies did not make any recommendations for boosting PPT benefits in most mainstream tourist destinations. However, some development researchers are starting to close this information gap by using value chain analysis (VCA) to map the tourism economy, its revenue streams and beneficiaries. This form of analysis can be used to address questions for policy makers who want to improve the pro-poor impact of tourism. While there are several factors that affect the degree of pro-poor benefit, some results are becoming clearer.

Although it must be remembered that the information on which it is based remains quite limited, the analysis should be taken into account when planning pro-poor interventions. The domestic sourcing of supplies for the tourism industry can be an especially important factor in its contribution to poverty reduction. The Cambodia PRSP, for example, states: "Estimates show that for every tourist dollar, 75 cents are returned to Thailand to import fresh vegetables, fruit, flowers, handicrafts and furniture." If such leakages are reduced, there are benefits for both industry profitability and the local poor.

BARRIERS

There will always be particular barriers that need to be overcome if poor people are to significantly benefit from tourism. The ODI lists 15 different types of barriers to consider in this regard. Policies, programmes or projects that attempt to incorporate pro-poor dimensions in tourism and other sectors can use this as checklist to ensure that potential barriers are identified, evaluated and addressed.

While some of these possible barriers to the poor benefiting need government intervention to be overcome (for example regulation and red tape, lack of pro-active government support) others can be overcome by those directly involved in the tourism industry. The industry can help overcome skill deficiencies by in-house training, it can help provide access to tourism markets and it can give information on product specifications and help link with local suppliers.

VOLATILITY

Hunger is neither seasonal nor temporary. Decent work depends on regular employment throughout the year, over a long period. However, in many destinations there is marked variation in tourist demand. This variation affects industry profit, job security and the tourist expenditure on which many poor people depend. Variation in demand is due to two main factors: seasonality and external shock.

Seasonality

Seasonal changes in tourist demand can be offset by marketing the destination in areas of the country where there are less extreme micro-climates. If the peak tourist period can be extended only a few weeks at either end through pricing and marketing, it can make a big difference to the destination's economy. Cooler mountain resorts can offset extreme heat in tropical countries during the dry season. Also, the seasonal downturn can be used for preparation and maintenance activities including staff recruitment and training, in appropriate segments of the industry.

External Shock

Tourism in particular destinations has suffered external shocks such as tsunamis, severe acute respiratory syndrome (SARS) and the threat of bird flu, as well as the wider effects of terrorist attacks, climate change and air travel fuel cost increases. However, it is remarkable how quickly tourism can regain lost ground after catastrophe. Infrastructure and accommodation may need to be repaired and improved. Security may need to be tightened. New marketing strategies may need to be developed. If these things are wellplanned, and if local labour is used where possible, the harm to the industry and to the poor can be reduced to a minimum. The Indonesian island of Bali is an example of one destination that has recovered quickly from recent external shock. Low-lying islands that risk being submerged as a result of climate change are a much more difficult problem whether or not they depend on tourism. This issue requires global as well as regional action.

Indicators

When intervening in the tourism industry to produce better results for poor people, it is critical that concrete outcomes are demonstrated so that further interventions can evolve. The way to demonstrate outcomes is by selecting good indicators before the intervention begins. Indicators are also important to show where policies may not have had the desired effects, and what mix of measures work best for the local industry.

Four Types

The World Bank identifies four different types of indicators. Under the source column, the "survey data" it refers to is usually the sample household surveys that support census information between census years. "Facility" and "community surveys" are usually undertaken by the institution or project concerned.

Selecting Indicators

- Selecting the right indicators–especially of outcomes and impact–needs a lot of thought. A good indicator: Is easy to understand and easy to measure. Indicators that are easy to understand are better for programme focus. If large surveys are needed, monitoring is more costly and requires more time.
- Is a direct and clear measure of progress. For example, immunization coverage is clearer than household expenditure on health, because an increase in health expenditure could be a good thing if it means that households have more resources to get healthcare. Or it could be a bad thing if it means that disease incidence or the cost of care has increased.
- Is relevant. It should directly relate to the measures undertaken. For instance, hotel operating costs depend on energy prices, and also on many other factors such as labour costs, marketing costs and occupancy rates. It might therefore not be a good indicator for progress on energy efficiency.
- Varies across areas, groups, over time and is sensitive to changes in policies and programmes. For instance, child malnutrition is more likely to vary quickly over time than life expectancy. Employment levels will be more sensitive than incidence of poverty.
- Is reliable and not easy to manipulate. Objective indicators are more reliable than indicators that depend on the interpretation of the user.
- Is gender disaggregated. Almost all changes affect men and women differently. Therefore the indicator should show both sexes separately as well as the total.

Pro-poor Tourism Indicators

The kinds of indicators that can be used to assess PPT outcomes and impacts depend on the interventions made. However, the following areas should be considered. The indicator measurements should be made both before and after the intervention has continued for a reasonable time. Often more reliable data can be obtained if confidentiality of the information can be guaranteed.

- *Movement from informal to formal employment*: This measures the number of people formally employed by the tourism sector (or enterprise) full-time and part time, before the intervention, compared with similar categories after the intervention. Of these, the number who previously worked in the formal economy, the informal economy, or who were unemployed prior to the intervention should be measured. A should be completed before the intervention and at 12-month intervals later to minimize seasonal variations. The data would be best collected through face-to-face interview questions matched with payroll totals to ensure complete coverage. For larger populations, samples rather than complete coverage could be used.

The example shows a 31.25 per cent ((75 ÷ 240) x 100) total movement from the informal to the formal economy, as indicated by the data in bold. If the intervention is designed to increase the number of people moving from informal to formal employment in the industry, then its success would tend to be demonstrated by a higher number than 75 at the bottom of column 4 in the later survey. Also note the different situation for men and women in the example.

- Income from formal employment. This measures total income from formal employment in the sector, before and after. A related indicator could measure average income per person formally employed (men, women, total). Data for such indicators may be more difficult to collect than for the informal-formal employment indicator above. This is because it involves questioning personal income as well as possibly payroll data. Confidentiality would have to be guaranteed.
- Earning from selling goods, service or labour, linked with other economic sectors. This measures income from tourism-related activities in other sectors, before and after and sex-disaggregated. For example, it would include profits made from craft and produce sales to the tourism industry, income from transport services, and income from work on infrastructure related to the industry.
- Profits arising from locally-owned enterprises with links to the tourism industry. This would require an estimation of the amount and proportion of profits accruing from the tourism linkage. Again confidentiality guarantees would be critical to its raw collection.
- Collective income from community enterprises, land rental or joint ventures. A starting point for accessing some of this data could often be local government who should be aware enterprise development in their area.

- Improvement of living and working conditions in the tourism sector, plus improvements in living and working conditions in linked sectors. Much of this information would have to be subjective or qualitative. For example respondents might be asked to rate their living and working conditions on 10-point scales relative to several criteria. Working conditions criteria could be based on core international labour standards and also include wage rates, hours worked and non-wage benefits.–Infrastructure. This measures (before and after) the value or quantity of infrastructure created or repaired, such as kilometres of roads, capacity of water reservoirs, number of homes linked to electricity, bridges constructed or extent of mobile telephone coverage. Some of this information may be available from planning or infrastructure ministries and agencies such as the World Bank may in involved in funding the provision of major infrastructure development.

A lot of information is available from household surveys conducted by planning ministries and used in poverty assessments between each national census. If programmes can use some of this information to support impact measurement, then the results may be more rigorous. Lastly, if indicators are consistent with those already established by the World Bank and the ILO, then they are likely to be more successful.

DECENT WORK AND THE MILLENNIUM DEVELOPMENT GOALS

The future of development programmes in any industry lies in closer integration of United Nations and other agencies at the national level. When developing programmes and projects, including those related to PPT, the ILO and its constituents must express proposals in a more integrated framework. Decent work programmes at the country level should be integrated into the PRSP process (and with the MDGs) to have the best impact. This is quite feasible in relation to both poverty reduction and the wider list of MDGs.

Poverty Reduction

The ILO's Decent Work Agenda directly relates to poverty reduction. The ILO itself summarized this relationship in 2005:

- Rights enable the empowerment of men and women to escape poverty;
- Employment involving productive work is the principal route out of poverty;
- Social protection safeguards against poverty;
- Dialogue, or employers' and workers' organizations participating in shaping government policy is key to poverty reduction.

Millennium Development Goals

The relationship between decent work and the full list of MDGs is more complicated. However, the Decent Work Agenda does contribute to all eight MDGs. Goal 1 (halving those with incomes of less than one dollar a day) and goal 8 (building a global partnership for development) are overarching goals towards poverty reduction. They both rely on decent work for their attainment. So does goal 7 on sustainable development. Goal 3 on gender equality is a condition for meeting all the MDGs, and gender mainstreaming is part of all ILO programmes. Decent work for parents and the elimination of child labour are essential to universal primary education. Social protection contributes directly to the health-related MDGs. Effective dialogue between government, employers' and workers' organizations supports inclusive policy reform. Institutions that foster social dialogue help good governance and social stability which are needed to achieve all of the MDGs.

Tourism Framework

Because PRSPs relate to the MDG framework, it is useful to outline how decent work fits with the MDGs in the particular context of tourism industry policy. The suggests how they all relate. The four decent work pillars head columns 2–5, while the eight MDGs head rows 3–10. The matrix outlines how examples of pro-poor measures in the tourism industry can fit within the two frameworks.

POVERTY REDUCTION STRATEGY PAPER CONTENT

Typically, PRSPs consist of an overall analysis of the economic development situation in the country, followed by several parts on measures planned by each sector. An example of such a PRSP part on tourism. At the end of the PRSP, there is usually a summary action plan in table form that outlines the measures to be taken, the resources devoted to them and the responsibility for their implementation. This summary action plan is the most important part of the document.

USES OF POVERTY REDUCTION STRATEGY PAPERS

PRSPs are not only the central document that determines key development measures; they also have several related uses.

PRSPs can be used:

- By the national government as a planning and budgetary framework;
- For World Bank and IMF loans and funding;
- For United National Development Assistance Framework (UNDAF) funding for a country;
- By international donors and non-government agencies as a framework for their own aid activities;

- As a monitoring and evaluation tool;
- As a framework for public consultation and discussion on priorities for poverty reduction.

For all these reasons, the ILO and its constituents need to get their PPT issues on the PRSP agenda if their proposals are to be taken seriously.

Lobbying

Lobbying can be useful to ensure national tourism administrations are involved in the PRSP process and also that poverty reduction is mentioned in national tourism policies and strategies. Lobbying can also help build support for PPT measures at all stages of the PRSP process.

Getting Issues Included

To ensure that an organization's issues are included in the PRSP, it is essential that it is clear about what measures it wants taken. In other words, organizations must first identify their priorities and strategies to achieve them.

Identify Priorities

Organizations can identify issues, priorities and strategies through workshops, possibly using input from studies like the Tanzanian example in the concept note part of this booklet. Priorities for PPT can be determined by identifying those that are both urgent and important. Priority issues identified (major problems) can be changed into priority objectives (positive objectives) by inversion. For example, a priority problem such as child labour is widespread in the industry can be inverted to the priority objective eliminate child labour in the industry.

Develop Strategies

Developing strategies to achieve priority objectives is best done in small groups that report back to the wider workshop. Ideas for strategies should be specific, practical and cost-effective.

It is also important to review the strategies selected to ensure men and women benefit equally. Select the best ideas to include in the summary.

For example, ideas to eliminate child labour in the industry might include:

- Set up a special labour inspectorate taskforce for the industry;
- Develop posters on the objective;
- Market the goal of eliminating child labour in tourist brochures;
- Set up discussions between schools, employers and unions in the industry.

Include Indicators

Where possible, the indicators to assess the net benefits to the industry and the poor should also be identified. Following the child labour example, an industry indicator could be based on the marketing of the campaign to tourists– by promoting the destination as one free of child labour, where instead children go to school. Tourists could be surveyed to find out of the industry campaign affected their decision to holiday at the destination.

Unacceptable work indicators include both:

- Children not in school by employment status (percentage by age);
- Children in wage employment activity rate (percentage by age). Child labour also relates to:
- MDG indicator No. 45 (youth unemployment rate);
- *Target 3*: Ensure that all boys and girls complete a full course of primary schooling.

Get Endorsement

The next step is getting the organization's plan endorsed. At this point, you have a draft list of objectives, strategies and indicators that your organization would like to see in the PRSP. Before any formal consultation on the list, get it endorsed by your organization's representative body. A trade union centre would put it before a meeting of delegates for endorsement. An employers' organization would go to its board of directors. Modify the list according to any substantial changes the representative body wants made before it proceeds through the PRSP process, so it truly represents the views of your organization.

Contact

Despite the intention that PRSPs should be locally owned and developed, often key staff from the World Bank write the final document, or are closely involved in its development. It is therefore most important for ILO staff and the social partners to identify, make contact with such people and discuss how to ensure that the measures they want to see for PPT are included in the summary action plan.

Securing Support

The final step before input to the PRSP process is securing support from other organizations that relate to the ILO (employer, worker, ministry and NGOs), and also from those external to the ILO that have most influence over the process. These latter groups will usually include the World Bank, the planning, commerce and tourism ministries, and the UNDP, especially if it is part of the "One UN" system in the country concerned. This networking and lobbying is a significant task that ideally should build on established relationships. However, it can be time and effort well-spent if it means that the PPT concept delivers the results intended.

7

The Demand for Recreation and Tourism

Understanding why human beings engage in recreational and tourism activities is an increasingly important and complex area of research for social scientists. Historically, geographers have played only a limited part in developing the literature on the behavioural aspects of recreational and tourists' use of free time, tending to have a predisposition towards the analysis of aggregate patterns of demands using quantitative measures and statistical sources. This almost rigid demarcation of research activity has, with a few exceptions, meant that behavioural research in recreation and tourism has only recently made any impact on the wider research community, with notable studies applying spatial principles to the analysis of recreational and tourism behaviour.

Within the recreational literature, the geographers' contributions have often been subsumed into social science perspectives, such as sociology, psychology and planning, so that the spatiality and placefulness of their contribution has been implicit rather than explicit. For this reason, this chapter discusses some of the key behavioural issues associated with recreation and tourism demand followed by an analysis of the major data sources which researchers use, emphasising how the geographer has used and manipulated them to identify the patterns, processes and implications of such activity.

Within the literature on recreation and tourism, there is a growing unease over the physical separation of the theoretical and conceptual research that isolates behavioural processes and spatial outcomes, and fails to derive generalisations applicable to understanding tourism in totality. According to Moore *et al.* (1995:74) there are common strands in the 'relationships between the various motivating factors applicable to both leisure and tourism'; and as Leiper (1990) argued, tourism represents a valued category of leisure, where there is a degree of commonality between the factors motivating both tourist and recreational activities and many of the needs, such as relaxation or being with friends, can equally be fulfilled in a recreational or tourism context. Although there is some merit in Leiper's (1990) approach, grouping leisure into one amorphous category assumes that there are no undifferentiated attributes which distinguish tourism from leisure. As Pigram and Jenkins (1999:19) confirm, 'the term recreation demand is generally equated with an individual(s) preferences or desires, whether or not the individual has the economic and other resources necessary for their satisfaction'.

In this respect, it is the preference-aspiratio-desire level, reflected in behaviour or participation in activities. It is interesting to note that Leiper's (1990) approach has a great deal of validity if one recognises that some tourism motivations may in fact differentiate tourism from leisure experiences, just as the reverse may be true, and that ultimately the particular range of motives associated with a tourism or recreational activity will be unique in each case despite a range of similarities. For this reason, the following discussion examines recreational demand, emphasising many of the explanations commonly advanced in the recreational literature followed by a discussion of the tourism context and the issues raised, bearing in mind the need to compare and contrast each literature base in the light of the arguments advanced by Moore *et al.* (1995) and Leiper (1990).

RECREATIONAL DEMAND

Human activity related to recreation and tourism is a function of an individual's or group's willingness or desire to engage in such pursuits. Yet understanding this dimension in recreation and tourism requires a conceptual approach which can rationalise the complex interaction between the desire to undertake leisure activities, however defined, and the opportunities to partake of them. As Coppock and Duffield (1975:2) argued: 'the success of any study of outdoor recreation depends on the synthesis of two contrasting elements: the sociological phenomenon of leisure or ... that part of leisure time which an individual spends on outdoor recreation [and tourism] and ... the physical resources that are necessary for the particular recreational activities.'

In other words, Coppock and Duffield (1975) ackno-wledged the need to recognise the interrelationship between human demand as participation or a desire to engage in recreation and tourism, and the supply of resources, facilities and opportunities which enable such demand to be fulfilled. The concepts of demand and supply have largely been developed and applied to conventional market economies, where the individual has a choice related to the consumption of recreation and tourism. According to Smith (1989:45):

Recreation geographers use the work [demand] in at least four different ways. The most traditional sense is a neoclassical definition: demand is a schedule of the quantities of some commodity that will be consumed at various prices.... A second definition of demand is that of current consumption ... [which] is of limited utility to recreation planners because it tells nothing about trends in participation or about current levels of unmet need. Demand is also used to refer to unmet need. This is sometimes referred to as latent demand. ... Finally, demand is used to describe the desire for a psychological experience. In contrast, Patmore (1983:54) acknowledges, 'leisure is far more easily recognised than objectively analysed ... the difficulties are only in part conceptual: equally important are the nature and limitations of available data', which this section will seek to explain in a recreation context.

According to Pigram (1983) there is a general lack of clarity in the use of the term *demand* in the recreational literature. One can distinguish between demand at a generic level, where it refers to an 'individual's preferences or desires, whether or not the individual has the economic or other resources necessary for their satisfaction' reflecting behavioural traits and preference for certain activities. At another level, there are the specific activities or participation in activities often expressed as visitation rates and measured to reflect the actual observed behaviour.

One factor that prevents observed demand equating with participation is the concept of latent demand (the element which is unsatisfied due to a lack of recreational opportunities). Knetsch (1969) identified the mismatch and confusion between participation and demand, arguing that one cannot simply look at what people do and associate it with what people want to do, so ideally any analysis of demand should also consider why people do not participate, and examine ways of overcoming such obstacles by the provision of new resources as well as understanding social and cultural barriers. As Pigram and Jenkins (1999:20) argued, 'In the real wòrld, recreation demand rarely equals participation.

The difference between aggregate demand and actual participation (or expressed, effective, observed, revealed demand) is referred to as latent demand or latent participation-the unsatisfied component of demand that would be converted to participation if conditions of supply of recreation opportunities were brought to ideal levels'. Attempting to summarise the factors which influence the decision to participate in recreation led Pigram (1983) which highlights the complex range of variables that affect the process.

Most research has examined effective demand which is actual participation rather than latent demand, and the geographers' contribution has largely been related to the spatial and temporal expression of demand in relation to supply (i.e. demand at specific sites). This is very much resource specific, and dates back to the geographical tradition of resource identification, use and analysis which can be traced to at least the 1930s. However, Coppock and Duffield (1975) also distinguish between passive recreation and active recreation, thereby beginning to differentiate between different forms of demand. While passive recreation is by far the most important type numerically, it is difficult to study due to its diffuse and often unorganised nature. Coppock and Duffield (1975:40) argued that Active recreation in the countryside differs from passive recreation in a number of ways. Not only are participants a minority of those visiting the countryside for outdoor recreation, but they are generally younger and differ in respect of a number of socio-economic characteristics: they often depend on particular (and sometimes scarce) recreational resources in the countryside ... yet as with passive recreation, information about such activities is scanty. This illustrates the necessity of trying to measure recreational demand together with gauging the types of factors which can facilitate and constrain recreational demand. But what motivates people to engage in recreational activities?

Argyle (1996) argues that part of the reason why people undertake leisure and recreational activities can be found in the process of socialisation and personality traits, where childhood influences such as parents and peers are forms of social influence and learning that affect future activity choice. In fact, nearly half of adult leisure interests are acquired after childhood, and personality factors influence preferences towards specific forms of recreation. However, understanding the broader psychological factors which motivate individuals to undertake forms of recreation is largely the remit of psychologists, being an intrinsic form of motivation (i.e. something one is not paid to undertake).

Crandall's list of motivations:

- Enjoying nature, escaping from civilisation
  - To get away from civilisation for a while
  - To be close to nature
- Escape from routine and responsibility
  - Change from my daily routine
  - To get away from the responsibilities of my everyday life
- Physical exercise
  - For the exercise
  - To keep in shape
- Creativity
  - To be creative
- Relaxation
  - To relax physically
  - So my mind can slow down for a while
- Social contact
  - So I could do things with my companions
  - To get away from other people
- Meeting new people
  - To talk to new and varied people
  - To build friendships with new people
- Heterosexual contact
  - To be with people of the opposite sex
  - To meet people of the opposite sex
- Family contact

  - To be away from the family for a while
  - To help bring the family together more
- Recognition, status
  - To show others I could do it
  - So others would think highly of me for doing it
- Social power
  - To have control over others
  - To be in a position of authority
- Altruism
  - To help others
- Stimulus seeking
  - For the excitement
  - Because of the risks involved
- Self-actualisation (feedback, self-improvement, ability utilisation)
  - Seeing the results of your efforts
  - Using a variety of skills and talents
- Achievement, challenge, competition
  - To develop my skills and ability
  - Because of the competition
  - To learn what I am capable of
- Killing time, avoiding boredom
  - To keep busy
  - To avoid boredom
- Intellectual aestheticism
  - To use my mind
  - To think about my personal values

A simplistic approach to recreational motivation is to ask recreationalists what actually motivates them. Crandall (1980) outlined 17 factors from leisure motivation research, derived from a synthesis of previous studies in this field, while Kabanoff (1982) identified a similar list of factors. It is apparent that relaxation, the need for excitement and self-satisfaction are apparent, though Argyle (1996) argues that specific motivations are evident in particular forms of recreation.

Torkildsen (1992:79), however, posits that homeostasis is a fundamental concept associated with human motivation where people have an underlying desire to maintain a state of internal stability. Human needs, which are 'any lack or deficit within the individual either acquired or physiological', disturb the state of homeostasis.

At a basic level, human needs have to be met where physiological theory maintained that all human behaviour is motivated. This leads to one of the most commonly cited studies in relation to recreation and tourism motivation-Maslow's hierarchy of human needs.

Table. Kabanoff's List of Leisure Needs.

Leisure needs scale	Items comprising scales	Item means	
1	Autonomy	Organise own projects and activities	2.78
		Do things you find personally meaningful	3.39
2	Relaxation	Relax and take it easy	3.20
		Give mind and body a rest	2.94
3	Family activity	Bring family closer together	2.81
		Enjoy family life	3.30
4	Escape from routine	Get away from responsibilities of everyday life	2.85
		Have a change from daily routine	3.12
5	Interaction	Make new friends	2.35
		Enjoy people's company	2.55
6	Stimulation	To have new and different experiences	2.66
		For excitement and stimulation	2.89
7	Skill utilisation	Use skills and abilities	2.89
		Develop new skills and abilities	2.61
8	Health	Keep physically fit	2.47
		For health reasons	2.46
9	Esteem	Gain respect or admiration of others	2.11
		Show others what you're capable of	2.15
10	Challenge/competition	Be involved in a competition	1.87
		Test yourself in difficult or demanding situations	2.31
11	Leadership/social power	Organise activities of teams, groups, organisations	1.79
		To gain positions of leadership	1.48

MASLOW'S HIERARCHY MODEL OF HUMAN NEEDS

Within the social psychology literature on recreation and tourism, Maslow's (1954) needs hierarchy remains one of the most commonly cited theories of motivation. It follows the principle of a ranking or hierarchy of individual needs, based on the premise that self-actualisation is a level to which people should aspire. Maslow argued that if the lower needs in the hierarchy were not fulfilled then these would dominate human behaviour. Once these were satisfied, the individual would be motivated by the needs of the next level of the hierarchy. In the motivation sequence, Maslow identified 'deficiency or tension-reducing motives' and 'inductive or arousal-seeking motives', arguing that the model could be applied to work and non-work contexts.

Despite Maslow's research shaping much of the recreation and tourism demand work, how and why he selected five basic needs remains unclear, though its universal application in recreation and tourism appears to have a relevance with regard to understanding how human action is related to understandable and predictable aspects of action compared to research which argues that human behaviour is essentially irrational and unpredictable.

While Maslow's model is not necessarily ideal, since needs are not hierarchical in reality because some needs may occur simultaneously, it does emphasise the development needs of humans, with individuals striving towards personal growth.

Therefore, Maslow assists in a recreational (and tourism context) in identifying and classifying the types of needs people have. Tillman (1974) summarised some of the broader leisure needs of individuals within which recreational needs occur, and these may include the pursuit of:

- New experiences (i.e. adventure);
- Relaxation, escape and fantasy;
- Recognition and identity;
- Security (freedom from thirst, hunger or pain);
- Dominance (to control one's environment);
- Response and social interaction (relating and interacting with others);
- Mental activity (to perceive and understand);
- Creativity;
- A need to be needed;
- Physical activity and fitness.

A different perspective is offered by Bradshaw (1972), who argued that social need is a powerful force, explaining need by classifying it as normative, felt, expressed and comparative need. Mercer (1973), Godbey (1976) and McAlvoy (1977) extended Bradshaw's argument within a recreational context, modifying the four categories of need by adding created, changing and false needs. Normative needs are based on value judgements, often made by professionals who establish that what they feel is appropriate to the wider population. Felt needs, which individuals may have but not necessarily express, are based on what someone wants to do and is a perceived need.

Expressed needs relate to those needs and preferences for existing recreational activities which are often measured but can only be a partial view of demand, since new recreational opportunities may release latest demand. Comparative needs are apparent where existing provision for the general population is compared with special groups (e.g. the elderly, ethnic minorities or disabled) to establish if existing provision is not fulfilling the needs of the special group. Created needs may result from policy-makers and planners introducing new services or activities which are then taken up by the population.

A false need is one that may be created by individuals or society, and which is not essential and may be marginal to wider recreational needs. Changing needs, however, are a recognition of the dynamic nature of human needs which change through time as individuals develop and their position in the life cycle changes. Thus what is important at one point in the life cycle may change through time as an individual passes through four key stages (Ken and Rapoport 1975):

- Youth (school years);
- Young adulthood;
- Establishment (extended middle-age);
- Final phase (between the end of work and of life).

Other researchers (e.g. Iso-Ahola 1980; Neulinger 1981) prefer to emphasise the importance of perceived freedom from constraints as a major source of motivation. Argyle (1996) synthesises such studies to argue that intrinsic motivation in leisure relates to three underlying principles:

- Social motivation;
- Basic bodily pleasures (e.g. eating, drinking, sex and sport);
- Social learning (how past learning explains a predisposition towards certain activities).

One useful concept which Csikszentmihalyi (1975) introduced to the explanation of motivation was that of flow. Individuals tend to find a sense of intense absorption in recreational activities, when self-awareness declines, and it is their peak experience - a sense of flow - which is the main internal motivation. The flow is explained as a balance resulting from being challenged and skill which can occur in four combinations:

- Where challenge and skill are high and flow results;
- Where the challenge is too great, anxiety results;
- If the challenge is too easy, boredom may occur;
- Where the challenge and skill level is too low, apathy may result.

But this does not mean that everyone always seeks recreational activities which provide forms of high arousal. Some recreational activities may just fulfil a need to relax, being undemanding and of low arousal. As Ewert and Hollenhurst (1989) reported, those who engaged in outdoor recreational sports with a high-risk factor (i.e. whitewater rafting) viewed the sport as providing a flow experience, and the study predicted that as their skill level improved they would increase the level of participation and risk. Yet even though this occurred the internal motivation of the group remained unchanged, where low and high arousal seem to be juxtaposed. Thus levels of arousal vary from time to time, a factor which can be used by adventure tourism operators to manage the adventure experience and increase the level of satisfaction of participants. Recreation may also lead to an enhanced self-image, where the identity becomes a basis for motivation because recreational activities can lead to a sense of belonging to a particular and identifiable group. Some activities may also require the development of special skills and enhanced self-esteem. Where recreational activities require a degree of competency, Bandura (1977) proposed that perception of one's ability to perform the skill is a motivator and may result in self-efficacy, a form of self-confidence and judgement of one's ability.

In spite of the significance of motivation, it is apparent that no single theory or even a clear consensus exists in relation to recreation. Instead, 'in theories of motivation need is seen as a force within the individual to gain satisfactions and completeness. There appear to be many levels and types of need, including the important needs of self-actualisation and psychological growth'.

An understanding of needs and intrinsic motivation and some of the ideas implicit in studies of recreational motivation may offer a range of insights into why people engage in recreational activities. But not only is it necessary to understand why people engage in recreation, but also what factors or barriers may inhibit them from participating. Torkildsen (1992) outlines the influences on leisure participation in terms of three categories: personal, social and circumstantial, and opportunity factors. These influences are also of value in understanding some of the constraints on recreation.

BARRIERS TO RECREATION

Within the wider literature on recreation and leisure, a specialist research area has developed, focused on constraints, namely those factors, elements or processes which inhibit people from participating in leisure activities. From the diverse range of studies published, two forms of constraint have been identified: intervening constraints, namely those which intervene between a preference and participation, and antecedent constraints, which influence a person's decision not to undertake an activity.

Although the constraints on recreation and leisure literature can be dated to the 1960s, the 1980s saw a range of studies published, a number of which have set the research agenda in recent years. In the initial formulation, Crawford and Godbey (1987) proposed that constraints were associated with intrapersonal, interpersonal and structural constraints. In the subsequent reformulation of their thinking, Crawford *et al.* (1991) proposed a hierarchical process model, with their three types of constraint integrated. As a consequence of their model, they proposed, which indicates that:

- Participation in leisure is a negotiation process, where a series of factors became aligned in a sequence;
- The order in which constraints occur leads to a 'hierarchy of

importance', where intrapersonal constraints are the most powerful in sequence ending with no structural constraints;

- That social class has a strong influence on participation and non-participation leading to a hierarchy of social privilege, i.e. social stratification is a powerful conditioning factor and may act as a constraint.

Table. Influences on Leisure Participation.

Personal	Social and circumstantial	Opportunity factors
Age	Occupation	Resources available
Stage in life cycle	Income	Facilities - type and quality
Gender	Disposable income	Awareness
Marital status	Material wealth and goods	Perception of opportunities
Dependants and ages	Car ownership and mobility	Recreation services
Will and purpose in life	Time available	Distribution of facilities
Personal obligations	Duties and obligations	Access and location
Resourcefulness	Home and social environment	Choice of activities
Leisure perceptions	Friends and peer groups	Transport
Attitudes and motivation	Social roles and contacts	Costs: before, during, after
Interests and preoccupations	Environment factors	Management: policy and support
Skill and ability - physical, social and intellectual	Mass leisure factors	Marketing
Personality and confidence	Education and attainment	Programming
Culture born into	Population factors	Organisation and leadership
Upbringing and background	Cultural factors	Social accessibility
		Political policies

This research has provided a framework for further evaluations of constraints (e.g. Samdahl and Jekubovich 1997, and subsequent criticisms by Henderson 1997). In fact, subsequent research by Jackson *et al.* (1993) suggested that the real key to understanding leisure constraints was embedded in the negotiation process: namely how an individual will proceed with experiencing an activity even when constraints are apparent. Ultimately, Pigram's (1983) model helped to frame the context in which participation may occur, and the way that process may be affected by underlying constraints on one's participation. It is against this background that one can appreciate the use of leisure time and leisure space in different cultures and among groups where leisure time in a western conception is inappropriate. For example, in a fascinating review of poor rural women's leisure experiences in Bangladesh by Khan (1997), it is evident that 'the conventional approach to leisure studies which has a myopic view of leisure as free or non-obligatory time' is meaningless due to blurring of boundaries between free or non-work time and obligatory activities which are often cumbersome and all-encompassing in everyday life.

At an empirical level, a range of notable studies have highlighted the prevailing constraints to recreation. For example, Kay and Jackson's (1991) notable study of 366 British adults' recreational constraints identified:

- 53 per cent who cited money as the main constraint;
- 36 per cent who felt lack of time was the main limitation;
- Conflicts with family or work, transportation problems and health concerns as other contributory factors.

A study in Alberta which surveyed 1,891 people asked respondents to rate 15 possible barriers to a desired activity, and the results highlighted social isolation, accessibility, personal reasons (lack of confidence or skill), costs, time and facilities as the main constraints. It has been proposed that such constraints have a specific ordering in terms of importance, with the most significant constraints being interpersonal ones, followed by structural ones (e.g. lack of time or money).

Yet such arguments have been queried by Shaw *et al.* (1991), who found that in a survey of 14,674 Canadians, of 11 constraints, only lack of energy and ill-health were associated with a lower rate of participation. Therefore, barriers may be negotiable or solvable, as Kay and Jackson (1991) suggest. Patmore (1983) summarises the main physical barriers to recreation in terms of:

- Seasonality;
- Biological and social constraints;
- Money and mobility;
- Resources and fashions;

with the availability of time also being a major constraint.

Coppock and Duffield (1975:8) recognised the principal variations which exist in terms of demand due to variable uses of leisure time budgets by individuals and groups in relation to the day, week and year.

Both Coppock and Duffield (1975) and Patmore (1983) use similar data sources (e.g. the UK's Pilot National Recreation Survey (British Travel Association and Univeristy of Keele 1967 and 1969) and sociological studies of family behaviour in the pioneering study by Young and Wilmott (1973)) to examine time budgets, variations in demand and constraining factors. One of the most important distinctions to make is that 'the weekend thus represents a large increase in the time that can be committed to leisure pursuits, which in turn affects the weekend time budget'. Yet when one looks beyond the day and week to the individuals and groups concerned, a wider range of influences emerge which are important in explaining recreation patterns. Argyle (1996) highlights the fact that one of the main reasons for examining constraining and facilitating factors is to understand 'how many people engage in different kinds of leisure, how much time they spend on it, and how this varies between men and women, young and old, and other groups'. This is because some groups such as 'women, the elderly and unemployed face particular constraints which may affect their ability to engage in leisure and recreational activities which people do because they want to, for their own sake, for fun, entertainment or self-improvement, or for goals of their own choosing, but not for material gain'.

SEASONALITY

Patmore (1983:70) argued that 'one of the most unyielding of constraints is that imposed by climate, most obviously where outdoor activities are concerned. The rhythms of the seasons affect both the hours of daylight available and the extent to which temperatures are conducive to participant comport outdoors.' This is reflected in the seasonality of recreational activity which inevitably leads to peaks in popular seasons and a lull in less favourable conditions. Patmore (1983) identified a continuum in recreational activities from those which exhibit a high degree of seasonality to those with a limited degree of variation in participation by season.

The first type, which is the most seasonal, include outdoor activities often of an informal nature which are weather dependent. The second, an intermediate group, is transitional in the sense that temperature is not necessarily a deterrent since a degree of discomfort may be experienced by the more hardened participants (e.g. when walking and playing sport). The final group is indoor activities which can be formal or informal, and have virtually no seasonality. In addition, the physical constraints of season, climate and weather inhibit demand by curtailing the periods of time over which a particular resource can be used for the activity concerned, although resource substitution (e.g. using a man-made ski slope instead of a snow-clad one) may assist in some contexts, but often the man-made resource cannot offer the same degree of excitement or enjoyment.

ACCESS TO RECREATIONAL OPPORTUNITY

Argyle (1996) observed that while many studies emphasised lack of money as a barrier to engaging in recreational activities, Coalter (1993) found that it had little impact on participation in sports. In fact, Kay and Jackson (1991) also acknowledged that money or disposable income was a barrier to undertaking activities which were major consumers of money (drinking and eating socially) whereas it had little impact on sport which was comparatively cheap. Income, occupation and access to a car combined have a significant impact on participation, and as Patmore (1983:78) succinctly summarised, 'those with more skilled and responsive occupations, with higher incomes, with ready access to private transport and with a longer period spent in full-time education tend to lead a more active and varied leisure life, with less emphasis on passive recreations both within and beyond the home'.

It is the car which has provided the greatest degree of personal mobility and access to a wider range of recreational opportunities in time and space since the 1960s in many developed countries (and earlier in some cases such as the USA and Canada).

For example, most car-owning households in UK studies have twice the propensity to participate in sport and recreation than non-car-owning households. Even so, Martin and Mason (1979:62) observe that 'one of the paradoxes of leisure is that while time and money are complementary in the production of leisure activities, they are competitive in terms of the resources available to the individual. Some leisure time and some money to buy leisure goods and services are both needed before most leisure activities can be pursued.'

GENDER AND SOCIAL CONSTRAINTS

The influence of gender on recreation remains a powerful factor influencing participation, a feature consistently emphasised in national surveys of recreational demand. As Argyle (1996:44) argues, 'there is an influential theory about this topic, due to a number of feminist writers, that women have very little or no leisure, because of the demands of domestic work and the barriers due to husbands who want them at home ... [and] that leisure is a concept which applies to men, if it is regarded as a reaction to or contrast with paid work'. Thus women with children appear to have less time for recreation, while those in full- and part-time employment have less time available than their male counterparts.

These general statements find a high degree of support within the recreational literature, with gender differences in part explained by the male free time occurring in larger blocks and in prime time.

Even so, studies by Talbot (1979) explore this theme in more detail. Rodgers (1977) documents the wide discrepancy in male:female participation in sport as a form of recreation within a European context where for every 100 females engaging in sport, there were 188 male participants in Britain, 176 in Spain, 159 in France, 127 in Belgian Flanders, 127 in Norway, 116 in the Netherlands and 111 in former West Germany.

While definitions and the variations in data sources may in part explain the variability, the presence of a gender gap is prominent. Age also exerts a strong influence on participation in recreation, with Hendry *et al.* (1993)

describing adolescence as the peak time of leisure needs. Therein lie two key explanations of participation and constraints. Stages in the life cycle present a useful concept to explain why women with young children appear to have fewer opportunities for recreation than adolescents. Likewise, physical vigour and social energy are traditionally explained in terms of a decline in the later stages of adulthood resulting in a decline in active recreation throughout later life. The Greater London Recreation Survey of 1972 (Greater London Council 1976) identified some of these traits in that:

- Activities exist where participation markedly declined by age (e.g. energetic sports like football);
- Activities occur with sustained participation through the life cycle (e.g. tennis and indoor swimming);
- Some activities exist where participation increased as a person got older (e.g. golf and walking).

In fact these results not only illustrate the importance of age (and to a degree gender), but also the need to consider the significance of the life cycle in relation to changes or 'triggers' (Patmore 1983). One such trigger is retirement, and while it is sometimes interpreted as a stressful life event, Long (1987) found that for 58 per cent of male retirees there was no change in their leisure activities, while 8 per cent undertook education, 3 per cent developed an interest in photography and 3 per cent partook of sport. What Argyle (1996:63) emphasises from studies of retirement are that 'people carry on with the same leisure as before, though they are more passive and more housebound, and do not take up much new leisure'.

CASE STUDY: THE GEOGRAPHY OF FEAR IN RECREATION AND LEISURE SPACES: GENDER-BASED BARRIERS TO PARTICIPATION

Since the 1980s there has been a growing interest in the role of fear, personal safety and the spatial implications in the urban environment. There has also been an accompanying interest in the gender dimensions of personal safety, which has important implications within an urban environment in relation to the use of public leisure resources such as open space and urban parks. In fact, the concern with such issues may be traced to the changes in the discipline of geography 'and transformative developments both resulting from, and contributing to, a number of new and competing philosophies with the social sciences'. In relation to leisure and recreation geography, this transformation effect can be related to the concern with gender relations and theoretical perspectives associated with the new cultural geography as a mechanism to conceptualise and theorise leisure space.

One of the central tenets of this approach is embodied in Green *et al.*'s (1990:311) comment where 'A significant aspect of the social control of women's leisure is the regulation of their access to public places, and their behaviour in such places'. These critical perspectives have only recently begun to emerge in tourism geography, where empirical, logical-positivist approaches to personal safety have paid little attention to gender and public places.

In conceptual terms, the analysis of the geography of fear, particularly the implications for gender, is a good illustration of the participation issues for particular groups of women. The application of this perspective to recreational and leisure spaces in the city reveals the male domination of public leisure space. The new cultural geographies have seen leisure and recreational geographers move away, albeit slowly, from a positivist paradigm and the model-building era as new perspectives were conceptualised and theorised. The rise of feminist perspectives in leisure studies by geographers is a notable development, with the impetus provided by landmark studies by feminist leisure studies.

One of the principal problems with the emergence of a new cultural geography is epitomised in Sharmar-Smith and Hannam's (1994:13) comments: 'Place is a deceptively simple concept in geographical thought. We want to make it difficult, uneasy.' Herein lie many of the criticisms of the new cultural geography: one must have a sound grounding in social theory, cultural studies and a knowledge of the new tenets underpinning the debates.

One consequence is that 'the new cultural geography as it has been referred to since the early 1990s demonstrates that space, place and landscape - including landscapes of leisure and tourism - are not fixed but are in a constant state of transition as a result of continuous, dialectical struggles of power and resistance among and between the diversity of landscape providers, users and mediators'. This means that the focus is on agency rather than structure, criticising earlier geographical studies of leisure and recreation which did not problematise space or recognise the human element in the landscape.

This perspective - and one has to recognise it is only one perspective in geographical research - emphasises the diversity, differences and nuances in cultural phenomena which is the antithesis of logical positivist geographical thought that searches for certainty, coherence and generalisations in relation to patterns, forms and processes of spatial phenomena. As a consequence the new interest in leisure and tourism as cultural phenomena in the 'post-positivist geography [is such] that the new cultural geography has emerged and become merged with sociological and cultural studies analyses which are now combining to investigate the multiplicity of behaviours, meanings, consumption trends and identities constructed in and through leisure and tourism', and this case study focuses on the sexuality dimension. Given the growing interest in feminism within the leisure constraints literature, and the concern with constraints to participation, it is timely to focus on the issue of fear, derived from Madge's survey of Leicester's urban park system.

IMPLICATIONS FOR SOCIAL EXCLUSION

Urban parks are estimated to be used by 40 per cent of the British population on a regular basis, but critics argue that urban parks as a recreational resource are being avoided by the general public. This is particularly acute for certain groups of the population (e.g. women, children and ethnic groups), where fear acts as a constraint on use. This adds a new dimension to the recreational constraints literature. Explanations of the growing neglect of urban parks within the UK have been related to a decline in public spending, from 54 per cent of leisure budgets in 1981 to 1982 to 44 per cent in 1991 to 1992, although these statistics need to recognise greater financial efficiencies derived from contracting out park services.

In the 1990s there was growing evidence that urban parks were not perceived as peaceful sanctuaries for recreational and leisure pursuits among the wider population. Burgess *et al.*'s (1988a) innovative Greenwich Open Space Project documented the dimensions of fear. Dimensions included antisocial behaviour among teenagers and vandalism that reduced local enjoyment and participation. Similar concerns of insecurity, fear and use of parks and open spaces have also been recorded in Australia, and North America. Additional research shows how women, black people, the elderly and the gay community may be excluded from using urban spacc as frccly as other subgroups of the population. As Burgess *et al.* (1988a: 472) remarked in the Greenwich context: 'many people expressed feelings of insecurity and vulnerability in open spaces, reflecting fears of personal attack and injury.

Among the Asian community, these feelings are exacerbated by the growth in incidence of racially motivated attacks in public open spaces.' The outcome, as Madge (1997:238) recognised, was that 'This fear, which reflects structural inequalities in society, is translated into spatial behaviour which usually involves a reluctance to occupy certain public spaces at certain times of the day'. For the geographer, it is the spatial manifestation of that fear and its implications for recreational resource use. Although the evolution and development of Leicester's urban parks are reviewed later, it is worth observing the socio-demographic context of Madge's study prior to outlining the principal findings.

Leicester, located in the East Midlands in the UK, is a medium-sized city with a population of 272,000 people. What is notable is its diverse ethnic mix: 72 per cent of the population are white, 24 per cent are Asian, 2 per cent Afro-Caribbean, 2 per cent Chinese and other 'ethnic groups'. Despite the city's urban-industrial development, it is widely acknowledged that the city has an enviable distribution of open space. By 1994, Leicester City Council was responsible for over 1200 ha of open space, which comprised 20 per cent of the total city area. This is a significant level of provision within an international context, and certainly enhances the city's green and open feel as a British city. In this context, Madge's (1997) analysis of the geography of fear was timely.

The sampling framework, namely face-to-face interviews with Leicester residents at on-street locations sought to derive a sample of city-wide park and open space use, with some 535 respondents interviewed. From the survey, ten main constraints emerged which influenced park use. In order of importance these were:

- Fear
- Weather
- Lack of time due to work
- Family constraints
- Lack of transport
- Lack of interest
- Limited awareness of facilities available
- Housework
- Distance of parks/too far away
- Physically unable to get to the parks.

Some 43 per cent of respondents attributed fear as a 'very important' factor constraining their use of parks. The gender difference was striking with 75 per cent of women compared to 50 per cent of men stating fear was a major constraint on park use. This is in line with Westover's (1985) finding in North America, where 90 per cent of female respondents felt unsafe if alone in parks. Studies of victimisation in Leicester (e.g. Willis 1992) recognise that women have a greater sense of insecurity due to their vulnerability to crime.

When ethnicity was examined, Asian groups expressed higher levels of fear compared with white and Afro-Caribbean groups reflecting victimisation statistics, racial abuse and attacks in the urban environment. In terms of age, those over 45 expressed the greatest levels of fear. As Madge (1997:241) rightly acknowledged: 'The result of fear of crime is, however, concrete: the elderly are less likely to use public parks for recreation.'

In terms of causes of fear, Madge (1997) observed that the main causes of fear of park use were: anxieties related to actual or potential bodily harm (e.g. mugging, sexual attack, loitering people, gangs of youths, dogs and racial attack). Women's fears were greatest in relation to fear of sexual attack by men. These findings reflected the prevailing levels of fear of sexual violence which women in Leicester harbour, particularly the high level of sexual harassment which was rarely reported (Women's Equality Unit 1993). In fact 77 per cent of female respondents were fearful of sexual attacks in parks, a much higher figure than in similar surveys in Edinburgh and Seattle. Fear of racial attack was also much higher for Afro-Caribbean and Asian groups than for white groups.

The implications of these findings are reflected in the behaviour and use of parks. Women tended to avoid large open spaces, unlit areas and those areas with dense undergrowth and trees. The onset of nightfall also elevated fear of using such places, especially if they were alone. As Madge suggested, 'Fear is a significant factor structuring the use of public parks in Leicester. The intensity and cause of fear varied with social traits of gender, ethnicity and age and affected spatial behaviour regarding use of parks. The geography of fear is mediated through a set of overlapping social, ideological and structural power relations which become translated into spatial behaviour.'

The findings of Madge's study highlight how a new constraint on leisure behaviour has specific gender, ethnic and social ramifications for recreational resource use. Although Madge (1997) criticises the existing recreational literature for neglecting this issue, fear is a more profound issue in urban environments than has hitherto been the case in recreational research. While Hoyles (1994) argued for a greater feminisation of public space, and Madge (1997) argued for increased informal surveillance to encourage public participation and use of parks and open spaces, creating safer parks is deeply embedded in more complex notions of creating safe cities. Koskela and Pain (2000) point to the problems and failures of designing out fear from the urban environment, given the extent to which fear of crime pervades city spaces.

In a review of urban public space in Tokyo and New York, Cybriwsky (1999) recognised the growth in the surveillance of public spaces to improve security which could lead to a return to private spaces and attempts to modify social behaviour in recreational spaces. This is a feature which Giddens (1990:20) recognised whereby 'surveillance is a means of levering the modern social world away from traditional modes of social activity'. Indeed, Koskela and Pain (2000:279) argued that 'Geographers and planners should take greater account of the complexity of fear. ... Places have some influence on fear, but perhaps of equal or greater significance is the ways in which fear shapes our understanding, perception and use of space and place.'

This is certainly a truism in the case of recreational use of urban parks in Madge's (1997) findings which have a wider application to urban recreational resource use in the developed world. A great deal of progress will need to be made in addressing fear of crime and recreational and leisure spaces in urbanised societies until Koskela and Pain's (2000:274) analysis that 'Green urban spaces and woodlands are commonly perceived as dangerous places and feelings of insecurity often have a deterrent effect on women's use of them' is no longer a valid assessment.

- The geography of fear is an important factor shaping participation by certain social groups in recreational activities.
- The problem of fear affects certain groups' participation patterns (e.g. the elderly and women) more than others.
- The creation of safer recreational open spaces is more problematic since it will involve greater surveillance, monitoring and control of informal leisure spaces.
- The new cultural geography, particularly the geography of gender,

provides invaluable insights to explain how women's leisure space is embedded in notions of fear, constraints on the use of urban space and the resultant inequalities.

RESOURCES AND FASHIONS

While models of participation and obstacles to recreation have attempted to predict the probability of people participating in activities, using variables such as age, sex, marital status and social variables (e.g. housing tenure, income and car ownership), predictions decline in accuracy when attempting to identify individual activities (e.g. golf). What such recreational models often fail to acknowledge is the role of choice and preference given a range of options. In this respect, geographical proximity to recreational resources and access to them is a major determinant. This is demonstrated by Burton (1971), who found that in Britain, people were three times as likely to use a recreational resource if they lived between half and three-quarters of a mile away, a feature emphasised by Patmore (1983) and Page *et al*. (1994) in research on urban parks.

This shows that the proximity to a recreational resource increased the propensity for use at a swimming pool, yet for leisure centres where attendees used cars to visit them, the distance-decay function had a less rapid decline in attendance in relation to distance. Outside urban areas, the occurrence of recreational resources are more varied in their spatial distribution, and recreational opportunities need to be closely examined in relation to demand and supply. To provide a number of detailed insights into the patterns of recreation in different countries, and how demand is influenced and constrained, a number of national recreational patterns are examined followed by a case study of regional demand.

MEASURING RECREATIONAL DEMAND

Most geographers acknowledge the continued lack of suitable data on recreational demand, as Patmore (1983:55) explains:

Prior to the 1960s sources were scattered and fragmentary, and lacked any coherent basis. The studies undertaken for the American Outdoor Recreation Resources Review Commission and published in 1962 gave the impetus for work in Britain. Two wide-ranging national surveys were carried out later in the latter part of that decade: the Pilot National Recreation Survey ... and the Government social survey's Planning for Leisure.... These surveys remain unique at national level.

Although such surveys also have a number of limitations - they were 'one-off' studies, the methods of data collection did not allow comparability of the data for each survey, and the results are often dated on publication due to the time required to analyse the results - they were a starting point for analysing demand. Yet since 1972 no major survey specifically focusing on leisure has been undertaken in the UK, although the General Household Survey (GHS), which normally occurs every four years, has included a number of questions on leisure.

PROBLEMS AND METHODS OF MEASURING RECREATIONAL DEMAND

When seeking to understand their recreational habits, asking individuals questions about their recreational habits using social survey techniques remains the most widely used approach. A landmark study by Rowntree and Lavers (1951) of *English Life and Leisure* provides a good illustration of the early use of a diverse range of research methods and sources to construct patterns of participation in leisure and recreation in post-war Britain. Even so, researchers recognise that precision is needed to identify participation, non-participation and the frequency of each.

For this reason, questions on surveys need to follow the type of format used on the GHS, to provide both a temporal and quantitative measure of demand.

Patmore (1983:57) cites the GHS, which begins by asking respondents: 'What ... things have you done in your leisure time ... in the four weeks ending last Sunday?' Survey data rarely record all the information a researcher seeks (e.g. respondents' recall ability may not accurately record the full pattern), or respondents have a different understanding of a term to that intended by the researcher. As a result, a variety of survey techniques are necessary to derive a range of complementary and yet unique insights into recreation demand.

Within the recreation literature, three techniques have primarily been used:

- A continuous record of recreation activities of a sample population for a given time period which involves respondents keeping a diary of activities (the time budget approach) (Zuzanek *et al.*'s (1998) cross-national survey of Dutch and Canadian use of time is a good source to consult).
- Questionnaire surveys which require respondents to recall activities either in the form of an individual case study, which are detailed and sometimes contain both qualitative and quantitative questions and which are inevitably small-scale due to the time involved in in-depth qualitative interviews.
- Questionnaire surveys which are large scale, enabling subsamples to be drawn which are statistically significant. Such surveys may be derived using simple and unambiguous questions which focus on a specific recreation activity or one that covers the entire spectrum of leisure activities (e.g. the GHS which surveyed 17,574 people in 1993 in Great Britain aged 16 and over). To illustrate how these techniques have been used and the way such data have been analysed, the time

budget approach and national surveys of recreational activities are now examined.

According to Coppock and Duffield (1975:5), 'recreation takes place in that portion of people's lives in which they are free (within constraints) to choose their activities, that is, their leisure time, [and] how they spend their time (time-budgets) is of paramount importance in any attempt to establish recreational demand, since it determines where recreational activities are possible'.

Therefore, time budget analysis is a vital tool in analysing demand. Time budgets provide a systematic record of a person's use of time. They describe the duration, sequence and timing of a person's activities for a given period, usually of between a day and a week. When combined with the recording of the location at which activities occur, the record is referred to as a space time budget.

Time budget studies provide for the understanding of spatial and temporal behaviour patterns which may not be directly observable by other research techniques either because of their practicality or their intrusion into individual privacy. Such studies are often undertaken through the use of detailed diaries which are filled in by participants.

However, this method has not been widely used in comparison with more traditional survey techniques due to the difficulty for individuals of accurately keeping records. For example, in 1966 and 1974 to 1975 the British Broadcasting Corporation used its Audience Research Department to recruit people to keep a diary for a full week with half-hour entries. Yet even in such a short time span, diarists' willingness to record information accurately declined towards the end of the week. However, pioneering research by Glyptis (1981a) used a diary technique which examined a sample of 595 visitors to the countryside. Respondents kept a diary record spanning three days and five evenings, recording the dominant pursuit in half-hour periods.

While respondents identified up to 129 different leisure activities, each cited an average of 11. The value of the study was that through the use of cluster analysis to statistically analyse the sample and to group the population for more detail of this technique), it identified the leisure lifestyles of respondents with distinct groupings, where people of different social classes engaged in similar activities. The value of such research is in the identification of factors beyond simplistic analogies of demand determined by biological, social and economic factors.

INTERNATIONAL PERSPECTIVES

The most useful survey of national surveys of leisure time and the recreational activities undertaken may be found in Cushman *et al.* (1996a) which reviews international data on leisure and the existence of cross-national comparative research. It is also useful since the origins and role of participation surveys are reviewed, a feature subsequently updated by Parker (1999) in the UK context.

THE UNITED KINGDOM

Since the publication of Patmore's (1983) detailed review of data sources for analysing leisure and recreation patterns in the UK, Veal (1992) updated the situation pointing to the GHS and the role of the Australian Commonwealth government in commissioning the first National Recreation Participation Survey in Australia in 1985 to 1986. This section examines demand at the national level in a number of countries to provide comparisons. However the most up-to-date and accessible source which documents these issues in the UK is the Office of Population and Censuses (OPCS) Social Trends. The 1999 edition compiles data from a wide variety of sources and examines:

- Use of time for leisure and other activities showing that men in full-time employment had around two more hours of free time than women in full-time employment.
- Participation in home-based leisure activities in the period 1977 to 1997 indicated that watching television remained the most important pastime, while other activities vary by age and sex (i.e. gardening is more popular among men aged 25 years or more).

Table. Participation in Home-based Leisure Activities: by Gender, in Great Britain 1977-97.

	1977	1987	1996-97
Males			
Watching TV	97	99	99
Visiting/entertaining friends or relations	89	94	95
Listening to radio	87	89	90
Listening to records/tapes/ CDs	64	76	79
Reading books	52	54	58
DIY	51	58	58
Gardening	49	49	52
Dressmaking/needlework/ knitting	2	3	3
Females			
Watching TV	97	99	99
Visiting/entertaining friends or relations	93	96	97
Listening to radio	87	86	87
Listening to records/tapes/ CDs	60	71	77
Reading books	57	65	71
DIY	22	30	30
Gardening	35	43	45
Dressmaking/needlework/ knitting	51	47	37

Note: Percentage in each age group participating in each activity in the four weeks before interview.

- Day visits form a popular activity in terms of leisure time and derived from the 1998 UK Day Visits Survey examined round trips from home to locations in the UK. Between 1994 and 1998, leisure day visits increased by 15 per cent, rising to 5.9 billion in 1998. The two most commonly cited reasons for day visits were to drive out for a drink to a restaurant or public house, or to visit friends and relatives. In terms of gender, males were more likely to go out for a drink than females while females would tend to visit friends and relatives more than males.
- In terms of tourism, Blackpool Pleasure Beach was the UK's most popular tourist attraction (7.1 million visits in 1998), with the British Museum the second most popular (5.6 million visits in 1998).
- In 1998, 56 million holidays of four nights or more were taken by British residents, a rise of 36 per cent on 1971. The number of domestic holidays taken fell slightly in the of consumption of high forms of culture (e.g. visiting museums, exhibitions and concert halls).

Table. Participation in the Most Popular Sports, Games and Physical Activities: by Gender and Age, in the UK 1996-97

	16-19	20-24	25-34	35-44	45-54	55-64	65 and over	All aged 16 and over
Males								
Walking	57	57	50	53	51	50	37	49
Snooker/pool/billiards	54	45	29	19	13	9	5	19
Cycling	36	24	19	18	12	8	5	15
Swimming	18	17	17	20	10	7	5	13
Soccer	47	28	17	10	2	1	-	10
Females								
Walking	45	43	44	45	49	43	25	41
Keep fit/yoga	29	28	24	20	14	12	6	17
Swimming	23	21	26	22	14	12	5	16
Cycling	14	11	10	12	7	4	2	8
Snooker/pool/billiards	24	17	6	3	1	-	-	4

Table. Day Visits from Home: by Gender and Main Activity, 1998.

Great britain	Percentages		
	Males	Females	All
Eat/drink	21	15	18
Visit friends	14	19	17
Walk/hill-walk/ramble	16	14	15
Shop	9	15	12
Entertainment	5	7	6
Indoor sport	7	4	5
Outdoor sport	8	3	5
Hobby/special interest	4	5	5
Drive/sightsee	3	3	3
Swimming	2	3	3
Leisure attraction	2	2	2
Watching sport	2	1	2
Cycling/mountain biking	3	1	2
Informal sport/games	2	2	2
Other	2	5	3
All visits	100	100	100

Table. Holidays Abroad: by Destination.

	1971	1981	1991	1998
Spain	34.3	21.7	21.3	27.5
France	15.9	27.2	25.8	20.2
United states	1.0	5.5	6.8	7.0
Greece	4.5	6.7	7.6	5.3
Italy	9.2	5.8	3.5	4.0
Portugal	2.6	2.8	4.8	3.6
Irish republic	-	3.6	3.0	3.5
Turkey	-	0.1	0.7	3.0
Netherlands	3.6	2.4	3.5	2.7
Cyprus	1.0	0.7	2.4	2.6
Belgium	-	2.1	2.1	2.3
Germany	3.4	2.6	2.7	1.8
Malta	-	2.6	1.7	1.3
Austria	5.5	2.5	2.4	1.3
Other countries	19.0	13.7	11.8	13.9
All destinations (=100%) (thousands)	4,201	13,131	20,788	32,306

1990s, compensated by overseas trips. The most popular destination remained Spain in 1998, with Europe the dominant destination for British holidaymakers.

The USA remains the most popular non-European destination.

- In 1998, people aged 65 or more were the least likely to go on holiday, with those aged 45 to 54 years of age the most likely to take a holiday overseas.
- In terms of sporting activities, men are consistently more likely than women to participate in sport. In 1996 to 1999, 71 per cent of men and 57 per cent of women participated in at least one sporting activity in the four weeks prior to being interviewed for the GHS.

POLAND

Poland is an interesting example, given the new roles for recreation in the post-communist state, since market reforms and ideological change has led to new roles for leisure post-1989. Although one consequence of austerity programmes to deal with budget deficits, a number of pre- and post-communist data sources exist to reconstruct leisure participation. The government Central Statistical Office (GUS) collects the majority of data. Jung (1996) noted that over the period between 1972 and 1990, participation trends showed:

- Listening to the radio and watching television remained the dominant activities in terms of participation.
- Former communist culture activities, such as going to the cinema, theatre and opera declined in importance from over half of the population in 1972 to under one-third by 1990.
- Economic and political reforms in the 1980s may account for a sharp decline in participation

More detailed time budget studies have been examined by Olszewska (1989), and Jung (1996) highlighted a number of key global influences upon leisure participation: a growing media influence on mass culture, outbound travel by the Polish population (and inbound tourism), despite the withdrawal of state social subsidies for holiday travel. The electronic mass media also had an impact on leisure consumption. In the post-communist era, problems associated with the commercialisation of leisure and a growing polarisation of wealth, less economic security, rising unemployment and increasing rates of crime provide a new context for leisure participation.

HUNGARY

Fukaz (1989) examined the Csepel project undertaken in Hungary, which in 1969 sampled 400 blue-collar workers in one of the country's largest metal factories. Further in-depth interviews were undertaken in the period 1969 to 1972, 1975 to 1979 and 1979 to 1982, to collect time budget data as well as in-depth case studies. The longitudinal nature of the survey up to 1982 allows changes to be charted through time, and a simulation sample in 1985 (not using the original 1969 workers) provided a further in-depth case study. While the

Csepel project is not representative of the Hungarian population, macro-economic changes in Hungarian society are reflected in the lifestyles of the population and these are reflected in the Csepel sample.

Over the period 1969 to 1985, hours of work in Hungary were reduced from 48 to 40 hours a week, which is often argued by researchers as a pre-condition for the expansion of leisure. But in Hungary the reduction in official hours of work was accompanied by increases in overtime working and the growth of second jobs. Fukaz (1989:41) argued that 'as Hungary's economy developed, the prestige of leisure appears to have grown.... Only 6.4 per cent in 1976 and 3.9 per cent in 1979 preferred work to leisure on Saturdays'. Yet the evidence from the Csepel study indicates that 'the main obstacles to a growth and enrichment of leisure in Hungary are not rooted in inadequate leisure education, or in a weakening or absence of leisure values. Rather, the barriers have been erected by objective material and financial conditions. The latter have discouraged individuals from using reductions in official work time to enhance their leisure' preferring to use the time in some cases for pecuniary reward.

In terms of leisure activities undertaken by the Csepel workers, these were largely related to passive forms of recreation. The most popular activities were watching television and just relaxing, though seasonal variations exist, with winter leisure being home-based but urban work patterns tend to dominate leisure in present-day Hungary. The growth of second home ownership has also characterised weekend and vacation leisure time for those families with access to such resources.

These three examples of recreational demand show that the patterns of leisure activities for each population exhibit a common range of characteristics, in terms of the predominance of passive activities, and the constraints of urban living which largely structure the time budgets of those in employment due to weekday work commitments. In other words, the patterns of demand highlighted in the three national surveys point to the existence of factors which facilitate and constrain recreational activities in each particular context.

Even so, it is important to recognise the current criticisms and concerns with national participation surveys observed by Cushman *et al.* (1996b: 12) as 'Recently surveys have had a "bad press" from academics, particularly in light of the growing popularity - and indeed orthodoxy - of qualitative research methods in the field'. As a result, qualitative researchers point to the shortcomings, limitations and somewhat outmoded approach of quantitative 'positivist' research methods. However, so far the discussion of demand has focused on national patterns, and therefore attention now turns to the regional level to examine the contribution the geographer can make to the analysis of demand within a regional geographic framework.

THE REGIONAL DEMAND FOR LEISURE AND RECREATION

Within the studies of national recreational demand reviewed in the previous section, it is clear that the analyses of geographical patterns of demand were relatively scant, given the tendency for national studies to lack a regional dimension. It is the spatial variations in demand which are of interest to the geographer, and a number of studies have been undertaken which utilise the geographer's spatial analytical approach to examine demand patterns. North-West England is one such area which has seen a significant contribution made to understanding the scale and nature of regional recreational demand including evidence in Rodgers' (1969) insights from the *Pilot National Recreation Survey*, Rodgers' (1977) contribution to leisure in the North-West and Rodgers and Patmore's (1972) *Leisure in the North-West*.

The North-West of England is an interesting region with a variety of socioeconomic contrasts ranging from the urban decline apparent in inner-city areas through to a range of country districts with high levels of prosperity akin to South-East England. What Rodgers (1993) explored was the changing political climate for leisure provision at national level, namely the rolling back of the frontiers of the state and changing social philosophy that active and creative leisure pursuits deserved to 'be promoted as widely as possible, with the support of public funding and subsidy, to an increasing emphasis on the concept that the provision of recreation is simply another service industry best left to the operation of the market for most efficient delivery at least cost'.

This marks a shift in political ideology: that leisure is no longer a significant welfare service to be delivered to all sectors of the population at free or subsidised prices due to the contribution it makes to enhanced quality of life. Thus the move to a market-driven approach requires local authorities as the principal planners of community-based leisure provision to recognise the existence of leisure markets which comprise different forms of recreational demand in time and space. Local leisure markets are diverse, where a multitude of factors may affect their composition.

For example, those where unemployment, social stress due to environmental factors and low rates of population growth exist may offer little commercial opportunity for the private sector despite real leisure needs. Yet if left to the market, such needs may not be served adequately due to the apparent lack of prosperity or ability of individuals to pay for a resource that poor people view as a luxury item when they cannot always command the financial resources to meet basic needs.

Thus, at a regional level, a detailed district-by-district assessment of the market is necessary to show which areas and markets may still require local authority support to avoid gross inequalities in access and provision from developing any further.

Rodgers (1993) used two principles to underpin an analysis of leisure markets:

- A significant proportion of demand is age-related, and changes through time will affect future needs;
- Aocio-economic well-being is a powerful determinant of the volume and pattern of demand in the present and the future.

By combining these factors in an overall assessment, Rodgers (1993) was able to develop a typology of districts and their ability to support a market-based approach to leisure provision. In terms of age-related markets, Rodgers (1993:119-20) identified four groups:

- The teenage-young adult, who is active and a major generator of recreational demand, especially active pursuits. Within the North-West, this group exhibits an almost universal decline;
- The family phase (aged 25 to 44 years), with a distinctive set of leisure interests;
- A post-family phase (aged 45 to 60 years), where active recreational interests are in decline but an interest in general leisure activities is strong;
- The elderly, with a significant range of passive leisure interests.

By analysing forecast population growth in each of these groups, Rodgers (1993:125) concluded that for planning future leisure provision the following characteristics needed to be incorporated into any geographical assessment of demand:

- A common feature of districts in the region is the absence of growth, except in the family phase. Rates of growth of 4 per cent above the national average are apparent in the age group 25 to 44 years for 1981 to 1991. The opportunities for market-driven provision include fitness training, outdoor pursuits in the countryside, water-sports and ten-pin bowling.
- In the post-family phase, growth rates are less than the national average, with a degree of localised growth in the industrial towns of Greater Manchester, West Lancashire and districts of North Cheshire though not in Merseyside. The most prominent activities are bowls, fishing, dance, keep fit and walking which are likely to have little appeal for private sector operators.
- The youth market exhibits a clear decline, except for areas where planned growth exists (e.g. new towns), with rates above the national average for Merseyside and parts of inner Manchester. In the period 1981 to 1991 a decline of 13 to 17 per cent exists in most districts, with the exception of Cheshire and West Lancashire.
- Among the elderly, trends are complex, but no patterns of growth are evident in traditional retirement areas.

- A number of extremes exist in subregional patterns of demand, with weaknesses in Merseyside which stretches beyond the inner-city districts. In East Cheshire (e.g. Congleton, Crewe and Nantwich) a profile of demand akin to the affluent South-East of England exists with different subgroupings of demand in other areas.

One of the most significant contributory factors to the size and nature of demand is clearly related to socio-economic contrasts. Social well-being is, according to Rodgers (1993:126), 'a strong influence on both the volume and structure of leisure demand and on the relative roles of public and commercial provision in meeting it'.

Using the Department of the Environment (DoE) Social Deprivation Index, which derives negative indices based on unemployment, overcrowding, single-parent and pension households, housing quality and ethnic origin, Rodgers (1993) ranked the districts in the North-West on this composite measure of social stress and also included levels of car ownership. The results were used to identify a range of geographically based leisure markets which were strong or weak in terms of demand, particularly in relation to their capacity to pay for recreational activities in a market-driven local leisure economy.

- Approximately 12 districts are in the top left quadrant, which represent areas of prosperity with comparatively little unemployment, high levels of car ownership and income generation and low levels of social stress. These districts exhibit some strength in demand despite a drop in numbers of people aged 13 to 24 years, while growth in the family and post-family sectors exists. These districts have the most appeal to commercial providers. Rodgers (1993:127) suggests that 'for large sections of the community and for many recreations a blend of private-sector and voluntary body provision, with local authorities acting largely with a market philosophy, might offer an effective formula. The case for massive direct subsidy is relatively weak, against the stronger conflicting claims of less fortunate areas' in the allocation of scarce public sector resources for recreation. Even so, pockets of target groups exist (e.g. housewives, the young and active elderly) who would benefit from some subsidy of their activities. In the north-west of the region, problems of access to recreational resources also exist in largely rural districts.
- A grouping which occupies the bottom right corner scores low on prosperity while the age-related markets show a major decline. This reflects the limited growth in a single age category and districts of population loss (e.g. Merseyside and some of the textile towns). Both the absolute numbers and spending power of the population are declining, where the case of recreational provision for social reasons is essential due to the concentration of disadvantaged groups (e.g.

the unemployed, the poor, single-parent families, the elderly and ethnic minorities). Dependence upon state benefits underpins the case for public subsidy for provision due to the multiple deprivation existing in such areas.

- A further six districts such as Hyndburn and Rochdale score high on low prosperity indices, with selective growth in family and post-family groups with a strong ethnic dimension. The welfare case for provision is also apparent in this category.
- The remaining districts exhibit relatively prosperous populations with limited growth potential, with limited justification for public funding of their recreational services.

While Rodgers (1993) admits the allocation of scarce public resources raises controversial decision-making choices, it does illustrate the value of a spatial analytical approach to recreation, if a wide range of data and factors are taken into account. In other words, this case study illustrates the geographer's ability to synthesise a wide range of complex data sources and concepts to derive a series of spatially contingent generalisations and groupings of the population for a region as diverse as North-West England.

Using concepts from social geography (e.g. social well-being and deprivation) and combining demographic data from districts across the region, the geographer is able to highlight the challenge for regional and local planners in the allocation of declining absolute public sector resources for recreational provision. Regional analysis epitomises the geographer's interest in places, and differences and similarities in both time and space. The greatest contribution geographical research has made is to the site-specific studies of demand, most notably site surveys. For this reason, the remaining focus of this section on recreation examines recreation site surveys.

THE SPATIAL ANALYSIS OF DEMAND AT THE MICRO LEVEL

Within the growing literature on geographical studies of recreation in the 1960s and 1970s, site surveys have become the most documented. As Glyptis (1981b: 277) indicated, 'numerous site surveys - mostly set in the format devised by Burton (1966) ... established the characteristics of visitors and their trips.

Social profiles, trip distances, modes of transport and the duration, purpose and frequency of visits are well documented.' Glyptis (1981b) also noted that the 1980s were ripe for behavioural analysis which had been neglected in relation to site surveys. While reviews of site surveys are too numerous to list, novel research methods which examine the behaviour rather than the socio-economic characteristics of recreationalists have remained less common in the published literature, although some reports have probed this area. Glyptis' (1981b) analysis of one 242 ha site - Westwood Common, Beverley near Hull (UK) - is one such example.

By employing participant observation methods to examine an undulating grassland area of common pasture land 13 km from the urban area of Hull, the spatial distribution of site use by recreationalists was observed and analysed. The main recreational activities observed at the site were sitting, sun-bathing, walking, picnicking, informal games and staying inside one's car. On a busy Sunday in summer, up to 2,000 visitors came to the site. Using dispersion maps, observational mapping permitted the visitor distributions to be located in time and space while length of stay (using car registration data) and maps of use for different days and times complemented traditional social survey methods to analyse visitor behaviour.

The site features, access points, availability of parking and location of landscape features and facilities permit a more detailed understanding of site use. Glyptis (1981b) used observations on five days in August and September between 11 a.m. and 6 p.m. to collate data. Visitor arrivals at the site during the weekend occurred between 12 noon and 2 p.m., and peak use occurred at 4.30 p.m., with the majority of visitors spending one to two hours on site.

The gradual increase in intensity of use by time of day varied by activity, with informal games and picnicking declining after Sunday lunch and walking increasing throughout the afternoon. Local users also displayed a preference to use the site at off-peak times, with increased patterns of dispersion and clumping through time. This reflects access roads, with visitors parking close to (within 15 yards) the site they visited. Visitors were also recorded going to landmarks and facilities (e.g.viewpoints) as well as buying refreshments (e.g. from mobile vans), with the density of use increasing through the day rather than the distribution.

Glyptis (1981c) devised a simple model to explain the dynamics of visitor dispersion. Thereafter, as the pace of arrivals slows, a degree of infilling and consolidation occurs. Then as people depart, dispersion occurs, with a more irregular pattern of distribution arising, although it may be affected by new arrivals in the afternoon who intensify the pattern. What Glyptis (1991:119) recognised was that even though 'sites clearly experience an increase in visitor density, visitor dispersion in a spatial sense remains fairly constant, even with space to spare and no restrictions on public access'.

Using nearest neighbour analysis, Glyptis (1981c) was able to measure the distances between groups of visitors, and that comfortable levels of tolerance exist for visitors in terms of proximity to other people, although the amount of personal space which recreationalists require may vary between different cultures. In fact, Glyptis (1991:119) remarked that 'as levels of use increase on a given day, the percentage occupancy of space actually decreases: visitors only ever use about a fifth of the space available to them, and at times of heaviest use they choose to occupy even less. In other words, site carrying capacity changes continually.'

This study also highlighted the significance of recreation sites with multiple uses, where a variety of recreational needs are capable of being met and, as Burton's (1974) survey of Cannock Chase, Staffordshire (UK) found, individual sites cannot be viewed in isolation: there are relationships between them and understanding them is vital to site management. Glyptis (1981c) highlighted a certain degree of consistency in visitor use of a site, explaining the patterns as a function of the resource base, visitor use and behavioural factors. It may be possible to accommodate or reduce capacity through simple modifications as 'the geographer is well placed to examine fundamental aspects of ... recreation, to diagnose issues in site management, and to propose solutions' (Glyptis 1981b: 285). Therefore, having outlined many of the factors and dimensions of recreational demand at a variety of spatial scales from the national, regional and local level, the discussion now turns to tourism demand.

TOURISM DEMAND

One of the fundamental questions tourism researchers consistently seek to answer is: Why do tourists travel? This seemingly simple proposition remains one of the principal challenges for tourism research. D.G. Pearce (1995a: 18) expands this proposition by asking 'What induces them to leave their home area to visit other areas? What factors condition their travel behaviour, influencing their choice of destination, itineraries followed and activities undertaken?' Such questions underpin not only issues of spatial interaction, but also lead the geographer to question:

- Why tourists seek to travel;
- Where they go;
- When they go and how they get there.

These basic issues have spatial implications in terms of the patterns of tourism, where tourism impacts will occur and the nature of management challenges for destinations which may attract a 'mass market' or be seeking to develop tourism from a low base. In other words, an understanding of tourism demand is a starting point for the analysis of why tourism develops, who patronises specific destinations and what appeals to the client market.

However, geographers are at a comparative disadvantage in answering some of the principal questions associated with tourism demand since 'geographers have not been at the forefront of this research which has been led by psychologists, sociologists, marketers and economists. Some of these researchers have touched on such issues as the potential significance of variations in motivation on destination choice'. However, tourist behaviour and the analysis of motivation has not traditionally been the logical positivist and empirical approach of traditional forms of spatial analysis on tourism with some exceptions. The area of tourist behaviour has a more developed literature within the field of social psychology than geography, and the emphasis in this section is on the way such approaches assist in understanding how tourist behaviour may result in the spatial implications for tourism.

The precise approach one adopts to the analysis of tourism demand is largely dependent upon the disciplinary perspective of the researcher. Geographers view demand in a uniquely spatial manner as 'the total number of persons who travel, or wish to travel, to use tourist facilities and services at places away from their places of work and residence', whereas in this context demand 'is seen in terms of the relationship between individuals' motivation [to travel] and their ability to do so' with an attendant emphasis on the implications for the spatial impact on the development of domestic and international tourism. In comparison, the economist emphasises 'the schedule of the amount of any product or service which people are willing and able to buy at each specific price in a set of possible prices during a specified period of time. Psychologists view demand from the perspective of motivation and behaviour', while Uysal (1998) reviewed the wider context of tourism demand. In conceptual terms, there are three principal elements to tourism demand:

- *Effective or actual demand* comprises the number of people participating in tourism, commonly expressed as the number of travellers. This is most commonly measured by tourism statistics which means that most official sources of data are measures of effective demand.
- *Suppressed demand* is the population who are unable to travel because of circumstances (e.g. lack of purchasing power or limited holiday entitlement) which is called potential demand. Potential demand can be converted to effective demand if the circumstances change. There is also deferred demand where constraints (e.g. lack of tourism supply such as a shortage of bedspaces) can also be converted to effective demand if a destination or locality can accommodate the demand.
- *No demand* is a distinct category for the population who have no desire to travel.

According to Cooper *et al.* (1993:16) the demand for tourism may be viewed in other ways using a number of other concepts:

- *Substitution of demand* where the demand for a specific activity is substituted by another activity;
- *Redirection of demand* where the geographical distribution of tourism is altered due to pricing policies of competing destinations, special events or changing trends and tastes.

Therefore, it is apparent that the analysis of tourism demand as an abstract concept remains firmly within the remit of tourism economics. However, the factors which shape the tourist decision-making process to select and participate in specific forms of tourism is largely within the field of consumer behaviour and motivation.

TOURIST MOTIVATION

According to Moutinho (1987:16), motivation is 'a state of need, a condition that exerts a push on the individual towards certain types of action that are seen as likely to bring satisfaction'. In this respect Cooper *et al*. (1993:20) rightly acknowledge that 'demand for tourists at the individual level can be treated as a consumption process which is influenced by a number of factors. These may be a combination of needs and desires, availability of time and money, or images, perceptions and attitudes'.

Not surprisingly, this is an incredibly complex area of research and it is impossible within a chapter such as this to overview the area in depth. Nevertheless, P. Pearce's (1993) influential work in this field outlined a 'blueprint for tourist motivation', arguing that in an attempt to theorise tourist motivation one must consider the following issues:

- The conceptual place of tourism motivation;
- Its task in the specialism of tourism;
- Its ownership and users;
- Its ease of communication;
- Pragmatic measurement concerns;
- Adopting a dynamic approach;
- The development of multi-motive perspectives;
- Resolving and clarifying intrinsic and extrinsic motivation approaches.

To date no all-embracing theory of tourist motivation has been developed which has been adapted and legitimised by researchers in other contexts. This is largely due to the multidisciplinary nature of the research issues identified above and the problem of simplifying complex psychological factors and behaviour into a set of constructs and ultimately a universally acceptable theory that can be tested and proved in various tourism contexts. As a result, Cooper *et al*. (1993:20) prefer to view the individual as a central component of tourism demand to understand what motivates the tourist to travel. Their research rightly acknowledges that:

No two individuals are alike, and differences in attitudes, perceptions and motivation have an important influence on travel decisions [where] attitudes depend on an individual's perception of the world. Perceptions are mental impressions of ... a place or travel company and are determined by many factors which include childhood, family and work experiences. However, attitudes and perceptions in themselves do not explain why people want to travel. The inner urges which initiate travel demand are called travel motivators.

If one views the tourist as a consumer, then tourism demand is formulated through a consumer decision-making process, and therefore one can discern four elements which initiate demand:

- *Energisers of demand*: Factors that promote an individual to decide on a holiday;

- *Filterers of demand*: Which means that even though motivation may prevail, constraints on demand may exist in economic, sociological or psychological terms;
- *Affecters*: Which are factors that may heighten or suppress the energisers that promote consumer interest or choice in tourism;
- *Roles*: Where the family member involved in the purchase of holiday products and the arbiter of group decision-making on choice of destination, product, and the where, when and how of consumption.

These factors underpin the tourist's process of travel decision-making although it does not explain why people choose to travel.

HIERARCHY MODEL AND TOURIST MOTIVATION

Within the social psychology of tourism there is a growing literature which has built upon Maslow's work (discussed earlier in relation to recreation) to identify specific motivations beyond the concept of needing 'to get away from it all' pioneered by Grinstein (1955), while push factors motivating individuals to seek a holiday exist, and pull factors (e.g. promotion by tourist resorts and tour operators) encourage as attractors.

Ryan's (1991:25-9) analysis of tourist travel motivators (excluding business travel) identifies the following reasons commonly cited to explain why people travel to tourist destinations for holidays, which include:

- A desire to escape from a mundane environment;
- The pursuit of relaxation and recuperation functions;
- An opportunity for play;
- The strengthening of family bonds;
- Prestige, since different destinations can enable one to gain social enhancement among peers;
- Social interaction;
- Educational opportunities;
- Wish fulfilment;
- Shopping.

From this list, it is evident that while all leisure involves a temporary escape of some kind, 'tourism is unique in that it involves real physical escape reflected in travelling to one or more destination regions where the leisure experience transpires ... [thus] a holiday trip allows changes that are multi-dimensional: place, pace, faces, lifestyle, behaviour, attitude.

It allows a person temporary withdrawal from many of the environments affecting day to day existence' (Leiper (1984) cited in D.G. Pearce (1995:19). Within most studies of tourist motivations these factors emerge in one form or another, while researchers such as Crompton (1979) emphasise that socio-psychological motives can be located along a continuum, Iso-Ahola (1980) theorised tourist motivation in terms of an escape element complemented by a search component, where the tourist is seeking something. However, Dann's (1981) conceptualisation is probably one of the most useful attempts to simplify the principal elements of tourist motivation into:

- Travel as a response to what is lacking yet desired;
- Destination pull in response to motivational push;
- Motivation as fancy;
- Motivation as classified purpose;
- Motivation typologies;
- Motivation and tourist experiences;
- Motivation as definition and meaning.

This was simplified a stage further by McIntosh and Goeldner (1990) into:

- Physical motivators;
- Cultural motivators;
- Interpersonal motivators;
- Status and prestige motivators.

On the basis of motivation and using the type of experiences tourists seek, Cohen (1972) distinguished between four types of travellers:

- The organised mass tourist, on a package holiday, who is highly organised. Their contact with the host community in a destination is minimal.
- The individual mass tourist, who uses similar facilities to the organised mass tourist but also desires to visit other sights not covered on organised tours in the destination.
- The explorers, who arrange their travel independently and who wish to experience the social and cultural lifestyle of the destination.
- The drifter, who does not seek any contact with other tourists or their accommodation, preferring to live with the host community.

Clearly, such a classification is fraught with problems, since it does not take into account the increasing diversity of holidays undertaken and inconsistencies in tourist behaviour. Other researchers suggest that one way of overcoming this difficulty is to consider the different destinations tourists choose to visit, and then establish a sliding scale similar to Cohen's (1972) typology, but which does not have such an absolute classification.

In contrast, Plog (1974) devised a classification of the US population into psychographic types, with travellers distributed along a continuum from psychocentrism to allocentrism. The psychocentrics are the anxious, inhibited and less adventurous travellers while at the other extreme the allocentrics are adventurous, outgoing, seeking new experiences due to their inquisitive personalities and interest in travel and adventure.

D.G. Pearce (1995) highlights the spatial implications of such conceptualisations, that each tourist type will seek different destinations which will change through time. However, criticisms by P. Pearce (1993) indicate that Plog's model is difficult to use because it fails to distinguish between extrinsic and intrinsic motivations without incorporating a dynamic element to encompass the changing nature of individual tourists. P. Pearce discounts such models, suggesting that individuals have a 'career' in their travel behaviour where people 'start at different levels, they are likely to change levels during their life-cycle and they can be prevented from moving by money, health and other people. They may also retire from their travel career or not take holidays at all and therefore not be part of the system'.

These are:

- A concern with biological needs;
- Aafety and security needs;
- Relationship development and extension needs;
- Special interest and self-development needs;
- Fulfilment or self-actualisation needs.

Cooper *et al*. (1993:23) argue that 'the literature on tourism motivation is still in an immature phase of development, it has been shown that motivation is an essential concept behind the different patterns of tourism demand'. From the existing literature on tourist motivation, the problems of determining tourist motivation may be summarised as follows:

- Tourism is not one specific product, it is a combination of products and experiences which meet a diverse range of needs.
- Tourists are not always conscious of their deep psychological needs and ideas. Even when they do know what they are, they may not reveal them.
- Tourism motives may be multiple and contradictory (push and pull factors).
- Motives may change over time and be inextricably linked together (e.g. perception, learning, personality and culture are often separated out but they are all bound up together) and dynamic conceptualisations such as P. Pearce's (1993) leisure ladder are crucial to advancing knowledge and understanding in this area.

Having examined some of the issues associated with what motivates tourists to travel, attention now turns to the process of measurement and recording tourist demand using statistical measures.

TOURISM STATISTICS

Ritchie argued that 'an important part of the maturing process for any science is the development or adaptation of consistent and well-tested measurement techniques and methodologies which are well-suited to the types of problems encountered in practice'. In this context, the measurement of tourists, tourism activity and the effects on the economy and society in different environments is crucial to the development of tourism as an established area of study within the confines of social science. Burkart and Medlik (1981) provide a useful insight into the development of measurements of tourism phenomena by governments during the 1960s and their subsequent development through to the late 1970s. While it is readily acknowledged by most tourism researchers that statistics are a necessary feature to provide data to enable researchers, managers, planners, decision-makers and public and private sector bodies to gauge the significance and impact of tourism on destination areas, Burkart and Medlik (1981:74) identify four principal reasons for statistical measurement in tourism:

- To evaluate the magnitude and significance of tourism to a destination area or region;
- To quantify the contribution to the economy or society, especially the effect on the balance of payments;
- To assist in the planning and development of tourism infrastructure and the effect of different volumes of tourists with specific needs;
- To assist in the evaluation and implementation of marketing and promotion activities where the tourism marketer requires information on the actual and potential markets and their characteristics.

Consequently, tourism statistics are essential to the measurement of the volume, scale, impact and value of tourism at different geographical scales from the global to the country level down to the individual destination. Yet an information gap exists between the types of statistics provided by organisations for and the needs of users. The compilation of tourism statistics provided by organisations associated with the measurement of tourism has established methods and processes to collect, collate and analyse tourism statistics (World Tourism Organisation (WTO) 1996), yet these have been understood by only a small number of researchers and practitioners. Thus this section attempts to demystify the apparent sophistication and complexity associated with the presentation of statistical indicators of tourism and their value to spatial analysis, since geographers have a strong quantified methods tradition, which is reflected in the use and reliance upon such indicators to understand spatial variations and patterns of tourism activity.

All too often, undergraduate and many postgraduate texts assume a prior knowledge of tourism statistics and they are only dealt with in a limited way by most tourism texts, and where such issues are raised they are usually discussed in over-technical texts aimed at a limited audience (e.g. Frechtling 1996). A commonly misunderstood feature which is associated with tourism statistics is that they are a complete and authoritative source of information (i.e. they answer all the questions posed by the researcher).

Other associated problems are that statistics are recent and relate to the previous year or season, implying that there is no time lag in their generation, analysis, presentation and dissemination to interested parties. In fact, most tourism statistics are 'typically measurements of arrivals, trips, tourist nights and expenditure, and these often appear in total or split into categories such as business or leisure travel'. Furthermore, the majority of published tourism statistics are derived from sample surveys, with the results being weighted or statistically manipulated to derive a measure which is supposedly representative of the real-world situation. In reality, this often means that tourism statistics are subject to significant errors depending on the size of the sample. The statistical measurement of tourists is far from straightforward, and Latham (1989) identifies a number of distinctive and peculiar problems associated with the tourist population:

- Tourists are a transient and highly mobile population, making statistical sampling procedures difficult when trying to ensure statistical accuracy and rigour in methodological terms.
- Interviewing mobile populations such as tourists is often undertaken in a strange environment, typically at ports or points of departure or arrival where there is background noise which may influence responses.
- Other variables, such as the weather, may affect the responses.

Even where sampling and survey-related problems can be minimised, one has to treat tourism statistics with a degree of caution because of additional methodological issues that can affect the results. For example, tourism research typically comprises:

- Pre-travel studies of tourists' intended travel habits and likely choice of destination (intentional studies);
- Studies of tourists in transit to provide information on their actual behaviour and plans for the remainder of their holiday or journey (actual and intended studies);
- Studies of tourists at the destination or at specific tourist attractions and sites, to provide information on their actual behaviour, levels of satisfaction, impacts and future intentions (actual and intended studies);
- Post-travel studies of tourists on their return journey from their destination or on-site experience or once they have returned to their place of residence (post-travel measures).

In an ideal world, where resource constraints are not a limiting factor on the generation of statistics, each of the aforementioned approaches should be used to provide a broad spectrum of research information on tourism and tourist behaviour. In reality, organisations and government agencies select a form of research which meets their own particular needs. In practice, most tourism statistics are generated with practical uses in mind and they may usually, though not exclusively, be categorised as follows:

- Measurement of tourist volume, enumerating arrivals, departures and the number of visits and stays;

- Expenditure-based surveys which quantify the value of tourist spending at the destination and during the journey;
- The characteristics and features of tourists to construct a profile of the different markets and segments visiting a destination.

However, before any tourism statistics can be derived, it is important to deal with the complex and thorny issue of defining the population - the tourist. Therefore, how does one define and differentiate between the terms *tourism* and *tourist*?

The terms *travel* and *tourism* are often interchanged within the published literature on tourism, though they are normally meant to encompass 'the field of research on human and business activities associated with one or more aspects of the temporary movement of persons away from their immediate home communities and daily work environments for business, pleasure and personal reasons'. These two terms tend to be used in differing contexts to mean similar things, although there is a tendency for the United States to continue to use the term 'travel' when in fact they mean tourism. Despite this inherent problem which may be little more than an exercise in semantics, it is widely acknowledged that the two terms are used in isolation or in unison to 'describe' three concepts:

- The movement of people;
- A sector of the economy or an industry;
- A broad system of interacting relationships of people (including their need to travel outside their communities and services that attempt to respond to these needs by supplying products).

From this initial starting point, one can begin to explore some of the complex issues in arriving at a working definition of the terms *tourism* and *tourist*. In a historical context, Burkart and Medlik (1981:41) identify the historical development of the term *tourism*, noting the distinction between the endeavours of researchers to differentiate between the concept and technical definitions of tourism. The concept of tourism refers to the 'broad notional framework, which identifies the essential characteristics, and which distinguishes tourism from the similar, often related, but different phenomena'.

In contrast, technical definitions have evolved through time as researchers modify and develop appropriate measures for statistical, legislative and operational reasons implying that there may be various technical definitions to meet particular purposes. However, the concept of tourism, and its identification for research purposes, is an important consideration in this instance for tourism statistics so that users are familiar with the context of their derivation. While most tourism books, articles and monographs now assume either a standard definition or interpretation of the concept of tourism, which is usually influenced by the social scientists' perspective (i.e. a geographical, economic, political, sociological approach or other disciplines), Burkart and Medlik's (1981) approach to the concept of tourism continues to offer a valid assessment of the situation where five main characteristics are associated with the concept.

- Tourism arises from the movement of people to, and their stay in, various destinations.
- There are two elements in all tourism: the journey to the destination and the stay including activities at the destination.
- The journey and the stay take place outside the normal place of residence and work, so that tourism gives rise to activities which are distinct from those of the resident and working populations of the places, through which tourists travel and in which they stay.
- The movement to tourist destinations is of a temporary, short-term character, with the intention of returning home within a few days, weeks or months.
- Destinations are visited for purposes other than taking up permanent residence or employment remunerated from within the places visited (Burkart and Medlik 1981:42).

Furthermore, Burkart and Medlik's (1981) definition of tourism as a concept is invaluable because it rightly recognises that much tourism is a leisure activity which involves a discretionary use of time and money, and recreation is often the main purpose for participation in tourism. But this is no reason for restricting the total concept in this way and the essential characteristics of tourism can best be interpreted to embrace a wider concept. All tourism includes some travel but not all travel is tourism, while the temporary and short-term nature of most tourist trips distinguishes it from migration. Therefore, from the broad interpretation of tourism, it is possible to consider the technical definitions of tourism.

TECHNICAL DEFINITIONS OF TOURISM

Technical definitions of tourism are commonly used by organisations seeking to define the population to be measured, and there are three principal features which normally have to be defined:

- Purpose of travel (e.g. the type of traveller, be it business travel, holiday-makers, visits to friends and relatives or for other reasons).
- The time dimension involved in the tourism visit, which requires a minimum and a maximum period of time spent away from the home area and the time spent at the destination. In most cases, this would involve a minimum stay of more than 24 hours away from home and less than a year as a maximum.
- Those situations where tourists may or may not be included as tourists, such as cruise passengers, those tourists in transit at a particular point of embarkation/departure and excursionists who stay less than 24 hours at a destination (e.g. the European duty-free cross-channel day-trip market).

Among the most recent attempts to recommend appropriate definitions of tourism was the World Tourism Organisation (hereafter WTO) International Conference of Travel and Tourism in Ottawa in 1991 which reviewed, expanded and developed technical definitions, where tourism comprises 'the activities of a person travelling outside his or her usual environment for less than a specified period of time and whose main purpose of travel is other than exercise of an activity remunerated from the place visited', where 'usual environment' is intended to exclude trips within the areas of usual residence and also frequent and regular trips between the domicile and the workplace and other community trips of a routine character, where 'less than a specified period of time' is intended to exclude long-term migration, and 'exercise of an activity remunerated from the place visited' is intended to exclude only migration for temporary work. The following definitions were developed by the WTO:

- International tourism: consists of inbound tourism.
- Visits to a country by non-residents and outbound tourism residents of a country visiting another country.
- Internal tourism: residents of a country visiting their own country.
- Domestic tourism: internal tourism plus inbound tourism (the tourism market of accommodation facilities and attractions within a country).
- National tourism: internal tourism plus outbound tourism (the resident tourism market for travel agents and airlines) (WTO, cited in Chadwick 1994:66).

In order to improve statistical collection and improve understanding of tourism, the United Nations (UN) (1994) and the WTO (1991a) also recommended differentiating between visitors, tourists and excursionists (day trippers). The WTO (1991a) recommended that an international tourist be defined as: 'a visitor who travels to a country other than that in which he/she has his/her usual residence for at least one night but not more than one year, and whose main purpose of visit is other than the exercise of an activity remunerated from within the country visited'; and that an international excursionist (e.g. cruise ship visitors) be defined as 'a visitor residing in a country who travels the same day to a country other than which he/she has his/her usual environment for less than 24 hours without spending the night in the country visited and whose main purpose of visit is other than the exercise of an activity remunerated from within the country visited'.

Similar definitions were also developed for domestic tourists, with domestic tourists having a time limit of 'not more than six months' (WTO 1991a; UN 1994). Interestingly, the inclusion of a same-day travel, 'excursionist' category in UN/WTO technical definitions of tourism makes the division between recreation and tourism even more arbitrary, and there is increasing international agreement that 'tourism' refers to all activities of visitors, including both overnight and same-day visitors (UN 1994:5). Given improvements in transport technology, same-day travel is becoming increasingly important to some countries, with the UN (1994:9) observing, 'day visits are important to consumers and to many providers, especially tourist attractions, transport operators and caterers'. Chadwick (1994) moves the definition of tourists a stage further by offering a typology of travellers (tourists) which highlights the distinction between tourists (travellers) and non-travellers (non-tourists) which is summarised.

It is also useful because it illustrates where technical problems may occur in deciding which groups to include in tourism and which to exclude. From this classification of travellers, the distinction between international and domestic tourism needs to be made. Domestic tourism normally refers to tourists who travel from their normal domicile to other areas within a country. In contrast, international tourism normally involves a tourist leaving their country of origin to cross into another country which involves documentation, administrative formalities and movement to a foreign environment.

DOMESTIC TOURISM STATISTICS

D.G. Pearce (1995a) acknowledges that the scale and volume of domestic tourism worldwide exceeds that of international tourism, though it is often viewed as the poorer partner in the compilation of statistics. For example, most domestic tourism statistics tend to underestimate the scale and volume of flows since certain aspects of domestic tourist movements are sometimes ignored in official sources. The 'visits to friends and relatives, the use of forms of accommodation other than hotels (for example, second homes, camp and caravan sites) and travel by large segments of a population from towns to the countryside are not for the most part included'.

This is supported by the WTO, who argue that 'there are relatively few countries that collect domestic travel and tourism statistics. Moreover some countries rely exclusively on the traditional hotel sector, thereby leaving out of account the many travellers staying in supplementary accommodation establishments or with friends and relatives'. Therefore, the collection of domestic tourism statistics requires the use of different data sources aside from the more traditional sources such as hotel records which identify the origin and duration of a visitor's stay.

To assist in the identification of who to include as a domestic tourist, the WTO (1983) suggests the following working definition: 'any person, regardless of nationality, resident in a country and who travels to a place in the same country for not more than one year and whose main purpose of visit is other than following an occupation remunerated from within the place visited.'

Such a definition includes domestic tourists where an overnight stay is involved and domestic excursionists who visit an area for less than 24 hours and do not stay overnight. In fact, Latham (1989:66) points to the variety of definitions which exist aside from those formulated by WTO and the following issues complicate matters further:

- *Purpose of visit*: All countries using this concept define a domestic tourist as one who travels for a purpose other than to perform a remunerated activity.
- *The length of trip and/or distance travelled*: Certain definitions state that travellers should, for example, be involved in an overnight stay and/or travel a prescribed minimum distance.
- *Type of accommodation*: For practical reasons, some countries restrict the concept of domestic tourism to cover only those persons using commercial accommodation facilities (after Latham 1989:66).

Problems in applying WTO definitions may also reflect an individual country's reasons for generating such statistics, which may not necessarily be to contribute to a better understanding of statistics *per se*. For example, WTO (1981) identified four uses of domestic tourism statistics:

- To calculate the contribution of tourism to the country's economy, whereby estimates of tourism's value to the Gross Domestic Product is estimated due to the complexity of identifying the scope of tourism's contribution.
- To assist in the marketing and promotion of tourism, where government-sponsored tourism organisations seek to encourage its population to take domestic holidays rather than to travel overseas for a discussion of this activity among Pacific Rim countries).
- To aid the regional development policies of governments which harness tourism as a tool for area development where domestic tourists in congested environments are encouraged to travel to less developed areas and to improve the quality of tourism in different environments.
- To achieve social objectives, where socially oriented tourism policies may be developed for the underprivileged which requires a detailed understanding of the holiday-taking habits of a country's nationals.

Regional and local tourist organisations also make use of such data to develop and market destinations and different businesses within the tourism sector. But how is domestic tourism measured? Burkart and Medlik (1981) argue that two principal features need to be measured: first, the volume, value and characteristics of tourism among the population of the country; second, the same data relating to individual destinations within the country. The WTO (1981, cited in Latham 1989) considers the minimum data requirements for the collection of domestic tourism statistics in terms of arrivals and tourist nights in accommodation classified by:

- Month;
- Type of grade of accommodation establishment;

- Location of the accommodation establishment and overall expenditure on domestic tourism.

Latham (1989) argues that it is possible to generate additional data from such variables including length of stay, occupancy rate and average expenditure. Many countries also collate supplementary information beyond the minimum standards identified by WTO, where the socioeconomic characteristics of tourists are identified, together with their use of tourist transport and purpose of visit, though the cost of such data collection does mean that the statistical basis of domestic tourism in many less developed countries remains poor.

The methods used to generate domestic tourism statistics are normally based on the estimates of volume, value and scale derived from sample surveys due to the cost of undertaking large-scale surveys of tourist activities. The immediate problem facing the user of such material is the type of errors and degree of accuracy which can be attached to such data. For example, Latham (1989) identifies the following sample surveys which are now used to supplement data derived from hotel records:

- *Household surveys*, where the residents of a country are interviewed in their own home to ascertain information of tourist trips for the purpose of pleasure. A useful example of a pan-European study is the EC Omnibus study. Even so, little progress has been made internationally to collate common data on household surveys since the OECD's attempt in 1967 to outline the types of data which national travel surveys should collect.
- *Destination surveys*, where high levels of tourist activity occur in a region or resort. Such studies frequently compile statistics on accommodation usage, sample surveys of visitors and may be linked to existing knowledge derived from household surveys.
- *En route surveys*, where tourists are surveyed en route to examine the characteristics and features of tourists. Although it is a convenient way to interview a captive audience depending upon the mode of transport used, the results may not necessarily be as representative without a complete knowledge of the transport flows for the mode of tourist transport being surveyed.

The problem of incomplete questionnaires or non-response may occur where such surveys require a respondent to post the form back to the surveyor.

INTERNATIONAL TOURISM STATISTICS

The two principal organisations which collate data on international tourism are the World Tourism Organisation (WTO) and the Organisation for Economic Cooperation and Development (OECD). In addition, international regional tourism organisations such as the Pacific Asia Travel Association and the ASEAN Tourism Working Group also collect international tourism statistics.

Page (1994b) reviews the major publications of the first two organisations in relation to international tourism, noting the detailed contents of each.

In the case of the WTO, the main source is the *Yearbook of Tourism Statistics*, which contains a summary of the most salient tourism statistics for almost 150 countries and territories. In the case of the OECD, their *Tourism Policy and International Tourism* (referred to as the 'Blue Book') is less comprehensive, covering only 25 countries, but it does contain most of the main generating and receiving areas. While the main thrust of the publication is government policy and the obstacles to international tourism, it does expand on certain areas not covered in the WTO publication.

In contrast to domestic tourism, statistics on international tourism are normally collected to assess the impact of tourism on a country's balance of payments, though as Withyman (1985:69) argued:

Outward visitors seem to attract less attention from the pollsters and the enumerators. Of course, one country's outward visitor is another country's (perhaps several countries) inward visitor, and a much more welcome sort of visitor, too, being both a source of revenue and an emblem of the destination country's appeal in the international market. This has meant that governments have tended to be generally more keen to measure inward than outward tourism, or at any rate, having done so, to publish the results.

This statement indicates that governments are more concerned with the direct effect of tourism on their balance of payments. Yet such statistics are also utilised by marketing arms of national tourism organisations to base their decisions on who to target in international campaigns. The wider tourism industry also makes use of such data as part of their strategic planning and for more immediate purposes where niche markets exist. Even so, Shackleford (1980) argued that the collection of tourism statistics should be a responsibility of the state to meet international standards for data collection (WTO 1996). However, it is increasingly the case that only when the economic benefits of data collection can be justified will national governments continues to compile tourism statistics.

Where resource constraints exist, the collection and compilation of tourism statistics may be impeded. This also raises important methodological issues related to what exactly is being measured. As Withyman (1985:61) argued: 'In the jungle of international travel and tourism statistics, it behoves the explorer to step warily; on all sides there is luxuriant growth. Not all data sources are what they appear to be - after close scrutiny some show themselves to be inconsistent and often unsuitable for the industry researcher and planner.' The key point Withyman (1985) recognises is the lack of comparability in tourism data in relation to what is measured (e.g. is it visitor days or visitor nights?) and the procedures and methodology used to measure international tourism. Frechtling (1976) concluded that the approaches taken by national and international agencies associated with international tourism statistics were converging towards common definitions of trip, travel and traveller.

Yet the principal difficulty which continues to be associated with this is whether business travel should be considered as a discrete activity in relation to tourism. Chadwick (1994:75) notes that 'the consensus of North American opinion seems to be that, despite certain arguments to the contrary ... business travel should be considered part of travel and tourism'. While BarOn (1984) examines the standard definitions and terminology of international tourism as used by the UN and WTO, research by Ngoh (1985) is useful in that it considers the practical problems posed by such definitions when attempting to measure international tourism and find solutions to the difficulties. Latham (1989) suggests that the main types of international tourism statistics collated relate to:

- Volume of tourists;
- Expenditure by tourists;
- The profile of the tourist and their trip characteristics.

As is true of domestic tourism, estimates form the basis for most statistics on international tourism since the method of data collection does not generate exact data. For example, volume statistics are often generated from counts of tourists at entry/exit points (i.e. gateways such as airports and ports) or at accommodation. But such data relate to numbers of trips rather than individual tourists since one tourist may make more than one trip a year and each trip is counted separately. In the case of expenditure statistics, tourist expenditure normally refers to tourist spending within a country and excludes payments to tourist-transport operators.

Yet deriving such statistics is often an indirect measure based on foreign currency estimates derived from bank records, from data provided by tourism service providers or more commonly from social surveys undertaken directly with tourists.

Research by White and Walker (1982) and Baretje (1982) directly questions the validity and accuracy of such methods of data collection, examining the main causes of bias and error in such studies. According to Edwards (1991:68-9), 'expenditure and receipts data apart, tourist statistics are usually collected in one of the five following ways':

- Counts of all individuals entering or leaving the country at all recognised frontier crossings, often using arrival/departure cards where high-volume arrivals/departures are the norm. Where particularly large volumes of tourist traffic exist, a 10 per cent sampling framework is normally used (i.e. every tenth arrival/departure card). Countries such as New Zealand actually match the arrival/departure cards, or a sample, to examine the length of stay.
- Interviews carried out at frontiers with a sample of arriving and/or

departing passengers to obtain a more detailed profile of visitors and their activities within the country. This will often require a careful sample design to gain a sufficiently large enough sample with the detail required from visitors on a wide range of tourism data including places visited, expenditure, accommodation usage and related items.

- Selecting a sample of arrivals and providing them with a self-completion questionnaire to be handed in or posted. This method is used in Canada but it fails to incorporate those visitors travelling via the United States by road.
- Sample surveys of the entire population of a country including travellers and non-travellers, though the cost of obtaining a representative sample is often prohibitive.
- Accommodation arrivals and nights spent are recorded by hoteliers and owners of the accommodation types covered. The difficulty with this type of data collection is that accommodation

As a government-sponsored survey which began in 1961, the International Passenger Survey now covers all ports of entry/exit to the UK. It is based on a stratified random sample of tourists arriving and departing from the UK by air and sea. According to Latham (1989:64), IPS' four principal aims are:

- To collect data for the travel account (which acts to compare expenditure by overseas visitors to the UK with expenditure overseas by visitors from the UK) of the balance of payments;
- To provide detailed information on foreign visitors to the UK, and on outgoing visitors travelling overseas.
- To provide data on international migration.
- To provide information on routes used by passengers as an aid to aviation and shipping authorities.

owners have no incentive to record accurate details, particularly where the tax regime is based on the turnover of bed-nights.

The final area of data collection is profile statistics, which examine the characteristics and travel habits of visitors. For example, the UK's International Passenger Survey (IPS) is one survey that incorporates volume, expenditure and profile data on international tourism.

METHODOLOGICAL ISSUES

Latham (1989) reviews the major types of questionnaire/social survey type of data collection used for tourism statistics. He reports that among state-sponsored tourism research in the United States, conversion studies are a popular method to examine and evaluate advertising campaigns and visitor surveys, to assess a sample of visitors to individual states. The use of other methods of data collection are also discussed (e.g. diary questionnaires, participant observation and personal interviews). Yet few studies consider the issue of sampling, sample design and the sources of error which may arise from such surveys.

In fact the lack of research on the reliability of the estimate from a sample survey (the standard error) is rarely discussed in most tourism surveys. In many cases, large tourism surveys focus on the logistics of drawing the sample and the bias which may be reflected in the results. Therefore, any tourism survey will need to pay careful attention to the statistical and mathematical accuracy of the survey, especially the survey design and the effect it may have on the results, a feature which is discussed in great detail by Ryan (1995).

Ryan (1995) provides an excellent review of survey design, questionnaire design, sampling and also an insight into the statistical techniques to use for different forms of tourism data. As a result it serves as an important reference point for issues of methodology and the technical issues associated with the statistical analysis of tourism data. Without reiterating the excellent features of Ryan's findings, it is appropriate to consider some of the main accuracy problems associated with the collection of domestic and international tourism statistics.

PROBLEMS OF ACCURACY

Ryan (1995) argues that errors in data collection can lead to errors in data analysis. Among the most frequently cited problems associated with domestic and international tourism statistics are:

- The methods by which the data are collected, which are influenced by administrative, bureaucratic and legislative factors in each country;
- Sample sizes which are too small and lead to unacceptable sampling errors and in some instances where the sample design is flawed;
- The procedures for collecting tourism statistics are not adhered to by the agency collecting the data.

In addition, Edwards (1991:68) argues that a 'fourth potential reason - arithmetic mistakes and data processing errors - only occasionally produce significant errors'. In fact, Edwards (1991:68) supports the cause of 'tourist statisticians [who] are both knowledgeable and conscientious, but are having to work with tools which they know could produce inaccurate or misleading data', concluding that for any set of tourist data, potential sources of error obviously depend on the method of collection employed. This, in turn, tends to be largely determined by the legislative and administrative framework and by the financial and manpower resources available.

In the case of tourist expenditure and receipts data, organisations such as the International Monetary Fund (IMF) issue guidelines for the compilation of balance of payments statistics. But errors may occur where leakage results from tourist services paid for in overseas bank accounts and in extreme cases, where a black market exists in currency exchange. Edwards (1991) suggests that a regular programme of interviews with departing tourists and returning residents may assist in estimating levels of expenditure.

Despite the apparent problems which may exist with tourism statistics, Edwards (1991:72) argues that data on arrivals and nights spent for most destinations outside of Europe appear reasonably reliable.

Within Europe, data for both inbound and outbound travel are fairly satisfactory for the UK. Greece, Portugal, Spain and [the former] Yugoslavia all appear to have usable frontier arrivals data. The most serious problems are in core continental European countries such as France, Germany, Italy and the Netherlands for which there are no adequate volumetric measures of travel in either direction.

Accommodation arrivals and nights data are clearly gross understatements for many European countries ... often expenditure and receipts data appear better indicators. Outside Europe, the major problems are also in relation to high volume land flows, as between Canada and the USA (in both directions), from the USA to Mexico and from Hong Kong to China.

Therefore, in view of these potential constraints, Edwards (1991) advocates that researchers should compile a range of data from different sources which will not only highlight the deficiencies in various sources, but also extend the existing baseline data. Although Edwards (1991) provides guidelines for comparative tourism research using a range of data for different countries, trends in tourism data remain one of the main requirements for travel industry organisations. Edwards (1991:73) lists key issues to consider in examining tourism trends (i.e. Have arrivals or accommodation data been changed in coverage or definition? Have provisional data for earlier years been subsequently revised? Has the reliability of the data changed and how are changing tastes in travel products affecting the statistics?). Even so, the analysis of trends remains the fundamental starting point for most research studies in tourism. Having considered the issues associated with how tourism statistics are generated, attention now turns to the ways in which geographers analyse such statistics, and variations in tourism activity at different scales.

PATTERNS OF TOURISM

D.G. Pearce's (1995a) seminal study on the geographer's analysis of tourism patterns offers an excellent synthesis reflecting his international contribution to the methodological development of spatial analysis of tourism. By using geographical methodologies and concepts, D.G. Pearce (1995a) uses statistical sources and primary data on tourist activity patterns to analyse the processes and patterns associated with the dynamics of domestic and international tourist activity. This section can only provide a limited evaluation of the geographer's approach to analysis of the presentation of spatially oriented insights on modern-day tourism demand.

The WTO provides the main source of data for international tourism, collated from a survey of major government agencies responsible for data collection. While most international tourists are expressed as 'frontier arrivals' (i.e. arrivals determined by means of a frontier check), arrival/ departure cards (where used) offer additional detail to the profile of international tourists, and where they are not used periodic tourism surveys are often employed. WTO statistics are mainly confined to all categories of travellers, and in some cases geographical disaggregation of the data may be limited by the collecting agency's use of descriptions and categories for aid of simplicity (e.g. rest of the world) rather than listing all categories of arrivals.

In terms of the growth of international travel, documents the expansion of outbound travel with constant growth in the 1960s in an age of discovery of outbound travel for many developed nations. The late 1960s saw international travel expanded by new technology in air travel (e.g. the introduction of the Boeing 747 jumbo jet and the 737 as well as the DC10) which led to rapid growth until the oil crisis in the early 1970s. Growth rates varied in the 1980s, with 'shock waves' to the upward trend being caused by events such as the Gulf Crisis, but international travel has maintained strong growth rates, often in excess of 5 per cent per annum. In contrast, international receipts from travel have outperformed arrivals, with consistent rates of growth (with the exception of the oil crisis and Gulf Crisis) of 10 to 20 per cent which is indicative of the powerful economic effect of tourism for countries. However, China is the notable success story in terms of growth in receipts while a number of European destinations (e.g. the Netherlands and Belgium) have retained the volume of arrivals but their ranking of expenditure has dropped.

As the world's largest tourism markets by expenditure, the USA and Germany have retained their prominence in the top two rankings, whereas Japan has increased its importance as an outbound high spending market as have a number of other Pacific Rim nations such as Taiwan, Singapore and South Korea until the 1997 Asian financial crisis (Hall and Page 2000). As a result of the growth of major outbound growth and travel within the Pacific Rim region, a case study of the outbound South Korean market is now examined.

CASE STUDY: TOURISM DEMAND IN EAST ASIA PACIFIC: THE CASE OF THE SOUTH KOREAN OUTBOUND MARKET AND ACTIVITY PATTERNS IN NEW ZEALAND

Prior to the Asian financial crisis, Korea represented one of the major outbound markets in the Asia-Pacific region. Outbound travel grew from 484,000 in 1985 to 725,000 in 1988 to 3.1 million in 1994, which quadrupled in a six-year period up to 1994. By 1995, outbound travel had reached 3.8 million, representing 9 per cent of the national population of 45 million. Within New Zealand, inbound Korean arrivals increased consistently between 1989 and 1995 as the fastest growing market and remained the focus of industry attention until the Asian financial crisis (New Zealand Tourism Board 1995), despite any substantive and detailed research to consider the needs, aspirations and impact of this market in New Zealand.

Holiday travel has remained a major reason to visit, while females outnumbered males in holiday travel by 54.4 per cent: 45.66 per cent in 1994 and VFR by 63.5 per cent: 36.5 per cent, highlighting the trend towards housewives comprising the majority of outbound female visitors. Male visitors dominated in the purpose of visiting in relation to business travel (91 per cent), to attend a convention (87.7 per cent) and official travel (91.3 per cent). The age profile of the most common outbound Korean tourist was the 31 to 40 age group followed by the 21 to 30 age group, with a significant proportion of 'honeymooners' and single female office workers. According to the 1994 Nationals Overseas Travel Survey, shopping was a major leisure activity for Korean tourists, with an average spends of US$413 per person on purchases such as cosmetics, alcoholic beverages, electronic goods, clothing and toys. McGahey (1996) observed that 40 per cent of these purchases were for gifts.

THE KOREAN INBOUND MARKET IN NEW ZEALAND

According to New Zealand's International Visitor Survey (New Zealand Tourism Board 1995), the Korean market was estimated to have generated NZ$225 million of spending at 1995 prices, equating to an average spend of NZ$2253 per person of NZ$345 a day, the highest amount for any inbound market. In the 12 months ended March 1996, Koreans comprised 8 per cent of New Zealand's international visitor market, increasing from 2,018 in 1987 to 4,184 visitors in 1990 to 61,583 in 1994. The significance of this market was reflected in the New Zealand Tourist Board's (1995) optimistic forecasts for a further doubling of visitor arrivals over the next five years and a target of 114,000 arrivals. However, the size of the impact of the Asian financial crisis on Korea can be illustrated by the 78 per cent drop in Korean visitors to New Zealand in December 1997 compared with the previous year, with there being an expected 75 per cent drop in arrivals from South Korea in 1998 over the previous year.

In contrast to the age profile of the entire Korean tourist outbound market, the main age group of visitors to New Zealand was dominated by the visitors aged 45 to 64 years, predominately those aged 55 to 64. Yet among those visitors aged under 24 years, females outnumber males as unmarried office workers or tertiary level students are more likely to travel than their male counter-parts, since the former enjoy relatively more leisure time.

Since group travel tends to predominate among the inbound Korean market, the length of stay in New Zealand was conditioned by two key factors. First, it is a medium long-haul destination, and second, Korean holiday entitlement was still limited to under ten paid days a year and is not available in one block. Therefore, the maximum length of stay for most outbound Korean tourists was less than one week. According to research (New Zealand Tourism Board 1995), Korean tourists perceived the main appeal of visiting New Zealand as its unspoiled natural phenomena such as hot springs in Rotorua and volcanic areas such as Mount Tongariro.

This reflects the limited spatial activity patterns which most inbound Korean tourists were likely to experience, typically including arrival and departure through Auckland International Airport, with time spent in Auckland, Rotorua, Waitomo Caves, Taupo and returning to Auckland. The following results report the findings of a survey to understand the interrelationship between the time constraints of Korean inbound travel and the spatial distribution of such visitors beyond the limited knowledge base derived from the 442 Korean tourists included in the New Zealand International Visitor Survey of 1995/1996.

KOREAN TOURISTS' ACTIVITY PATTERNS IN NEW ZEALAND

Using a time budget methodology, a survey in July 1996 was employed to produce a systematic record of a person's use of time over a given period to hereby understand the sequence, timing and duration of the tourist's activities in relation to the location of the activities. The technique provides a systematic record of a person's use of time over a given period, typically for a short period ranging from a single day to a week. One of the fundamental assumptions in using this research method is that tourist behaviour and activities are the result of choices, a point illustrated by Floor (1990). D.G. Pearce (1987a) argues that there has been a comparative neglect of tourist activities by tourist researchers, compounded by the lack of available data. Where questionnaire surveys have addressed such issues, the results have often failed to provide a comprehensive assessment of tourist activities, both formal/informal and the relative importance of each. Thrift (1977) provides an assessment of three principal constraints on tourists' daily activity patterns, which are:

- *Comparability constraints* (e.g. the biologically based need for food and sleep);
- *Coupling constraints* (e.g. people need to interact and undertake activities with other people);
- *Authority constraints* (e.g. where activities are controlled, not allowed or permitted at a certain point in time).

Thus both Chapin (1974) and Thrift (1977) identify choices and constraints which will influence the specific activities and context of tourists' daily activities. The use of time budgets via diaries to record tourists' activity patterns has been employed in a number of contexts as research by Gaviria (1975), Cooper

(1981), P.L. Pearce (1981), D.G. Pearce (1986) and Debbage (1991) indicates. Methodological issues raised by these studies highlight the problem of selecting appropriate temporal measures to record tourists' activities. P.L. Pearce (1981) used three main time periods (morning, afternoon and evening) with Gaviria (1975) selecting quarter-hour periods and Cooper (1981) using five time sequences. While the recording of activities by time is a demanding activity for tourists, D.G. Pearce (1986) argues that the main methodological concerns for such surveys are the type of technique to be used; the period to be covered; and the type of sample selected. In addition, Chapin (1984) argues that such studies may choose to use three main survey techniques, which are:

- *A checklist technique*, where respondents select the list of activities they engage in from a pre-categorised list;
- *The yesterday technique*, where subjects are asked to list things they did the previous day, where and when they did them;
- *The tomorrow technique*, where participants keep a diary on what they do, where and when they undertake them.

Although time budget studies may still be viewed as experimental in tourism research, they do offer great potential to gain a detailed insight into tourist activity patterns.

THE SURVEY

During three weeks in July 1996, a time budget survey was developed using the 'yesterday technique' and the time sequencing technique advocated by P.L. Pearce (1981) as part of a more detailed survey of inbound Korean tourists. The complete survey was designed to be completed by Korean tourists during their tour of the North Island of New Zealand and four sites were selected as distribution points for the surveys during the tourists' initial familiarisation point of their tour in Auckland and Rotorua. Two major hotels and two Korean restaurants were selected to provide a degree of close contract with Korean tourists in a familiar environment. Due to the highly organised nature of the Korean itineraries, a one-page diary was distributed at the key sites over a three-week period.

One immediate problem facing the use of the budget approach was in soliciting responses. While a Korean researcher approached the respondents on a random basis, it was essential to keep the survey to one A4 page to encourage participation. As a result, only time-budget questions could be included and key demographic data were omitted (a separate survey by the authors was undertaken examining demand issues among Korean tourists which did consider the profile of visitors).

However, from participant observation conducted during the data collection, it is apparent that the sample of 78 tourists who were prepared to participate in the time budget exercise were typical of the Korean tourist then visiting

New Zealand, being largely aged 31 to 50, being of middle-class status, earning between NZ$40,000 and $60,000 a year and undertaking a multi-destination product.

ACTIVITY PATTERNS OF KOREAN TOURISTS

According to D.G. Pearce (1995a), few data are collected to examine circuit tourism which this market is following, since they adhere to a predetermined circuit pattern. Data exist in a New Zealand context on the touring patterns of international tourists which builds on Forer and Pearce's (1984) innovative study of coach tours by nights spent at key nodes and inter-regional flows.

Forer and Pearce (1984) established the Auckland to Rotorua and Taupo axis by examining tour group itineraries for package tours. While it is apparent that a great deal of continuity and similarity exists in terms of the Korean tour group itineraries which follow a series of linear routes, activity patterns of the tour groups and their specific time budgets remain largely unresearched. One immediate feature which emerges from the 78 completed schedules is that the activity patterns of the visitors closely follow the tour itineraries. The respondents were undertaking three commonly used itineraries developed by tour companies which comprised:

- *Itinerary* 1: Auckland to Rotorua and return to Rotorua (12 tourists).
- *Itinerary* 2: Auckland to Rotorua and Waitomo Caves and return to Auckland (39 tourists).
- *Itinerary* 3: Auckland to Rotorua and Waitomo Caves to Taupo and return to Auckland.

Both itinerary 1 and 2 record only a limited amount of free time, being the shortest tour schedules among inbound visitors to New Zealand. The typical itinerary commences at 07:00 and finishes at 18:00 to 19:00 hours, with sightseeing comprising the major activity (30 to 32 per cent), undertaken over two nights and three days. During the 53 to 59-hour period, respondents spent their time:

- Sleeping (33 per cent);
- Touring (30 per cent);
- Free time (14 per cent);
- Transfers (12 per cent);
- Eating/meals (11 per cent).

On the basis of these results, three types of Korean tourists could be identified based on time budget research by Ashworth and Dietvorst (1995):

- *Organised sightseeing oriented visitors*, who comprise the large majority of visitors, with a city tour in a chartered coach during the day, interspersed with shopping before or after meals and a limited amount of free time spent walking around attractions and taking photographs. Evenings were spent at the accommodation base to rest after the day's activities.

- *Shopping and conviviality oriented tourists*, where shopping activities were conducted near to the accommodation base in the morning. The age profile of this group was younger (typically under 40 years of age), in search of specialist markets, tourist attractions and not venturing far from the accommodation base. In the evening, this group spent their leisure time at a wide variety of fun-related facilities (e.g. at a pub, gambling at the Casino in Auckland or at a night-club). In Rotorua, this group spent most of their free time at Korean pubs in the central tourist district.
- *Health and sports oriented tourists*, comprising the majority of the senior group (aged 50-plus) and a number of business travellers who pursued largely 'private' leisure activities. While no 'typical' activity patterns could be discerned during the day, with some preferring walking or going shopping, the time spent on these activities was much less than the two former groups. In the afternoons, sports activities dominated (e.g. golf and fishing) and in the early evening they frequented health facilities followed by relaxation for the remaining part of the evening.

While the results from the Korean case study indicate that removal of travel restrictions in 1989 has significantly increased outbound travel, there were significant 'pull' factors promoting Korean travel to New Zealand (e.g. immigration policy, no-visas agreement, new air services and 15,000 Korean residents living in Auckland promoting VFR traffic) which can be related to the motivational literature and the unique attractions available in New Zealand. The analysis of tourist activity patterns shows that in urban areas, Korean visitors do not venture far from their accommodation base. This limits the flow and distribution of visitors, with a tendency for bunching and concentration at key nodes around Auckland, Rotorua and Taupo.

Concerns over a saturation of tourists at key attraction sites accentuates the problem of managing the geographical patterns of this short and concentrated experience of New Zealand tourism. Many attractions are unable to cope with the arrival of large numbers of tour groups simultaneously, as this highly organised and almost regimented form of tourism is posing significant strains on the visiting infrastructure. In this respect, a spatial analysis of activity patterns and time budgets illustrates not only the shape of existing demand, determined by tour operators and group leaders, but also the geographical interaction and time constraints under which these tourists visit New Zealand have clear spatial implications for the type of tourism experience they require in time and space.

- Developing tourism from new markets in East Asia Pacific highlighted the fickle nature of tourism as an economic activity: a currency crisis led the Korean outbound market to New Zealand to decline dramatically.

- Packaged tourist itineraries have a strong influence on the activity patterns of tourist groups. This conditions the geographical patterns of consumption in time and space for tour groups.
- Even within tour groups, time budget research identified the diversity of motivations in relation to the reasons for undertaking a tour.
- Within urban areas, the Korean visitor has a tightly defined spatial search area which constrains the flow and distribution of their activities in time and space.
- Specific research tools such as time budget surveys, when linked to spatial patterns of activity, can yield a great deal of important information for tourism planners and commercial operators about the tourists' use of time and space.

PATTERNS OF DOMESTIC TOURISM

According to the WTO, domestic tourism is estimated to be up to ten times greater in volume than international tourism and yet comparatively little research has been undertaken on this neglected area of tourism activity. D.G. Pearce (1995a: 67) argues that this may be attributed 'to the less visible nature of much domestic tourism, which is often more informal and less structured than international tourism, and a consequent tendency by many government agencies, researchers and others to regard it as less significant'.

This problem of neglect is compounded by a paucity of data, since it is not a straightforward matter of recording arrivals and departures. It requires an analysis of tourism patterns and flows at different spatial scales to consider spatial interaction of tourists between a multitude of possible origin and destination areas within a country as well as a detailed understanding of inter-regional flows. Where government agencies and other public sector organisations undertake data collection of domestic tourism 'the results are not often directly comparable, limiting the identification of general patterns and trends'. For this reason, the innovative research undertaken by D.G. Pearce (1993b) is worthy of attention here since it comprises one of the few systematic analysis of domestic tourism in a country, which in this case is New Zealand.

As D.G. Pearce (1995a: 67) rightly acknowledges, 'there are still few examples of comprehensive inter-regional studies where the analysis is based on a complete matrix of both original and destination regions ... [since] few appropriate and reliable sets of tourism statistics exist which might be used to construct such a matrix'. Nationwide surveys are undertaken which are weighted to reflect the population base. One of the few comprehensive studies which yielded an origin-destination matrix is the somewhat dated New Zealand Domestic Travel Survey (NZDTS), established in 1983 (New Zealand Tourism Board 1991a) and recently updated.

THE NEW ZEALAND DOMESTIC TOURISM SURVEY

Domestic tourism data are harder to collect than those for international visitors, simply because no frontiers are crossed or formal registers required. Domestic travel estimates can thus only be made by factoring up from representative surveys of the population. As with all surveys, sample size and representativeness are critical, so that a manageable (and affordable) sample size of a thousand or so will give reasonably accurate figures for national trends but is useless at a regional level. The domestic travel surveys of the 1980s carried out by the NZTP were based on a sample of 12,000 interviews.

This gave confidence limits of +/" 0.9 per cent at the 95 per cent level and so was extremely reliable for national estimates. Even so, the authors of the research noted that potential error limits increase very quickly as sample sizes reduce and particular care should be taken in interpreting results for small subgroups of the sample. They went on to remind us that when a large proportion is being sampled and the sample result is projected, the sampling error is magnified also, and that a sampling error may run into very large numbers when expressed as a projection, even though, expressed as a percentage, it may appear to be quite small. The implication of this is that even regional statistics derived from a national survey may be quite inaccurate.

In 1999, New Zealanders are estimated to have made 16.6 million trips with at least one night away, comprising a total of 52.9 million nights; they spent NZ$4.1 billion on overnight trips. In addition, they made 44.3 million day trips of more than 40 km each way and spent a further NZ$2.8 billion on them (Forsyte Research 2000). As well as easily equalling the expenditure of international tourists, albeit in local currency, domestic travellers provide the essential base for most tourism infrastructure. These domestic tourism figures were derived from a major 1999 study carried out by Forsyte Research on contract to the former Public Good Science Fund. The primary focus of the research was to determine the direct economic impact of domestic tourism in New Zealand. A secondary objective was to measure domestic travel patterns for both overnight and day trips for 1999, to a level that allowed regional analysis. This was the first study of its scale since the last of the domestic travel survey series, noted above, carried out by AGB McNair in 1989/90 and the first to measure day trips in addition to overnight trips. Prior to this, the only recent research was a pilot survey carried out by Simmons (1997). The Forsyte sample was substantial, at 17,037, and provides high-grade data.

In all, almost 70 per cent of domestic travel in New Zealand was to the North Island, or within it. Canterbury, and then Otago, were the major destinations in the South Island. Regional flows, in net person nights, show a more interesting picture. The North Island is a net exporter of some two and a half million person nights to the South. Within the North Island, Auckland and Wellington are the main deficit regions, exporting a total of almost nine million person nights. The major beneficiaries are Northland, Waikato and the Bay of Plenty. In the South Island, the main beneficiaries are Otago and Nelson, followed by Marlborough and the West Coast. Canterbury is the only deficit region.

About half of all travel (46 per cent) is for holidays and leisure, with an average duration of 3.8 nights, and one-third (35 per cent and 2.9 nights) for visiting friends and relatives; a further 12 per cent is business travel, with an average stay of 2.5 nights. Of course, the economic impacts will not fall in direct proportion to the type of travel. Accommodation used is, overwhelmingly, the private home of a friend or relative or a borrowed second home. Motels are the commonest form of commercial accommodation with a total of 14 per cent; hotels attract only 7 per cent, many of whom would be business travellers (Forsyte Research 2000; Hall and Kearsley 2002).

Overall patterns of expenditure are split between the two islands broadly proportionately to visitor numbers, but the average amount spent per night varies considerably by region, with Wellington and Auckland the highest and Northland, Gisborne and Marlborough the lowest. As a result, Auckland has the largest total receipts at over NZ$700 million, followed by Waikato, Wellington and Canterbury. In total, the North Island receives almost NZ$2.8 billion and the South NZ$1.29 billion.

Even the least earning region, Gisborne, receives nearly NZ$47 million, although in Gisborne's case there is a small net outflow. In terms of regional flows of income, the North Island is an exporter of money, to the value of NZ$212 million, to the South. Auckland shows the largest net deficit by far ("NZ$453 million). In the South Island, every region is a net beneficiary, so that domestic tourism is a major economic sector and a powerful agent of income redistribution on a regional basis. In aggregate, a quarter of all expenditure is on accommodation and just over a quarter is on food. Shopping of all types consumes one-fifth of expenditure, while transport, recreation and alcohol account for about 10 per cent each. Business travel is getting on for three times the cost of other trips per night, and is heavily weighted towards travel and accommodation costs when compared with other sectors, both proportionately and in real terms. VFR travel is slightly more demanding of travel expenditure than are holidays, but accommodation costs, not surprisingly, are considerably less.

The analysis of behavioural issues in recreational and tourism research indicates that 'in behavioural terms then, there seems little necessity to insist on a major distinction between tourism and leisure phenomena. Therefore, it should follow that a greater commonality between the research efforts in the two areas would be of advantage' although different social theoretical approaches exist towards the analysis of recreation and tourism phenomena. As a result, Moore *et al.* (1995:79) conclude that 'there is little need, if any, to take a dramatically different approach to the behavioural analysis of tourism and leisure'. One needs to view each activity in the context of the everyday life of the people involved to understand how each is conceived. There is a clear distinction within the literature between what motivates recreationalists and tourists, and comparative studies of similar groups of people and the similarities and differences between these motivations has yet to permeate the research literature. While geographers have focused on recreational and tourist behaviour in relation to demand issues, the analysis has largely been quantitative, site specific, and has not adapted a comparative methodology to examine the recreation-tourism continuum.

8

Tourism's Relationship with the Political Environment

CHANGING PERSPECTIVES ON TOURISM'S RELATIONSHIP WITH THE POLITICAL ENVIRONMENT

The reliance of tourism upon the natural and cultural resources of the political environment means that its development induces change which can either be positive or negative. Today there is a growing interest in the political environmental effects of tourism from governments, non-governmental organisations (NGOs), the private sector, academics and the public. This interest is reflective of a marked change in attitudes to our interaction with the political environment that has occurred during the second half of the twentieth century.

Society's concerns after the Second World War rested primarily with rebuilding the economies of Europe and political environmental priorities were subsequently low. By the late 1960s, as the effects of the pursuit of economic growth upon the political environment became more evident, political environmental issues began to gain more prominence. The first break-up of a major oil-tanker, the Torrey Canyon, leading to the release of oil onto the south-west coast of England caused a high level of public concern and highlighted the fact that increased consumer consumption was not free of political environmental risk.

The increasing industrialisation of farming in the USA was also heavily criticised in Rachel Carson's (1962) book, *Silent Spring*, for the ecological damage caused by the use of agro-chemicals on farmland. This book subsequently had a major influence on public consciousness and eventually on regulatory policy, with the banning or restriction of use being placed on twelve of the pesticides and herbicides Carson identified as being most dangerous, including the notorious DDT. Academic interest in the political environment was also heightened during the 1960s, and the disciplines of chemistry, physics, mathematics, ecology and biology began to be applied to the political environment in an integrated manner within the field of political environmental sciences. However, tourism remained largely immune from political environmental criticism, the image of tourism being predominantly one of an 'political environmentally friendly' activity, the 'smokeless industry'. This perception was enhanced by the imagery of tourism, embracing virtues of beauty and virginity, as portrayed in landscapes of exotic beaches and mountain areas framed in sunshine.

Nevertheless, there were one or two dissenting observations about the 'smokelessness' of tourism. Milne (1988) comments that in 1961 there was concern being expressed over the possible ecological imbalance that could result from tourism development in Tahiti in the Pacific. The observation of the effects of increasing numbers of people descending upon beautiful areas in the 1960s led Mishan (1969:141) to write:

Once serene and lovely towns such as Andorra and Biarritz are smothered with new hotels and the dust and roar of motorised traffic. The isles of Greece have become a sprinkling of lidos in the Aegean Sea. Delphi is ringed with shiny new hotels. In Italy the real estate man is responsible for the atrocities exemplified by the skyscraper approach to Rome seen across the Campagna, while the annual invasion of tourists has transformed once-famous resorts, Rapallo, Capri, Alassio and scores of others, before the last war no less enchanting, into so many vulgar Coney Islands.

By the 1970s people were becoming more aware and concerned over political environmental issues. In 1972, the results of research by a group of scientists and business leaders into population growth, resource use and other political environmental trends were published in the 'Limits to Growth: A Report for the Club of Rome Project'. Predictions in the report of pollution, resource depletion and heightened death rates resulting from a lack of food and health services, raised public consciousness over political environmental issues. In 1979, the near meltdown of the nuclear reactor at Three Mile Island in Pennsylvania, and the subsequent threat of a major political environmental catastrophe, alerted the public to the dangers of the civil nuclear power programme.

Opposition to nuclear power became a central focus of the political environmental movement in the 1970s, based upon both the political environmental consequences of the programme and its strong link to the development of nuclear weapons. During the 1970s, questions about the political environmental impacts of tourism began to be raised more widely, as tourism expanded internationally and the negative effects of its development became more obvious.

Recognition of the problems that could be caused by tourism led the Organisation of Economic Cooperation and Development (OECD) to establish in 1977 a group of experts to examine the interaction between tourism and the political environment. Negative effects on the political environment from tourism such as the loss of natural landscape, pollution, and the destruction of flora and fauna were already being noted. These concerns were also expressed in academic circles, with the publication of *The Golden Hordes* by Turner and Ash (1975), in which the whole process of tourism development was questioned.

By the 1980s, global political environmental problems resulting from the human actions had begun to become popular media items. Global warming, associated with the burning of the earth's carbon stocks for energy and the associated release of CO_2 had become a major concern, as had the depletion of the ozone layer.

The predicted climatic changes associated with global warming, and the increased risk of skin cancer resulting from the depletion of the ozone layer, became matters of both interest and concern to many members of the public. There was a growing realisation that the pursuit of economic growth and increased material consumption was having a profound effect upon our political environment and threatening the long-term well-being of humankind. Concern was also being increasingly and vociferously voiced over the depletion of the tropical rain forests of the world for agriculture and logging.

Nuclear power remained a concern as the world had its worst nuclear disaster at Chernobyl in the Ukraine in 1986 and the effect of the nuclear fall out was felt all over Europe. It is not a coincidence that in 1989 the Green Party in the United Kingdom recorded 15 per cent of the vote in the European elections.

During the 1980s, the spread of mass tourism beyond the Mediterranean basin into new areas, including south-east Asia, Africa and the Caribbean, meant that there was increasing focus on tourism as a form of economic development in less developed countries. Besides economic aspects of development, this focus also included concern over the political environmental and cultural consequences of tourism development. The awareness that tourism could have negative effects was increasingly being recognised by NGOs.

Pressure groups such as Tourism Concern, the UK-based campaigning group for humane tourism development, and the Ecotourism Society in the USA were established in the 1980s to promote ethically based tourism for both indigenous peoples and nature. Local pressure groups, concerned by the effects of tourism development on their physical and cultural political environment were also formed, such as the Goa Foundation in India.

The Goa Foundation have opposed tourism because of the loss of access to resources for local people and other associated human rights violations associated with its development, as is described later in this chapter. There was also evidence of increasing dissatisfaction by tourists with areas that were perceived as being overdeveloped or having lost their original attractiveness.

For instance, Barke and France (1996:302), commenting on the problems facing tourism in the Costa del Sol region of Spain in the late 1980s, state:

'Political environmental decay and poor image have combined with overcrowding and low safety and hygiene standards, together with the popularity of cheaper forms of accommodation and catering, to reduce the perceived attractiveness of the region.'

During the 1990s, new political environmental concerns became prominent, reflecting both local and global concerns. An ethical dimension was increasingly introduced into political environmental campaigning over the rights of non-human life, with high profile and sometimes violent actions being taken for the liberation of animals from experimentation. Protests against road building became a central focus for political environmental campaigners in Britain and other European countries as concerns over the loss of countryside and nature grew.

The enthusiasm and popular support for this campaign led the British government to a major rethink of its strategy over transport, particularly the role of the private motor car and road building, leading to the cancellation of numerous road-building projects. Green politics in Europe gained increasing recognition through formal political routes in the 1990s, notably the formation of a governing red-green coalition in Germany, and by the end of the decade green politicians were in charge of the political environment ministries of Germany, France, Italy and Finland.

Concerns over the practices employed by farmers were also heightened with the outbreak of bovine spongiform encephalopathy (BSE) in Britain, which not only threatened animal life, but could also be transmitted to humans in the form of Creutzfeldt - Jakob disease (CJD). Worries over genetically modified crops were also raised in Europe and there was a subsequent increased demand for organically produced vegetables, fruits and meats.

Major protests were also made over the global inequality in world trade and the role of the World Trade Organization in encouraging the removal of trade barriers and import tariffs. By the end of the 1990s, tourism development had for the first time been attacked directly by eco-warriors. Ski facilities were burnt down in Vail in Colorado at the beginning of 1999 because of their possible impacts upon wildlife. In the 1990s, the tourism industry began to take action over the political environment, with many tour operators, hotels and airlines attempting to improve their political environmental credibility.

Growing concern over the use of the political environment for tourism also found its way into the popular press; for example, the English newspaper the *Guardian* raises political environmental issues associated with tourism almost on a regular basis in its weekend travel section.

Tourism and the need for a more sustainable approach to its development also led non-governmental organisations not directly associated with tourism, such as the World Wide Fund for Nature, Voluntary Service Overseas and Oxfam, to become increasingly interested in tourism development. A growing number of tourists also became more interested to varying degrees in the political environmental aspects of tourism. 'Green tourism', 'eco-tourism' and 'sustainable tourism', became favourite phrases in the industry. A summary of the changing attitudes of society towards the political environment and tourism over the last five decades is shown.

THE POLITICAL ENVIRONMENTAL IMPACTS OF TOURISM

This section of the chapter discusses the political environmental impacts of tourism. As will be illustrated tourism will have either negative or positive impacts upon the political environment; rarely, if ever, will it have a neutral relationship with the political environment.

Although the discussion will attempt to be as holistic as possible, our knowledge of the impacts of much of human action upon the political environment, and subsequently the amount we know about the effects of tourism, is limited. The limitations of the discussion that need to be taken into account can be summarised as follows.

- Research into impact studies is relatively immature and a true multidisciplinary approach to invest-igation has yet to be developed.
- Research into the political environmental consequences of tourism tends to be reactive and therefore it is not always easy to establish a baseline against which to monitor changes.
- It is not always easy to separate out the environm-ental impacts attributable to tourism from the effects of other economic activities or anthropogenic factors, such as human habitation, and non-anthropogenic causes, such as natural political environmental change.
- It is not always possible to separate the source of impacts upon the political environment between local residents and tourists.
- The consequences of tourism are difficult to assess because tourism development is often incremental and the effects are cumulative.
- Spatial discontinuities are inherent to tourism. For example, the effects of air pollution caused by air and car emissions associated with tourism may contribute to acid rain which destroys forests hundreds of kilometres away.

The impacts of tourism upon the political environment can be separated into two broad categories of negative and positive changes. To provide a structure to the discussion, the first part of the following section deals with the negative consequences of tourism and the second part with the positive effects for the political environment.

This ordering is reflective of much of the observation and commentary that has been expounded on the impacts of tourism, which has raised awareness of the negative political environmental aspects that can result from tourism development, whilst the positive political environmental aspects are less well defined. This imbalance in the literature is also a reflection of the fact that any change to the natural political environment by human action is likely to be viewed as harmful, involving at the very minimum damage to individual flora and fauna, and sometimes threatening the existence of species and whole ecosystems.

However, it should be realised that within the context of the discussion on impacts, the extent to which we determine impacts to be either positive or negative ultimately relies on value judgements. From an anthropocentric viewpoint, these judgements need to be balanced with the consideration that through the usage of natural resources for development, the standard of living for humans can be improved.

This is a particularly relevant consideration for societies that live in material poverty and struggle to meet their basic needs for food, clean water and shelter. Nevertheless, this is not to condone the negative effects of tourism upon the political environment, as in many situations these result from a mixture of human ignorance and greed, rather than from a philanthropic desire to improve the living conditions of human beings.

THE NEGATIVE IMPACTS

There are a broad range of negative physical and cultural political environmental impacts resulting from tourism development, which can be categorised into three major types of concern: resource usage; behavioural considerations; and pollution.

RESOURCE ISSUES AND TOURISM

The development of tourism requires physical resources to facilitate its expansion. One of the most noticeable developmental aspects of tourism in generating and destination areas is airport construction. Airports are an essential part of the international tourism system and can generate major employment opportunities for local people. The expansion and development of airports is also beneficial to the tourist by offering easier access to a wider choice of destinations.

However, the resultant effects for the political environment, including the people who live near to airports, are not always as beneficial. For instance, airport development and expansion often involves the transformation of agricultural and recreational land which is covered by runways and terminal buildings. According to Friends of the Earth (1997), major international airports, like Heathrow in London, have paved areas equivalent to 320 kilometres of three-lane highways or motorways. In destination areas the extensive amount of land used for both airport and seaport development can also be problematic.

For example, in 'small island developing states' (SIDS), the loss of agricultural land for airport and seaport development can lead to an increased reliance upon food imports to meet local needs. The development of an airport also requires additional infrastructure, such as new roads and railways, which again necessitates land-use changes and adds to the pollution of surrounding areas. As the demand for international tourism increases, the demand for the expansion of airports is likely to grow.

According to Whitelegg (1999), air transport demonstrates the biggest growth rate of any form of transport and the International Air Transport Authority (IATA) estimate that the rate of growth in air passengers will continue at 5 per cent per annum until the year 2010.

Within destinations, the development of the tourism superstructure, such as hotels and attractions, and its associated infrastructure, also requires land. Tourism is often a competitor for land use with other economic activities, such as agriculture, and in some cases extractive industries like logging and mining.

Subsequently, the use of land for tourism development is at the denial of other forms of economic activity, thereby incurring what economists refer to as 'opportunity costs', that is the potential economic benefits resulting from another type of development other than tourism are denied. The danger of unplanned and unregulated tourism development, in response to market conditions in which there is a high demand for tourism, can mean there is an overuse of resources for tourism and a lack of development of other forms of economic activity.

This can lead to an economic overdependence upon tourism and a lack of diversification of the economic base. The danger of this situation is that if tourism demand to a destination decreases, there is a lack of development of other economic sectors to support the local economy. This is likely to lead to high levels of unemployment and associated social problems.

Another key natural resource that is essential for tourism is water. The addition of hundreds or thousands of bed spaces in a destination, combined with the lifestyle demands of western tourists, such as a daily requirement for showering, clean sheets and bath towels, means that tourism is responsible in some destinations for the consumption of copious amounts of water compared to the needs of the local population.

Salem (1995) remarks that 15,000 cubic metres of water will supply 100 luxury hotel guests for 55 days, whilst the same amount will supply 100 nomads or 100 rural farmers for three years, and 100 urban families for two years. The effects of the development of tourism in areas where water resources are limited can mean that local people are denied the access to the water resources they previously used, for example to irrigate crops.

They may find that streams previously used for irrigation have been diverted further upstream to service tourism development, or that the water-table level has been lowered by overextraction to service tourism establishments, rendering their wells useless. Where it is impossible to continue to extract enough fresh water locally, hotels can pay to have the water imported, whilst local people suffer water shortages. Unsurprisingly, access to water resources has sometimes led to conflict over tourism development between the developers and the local community.

CONFRONTATION OVER WATER RESOURCES

In Tepotzlan in Mexico, the place from which Zapata led the peasant army in the Mexican Revolution of the early twentieth century, the residents who are mostly Nahua Indians protested against plans to build a golf course, five-star hotel and 800 tourist villas. Apart from the fact that such a development will be exclusive of local people in terms of employment opportunities, it is calculated that the development will use up to 525,000 gallons of water a day, threatening shortages in the town. Using slogans of 'Zapata lives' and 'Land and Liberty', the locals took over the town hall periodically, and barricaded the streets with barbed wire and boulders in protest against the scheme.

In Goa, in India, tourism development has also caused discord over resource issues between developers and local people. This has resulted in local people organising protest groups against tourism development and open antagonism towards tourists.

CLASHES OVER RESOURCES IN GOA, INDIA

The development of tourism in Goa raises many issues over the interaction between local people and tourism. Goa is a state in western India facing the Indian Ocean. It possesses the typical 'exotic' image of paradise for westerners with over 65 kilometres of sandy beaches and coconut palms. The area began to develop its international tourism (it was already very popular for domestic tourism) potential in the 1980s with the first German charter arriving in 1987.

The development of tourism has been characterised by investment from outside the region and the building of large four- or five-star hotels. Unfortunately, this style of development has meant that tourism has excluded some local people from the resources that they need for their livelihoods. Nicholson-Lord (1993) gives examples of the 'Cidade de Goa Hotel' which built a 2.4-metre wall around a beach to deny local people access, and the Taj holiday village and Fort Aguada beach resort hotels, where guests are guaranteed water twenty-four hours a day whilst nearby villagers are denied access to the pipeline for even one to two hours a day.

Many villagers face electricity and water shortages, with one five-star hotel consuming as much water as five villages, and one fivestar tourist consuming twenty-eight times more electricity than a Goan. Many of the hotels were also built directly on the beach, damaging the dunes, and human sewage was put directly into the water without being treated. The extent of the feeling of exclusion of local people from the benefits of tourism has led to the growth of protest groups against tourism development, notably the Jagrut Goenkaranchi Fauz (Vigilant Goan's Army) and the 'Goa Foundation', an political environmental group.

Occasionally there has been open aggression towards tourists, such as the pelting of German tourist buses with rotten fish in the late 1980s, and ten tourists were beaten up by a group of villagers in Nuven village after knocking down two pedestrians.

Besides possibly having restricted access to water resources, local people may also find that they are excluded from other areas that they used to use for natural resources and recreation, such as beach areas. A typical sign on beaches that have been privatised to accompany up-market hotel development, especially in less developed countries, taken on the island of Langkawi in Malaysia.

Tourism development can also lead to the displacement of people from their homes, particularly of poorer people in less developed countries, many of whom possess no rights of land ownership and have limited or no access to legal representation. One of the most notable examples of the displacement of indigenous people associated with tourism was the exclusion of the Maasai people from their traditional lands, when the Maasai Mara reserve in Kenya was established. However, the exclusion and displacement of local people from lands for tourism development is not something that is specific to Kenya.

The development of the Chitwan National Game Reserve in the Terai area of Nepal was also achieved by the exclusion of local people, and on the island of Langkawi in Malaysia, the compulsory reclamation of land by the state government led to the splitting up of a long established community and a loss of livelihood for many villagers. Displacement of people from the land for the development of 'golf villages' in South-East Asia has also occurred.

The development of these golf villages usually involves the transformation of agricultural land, the development of condominiums, conference centres and other leisure facilities. Their size can be up to 80 times the size of a typical European golf course. It is difficult to have a global perspective on the numbers of people that may be displaced from the land for tourism development. However, it is evident that tourism development can be an exclusive process, and as landowners and entrepreneurs become aware of the financial opportunities to be gained from tourism, then the pressure on local tenants to leave their land is likely to increase.

CORAL REEFS AND GAME PARKS, ISSUES OF TOURISM DEVELOPMENT IN KENYA

The country of Kenya in east Africa is endowed with natural resources that should make it an attractive tourism destination for decades into the future. It has both fantastic game reserves, a beautiful coastline with coral reefs, and cultural diversity. However, many of these resources are being put under threat from tourism development. The most popular area for holiday tourism in Kenya is along the coast, north and south of Mombassa.

The coast has a diverse range of ecosystems including coral and mangrove swamps. However, the development of tourism has placed the coral under threat from sewage pollution from hotels, tourists walking on the coral and killing it, local people breaking it off to sell as souvenirs to tourists, and boats dragging their anchors through it. Mangrove swamps which form the basis of another vital ecological chain are also being cleared in an unsustainable fashion.

They are being cut for construction poles, timber and fuel wood, as well as being removed for aquaculture farms. As a result of the demand by tourists for lobsters, crabs, prawns and fish, there has been overfishing and a decline in fish stocks, and subsequently lobsters and prawns now have to be imported from Tanzania.

Nor is tourism faring much better in some of the safari parks in Kenya, tourists being attracted by the 'Big Five' game animals: elephant, rhino, buffalo, lion and leopard. Indigenous people were displaced to create the parks in the 1940s, notably the Maasi people from the Maasi Mara park. This has radically altered their way of life and resulted in some of the Maasi having to migrate to the coast to sell their handicrafts to tourists. The consequences for the wildlife of increasing numbers of tourists in some of the parks have been the disruption of their breeding and eating patterns.

Tourists are taken too close to the animals, elephants have been poisoned from eating zinc batteries thrown out in the rubbish from the tourist lodges that have been established, and there is also erosion of the vegetation from the excessive numbers of minibuses crossing the parks threatening the grazing of herbivores. Other problems in the parks include the pollution of water through lack of adequate sewage and other waste disposal facilities.

This has led to wild animals and vultures feeding on the waste food and drinking from open sewers. Besides adversely affecting the access of local people to resources, the physical political environment can also be threatened by tourism development. A natural feature of many holiday destinations is the beach, but even it may be used as material for hotel construction ultimately leading to its disappearance.

For example, in Antigua in the Caribbean, miles of pristine sand have been removed by sand-mining companies for use in constructing tourism projects, and sand has also been shipped to the Virgin Isles to build other beaches.

Similarly, coral reefs, the second most biologically diverse ecosystem on the earth after tropical rainforests and subsequently a great attraction for tourists, have come under threat from tourism development. Coral reefs are home to approximately 25 per cent of all marine species despite covering only 0.17 per cent of the ocean floor.

Their growth requires specific political environmental conditions, including a water temperature of between 25 and 29 degrees centigrade, a relatively shallow platform of less than a 100 metres below sea-level to grow upon, highly oxygenated water, and areas free from sediment or pollution. There are three main types of coral reefs: 'fringing reefs', which connect directly with the shore; 'barrier reefs', which are separated from the shore by a lagoon; and 'atolls', which consist of a ring of coral reefs around a lagoon. The reefs are composed of a thin veneer of living corals that exist on the top of the skeletons of previous biological growths.

Coral is placed under threat from different aspects of tourism, including the construction of tourist facilities, inadequate sewage disposal measures to deal with human waste, and the behaviour of local people and tourists. Coral reefs have been mined for building materials in Sri Lanka, India, Maldives, east Africa, Tonga and Samoa. Besides being used for building materials, reefs may also be placed under threat from the dust created by construction which gets blown onto the reef, for example as in the Red Sea off the coast of Egypt.

The addition of untreated sewage into the water results in nutrient enrichment or eutrophication, which stimulates the growth of algae, which can cover coral reefs, in effect suffocating them. For instance, the discharge of partially treated sewage into the sea off the Hawaiian island of Oahu stimulated the growth of the alga *Dictyosphaeria cavernosa*, which overgrew and killed large sections of the reef.

Similarly parts of the Great Barrier Reef off the coast of Australia are being destroyed by the proliferation of 'crown-of-thorns' starfish, *Acanthaster planci*, which feed on the reef and have become abundant as a consequence of pollution and overfishing of their predators.

According to Jenner and Smith (1992) millions of starfish have been observed, each one able to eat its own area of coral in a day, and as much as one-third of the Great Barrier Reef has been adversely affected to some degree. The Queensland tourism industry has been devastated, and the world's first floating hotel called the 'Barrier Reef Floating Hotel' operated for only a few months in 1988, before being towed back to Ho Chi Minh City from where it had come owing to a lack of tourist demand. The behaviour of local people and tourists towards the reefs can also damage the coral. One country in which tourism has resulted in negative effects upon its coral reefs, and other types of natural resources is Kenya.

According to Pattullo (1996) over 90 per cent of the world's coral reefs are said to have been damaged by various forms of human activity. The extent of tourism's involvement in this damage is generally thought not to be large compared to other industrial sectors, although as Goudie and Viles (1997) point out, 73 per cent of the coral reefs off the coast of Egypt are thought to have been adversely affected by tourism.

Nevertheless, the blame for the demise of the world's coral reefs cannot solely be laid at the door of tourism. Tourism is a contributory factor to the destruction of coral reefs along with other natural and human causes. These include storms and hurricanes, El Niño, overfishing, increased sedimentation produced by the deforestation of land and industrial pollution.

Hurricanes can kill living coral by flinging it up to the top of the reef, whilst El Niño which is an ocean current occurring off the coast of Peru every two to ten years, causes changes in ocean currents and sea temperatures. Changing sea temperatures have also been attributed to the effects of global warming.

The raising of sea temperatures can threaten the food supply of coral, which is dependent upon microscopic algae called *Zooxanthellae* turning the sun's energy into sugars, to provide energy for the coral polyps. The algae are very temperature sensitive, and as the temperatures of the ocean rise the algae will leave the polyps denying them food, which may subsequently lead to the mass death of the corals. It is thought that with continued global warming and increasing ocean temperatures, this process of coral bleaching may occur more regularly.

Additional threats for coral are also posed by more aggressive kinds of human actions. The reefs of French Polynesia in the tropical Pacific face the constant threat of nuclear bomb testing by the French, whilst the residual radiation remaining on some of the atolls from the American and British nuclear tests in the 1960s means they cannot be used for habitation or tourism. Industrial activity can also threaten the well-being of coral, for instance increased silting as a consequence of dredging for tin poses a threat to coral reefs in Thailand. The destruction of coral reef not only means a loss of biodiversity but also threatens other political environmental resources upon which tourism depends.

In the same way that tourism was likened to a spider's web, major natural features such as coral, form part of interlinked and complex ecosystems. Coral not only provides an abundance of food for fish but also acts as a natural breakwater to help protect coastline and beach areas from erosion. Without this natural breakwater, beach erosion will occur at a much quicker rate than normal, especially where palm trees, the roots of which help to stabilise the beach, are removed to make space for hotel construction.

The potential damage that unaware and unplanned tourism development can do to coral and beach political environments, developed from the work of Edington and Edington (1986). An actual example of the type of construction, which is a photograph of tourism development on the coastline of the Indian Ocean. The construction of tourist facilities would seem to be happening at a rapid pace, leading to the removal of palm trees, and destabilising the beach area.

Another important ecosystem in terms of making the earth a habitable place to live for humans, are coastal and inland wetlands, which cover approximately 6 per cent of the world's surface. Wetlands not only house a wide range of biodiversity and act as vast carbon-storing areas for the world, but also operate as a form of local flood control measure by absorbing vast amounts of water at times of high rainfall, and discharging it to adjacent areas in a slow and measured way.

However, the restricted availability of land for tourism development in coastal areas, combined with the engineering ability to reclaim wetlands, means that wetlands are increasingly being used for tourism development. For instance, in the Languedoc-Rousillon region of France, five new coastal areas were developed on reclaimed wetland sites, in response to the lack of available land for building on the French Riviera. One of the coastal areas, 'La Grande Motte', has subsequently become the third largest French resort in the Mediterranean after Cannes and Nice. The engineering project was enormous, involving the draining, dredging and filling of coastal marshes and saltwater lagoons, leading to the complete disappearance of the wetland fauna.

A similar scheme to reclaim wetlands including mangrove swamps has taken place in the Caribbean, to accommodate the Sir Donald Sangster International Airport in Jamaica. After coastal areas, the second most popular location for tourism is in mountain areas. Just as tourism has resulted in detrimental political environmental effects in coastal areas, it has also caused negative impacts in many mountain areas. Mountain areas are physical political environments which are sensitive to change, characterised by short growing seasons as a result of the cold temperatures, and soils which tend to be thin and nutrient deficient. The combination of these factors makes subsequent regeneration of damaged vegetation difficult.

Mountain areas have become popular destinations for activity-based tourism, and mountain systems worldwide are being used increasingly for activities such as downhill skiing and snowboarding, mountain biking, paragliding, white water rafting and trekking. One particular form of mountain tourism that is very popular, estimated to account for 3 to 4 per cent, or approximately 24 million of the recorded total of international tourist arrivals in 1997, is wintersports.

The economic benefit associated with sports such as downhill skiing and snowboarding has meant that their development has actively been encouraged through government policy in some countries, as a means of developing upland rural areas. Although the development of downhill skiing has aided the creation of economic prosperity in many mountain areas, it has also resulted in many negative consequences for the physical political environment.

The development of mountain tourism requires the construction of hotels, apartments and associated infrastructure, placing increased pressure on land resources and animal habitats. The removal of trees to create ski runs, besides resulting in a loss of habitat for wildlife, also means that rainfall falling on the mountain slopes is not absorbed in the same quantity as before. The removal of trees causes a loss of cohesion and stabilisation of the soil by the tree roots, and subsequently the mountain slope is more prone to slippage.

The combined effects of increased amounts of water running across the surface of the slope, its weakened stability and the force of gravity, has led to mountain areas becoming vulnerable to landslides. The effects of these landslides can be quite dramatic, sometimes involving the loss of human life. For example, Simons (1988) describes the avalanches of mud that swept down mountainsides during the summer of 1987 in northern Italy and southern Switzerland, in which 60 people died, 7,000 were made homeless and 50 towns and villages and holiday centres were wrecked.

The cause of these landslides was attributed to the removal of mountainside forest for ski development. Another mountain area to suffer deforestation and subsequent landslides as a consequence of tourism is Nepal. These landslides can be on a large scale, sometimes leading to whole mountainsides tumbling into valleys. The landslide in this photograph occurred at Tatopani in the Annapurna area of Nepal, and was on such a scale it dammed the powerful Kali Gandaki River behind it, necessitating the dynamiting of the blockage to let the river flow.

A major cause of deforestation in the Annapurna area is the influx of mountain trekkers into the area during the last thirty years. The traditional resource used in the mountain valleys of the area for cooking and to heat water is wood. The continued growth in the number of trekkers to the area has put increased pressure upon forest resources as trekkers demand hot food and often a shower every day.

HUMAN BEHAVIOUR TOWARDS THE POLITICAL ENVIRONMENT

An integral part of the tourism system is tourists and local people. The behaviour of both groups will be highly influential in determining the extent to which the consequences of tourism upon the non-human world are either negative or positive. The behaviour of tourists to the culture of the destination they are visiting will also be influential in determining whether tourism is viewed as a positive or negative force for change by local people.

A major natural attraction for tourists is wildlife but wildlife can be adversely affected by certain aspects of human behaviour. The viewing of wildlife species in their natural habitats has become an attractive activity for an increasing number of tourists, resulting in the intrusion of humans into political environments which had previously been the exclusive preserve of wildlife.

Ironically, the desire of the tourist to enhance their perceptions of nature by observing wildlife at close quarters can bring disruption to the natural behaviour of the wildlife they want to see. According to Duffus and Dearden

(1990) cited in Roe *et al.* (1997), the extent of the impact of tourism on wildlife can be related to the type of tourist activity and the level of tourism development. Mathieson and Wall (1982) also add that the resilience of wildlife to the presence of humans will influence the degree to which tourism proves harmful to a particular species.

THE POLITICAL ENVIRONMENTAL IMPACTS OF TREKKING IN NEPAL

Nepal is a small land-locked country situated between India and the People's Republic of China and is one of the world's poorest nations with a large foreign debt. It possesses outstanding natural resources for tourism, notably the Himalayan mountain range, and is becoming an increasingly attractive tourism destination for international travellers. The number of international arrivals has risen from 6,179 in 1962 to 393,613 in 1996.

One type of tourism that Nepal has become renowned for is trekking, with 23 per cent of the tourists who go to Nepal participating in this activity. The most popular trekking area is Annapurna, with 59 per cent of all trekkers going there, compared to 19 per cent who go to the Everest Region and 9 per cent who go to Langtang. The Annapurna area is rich in biodiversity containing both rare fauna and flora.

However the arrival of over 40,000 trekkers per annum has put extra pressure upon the natural resources of the area. Unplanned development has led to the construction of 700 tea houses and lodges in which trekkers can stay. Large areas of the outstandingly beautiful rhododendron forests that grow in the area have been removed to provide timber for construction, and fuel to heat food for tourists, and provide them with hot water for showers. Deforestation of the mountains has resulted in tremendous landslides becoming a regular feature of the area.

Waste disposal problems are also an issue. Inadequate sanitation facilities results in pollution of water supplies, and non-biodegradable litter is thrown into streams and piled in rubbish heaps on the edge of settlements, again leading to pollution and hygiene problems. Cultural problems have also been created in the area, with children begging from trekkers, and the development of an inferiority complex amongst some local people in comparison to the 'richer' tourist.

For example, the type of safari tourism practised in the Serengeti Park on the Kenyan/Tanzanian border is representative of a highly developed level of tourism, involving local operators taking tourists into the park in minibuses, and animals being surrounded by thirty or forty vehicles full of tourists taking photographs.

The invasion of the territorial space of the animals, and the associated increase in noise levels, raises the stress levels of animals which is disruptive to their breeding and eating patterns. For example, cheetahs and lions are reported to decrease their hunting activity when surrounded by more than six vehicles. The drivers of the minibuses are encouraged to ignore laws governing the proximity of their vehicles to the animals by the extra tips they receive from tourists for getting close to them.

Sometimes the threat to wildlife from tourism can be more direct, especially in communities where the level of political environmental education is low, and an insensitive view of the political environment is held by locals. For example, commenting on the backpacker operations that take tourists into the rainforest in Ecuador, Drumm (1995:2) writes:

Only 20% of local guides have completed secondary education, and very few are proficient in a language other than Spanish. Together with a social context which embues them with a settler frame of mind, antagonistic to the natural political environment, the negative impacts of this operation are significant. Hunting wild species for food and bravado is commonplace during tours as well as the occasional dynamiting of rivers for fish. The capture and trade in wildlife species including especially monkeys and macaws is also very common.

Besides wildlife, other natural resources may be placed under threat from the action of local people. For instance, coral is damaged by local people who break it off to sell as souvenirs, as in the Bahamas and Granada, where rare black coral is made into earrings for sale to tourists. Local operators taking tourists out in boats to visit reefs sometimes drag their anchors through the coral causing localised damage, whilst tourists harm the coral by touching and standing on it. Additionally, shells are sometimes collected by local people to sell to tourists, as in areas of the Red Sea, the Caribbean and off the coast of Kenya. Key factors influencing the attitudes of local people to the surrounding political environment, are poverty levels, economic opportunity and the extent of the provision by government and the private sector of political environmental education.

Careless behaviour by tourists can also adversely affect wildlife and ecosystems. A common problem associated with tourists is littering, which can potentially result in the death of animals eating the litter, and also lead to the attraction of predators of endemic species into areas where they would not normally go. For example, elephants have been killed by eating zinc batteries thrown onto rubbish heaps surrounding the outskirts of lodges in the Maasai Mara in Kenya.

In the Cairngorm mountains in Scotland, foxes who are predators of the indigenous ptarmigan and grouse have been enticed into the area, leading to a decline in bird numbers. However, as Shackley (1996) points out, although tourism can be detrimental to wildlife, the habitat of much wildlife is under a more widespread threat from other phenomena, such as agricultural development, urban expansion, and extractive industries like logging and mining. The behaviour of tourists can also cause cultural changes in the societies they visit. One of the possible consequences for cultures that are exposed to tourism, especially in less developed countries where there is likely to be a marked difference between the lifestyle of the tourist and the local population, is what anthropologists term the 'demonstration' effect. According to Burns (1999:101) the 'demonstration effect' applied within the context of tourism can be explained as:

This effect refers to the process by which traditional societies, especially those who are particularly susceptible to outside influences such as youths, will 'voluntarily' seek to adopt certain behaviours (and accumulate material goods) on the basis that possession of them will lead to the achievement of the leisured, hedonistic lifestyle demonstrated by the tourists.

Seemingly there exists a desire for some groups living in non-western cultures, to imitate western lifestyles by acquiring the same symbols, a phenomenon also referred to as 'blue-jean' culture. The imitating of western lifestyles may however, go beyond the purely superficial, to appropriating the more materialistic and individualistic values of western society. The adoption of such values will undoubtedly cause change in societies whose previous cultural value systems are likely to have emphasised religion, co-operation, the family and the community.

The copying of tourists' fashions can also lead to cultural conflicts between different groups in communities. For example, post-pubescent Muslim girls living on the Mombassa coast in Kenya who see western women dressed in bikinis, may wish to dress the same way, even though their religion dictates they should be completely covered. In societies with strong traditional values, such a situation is likely to result in conflict with the elders and men of the community.

Another criticism that is often made of tourism's effect upon local cultures is that it can lead to their commerc-ialisation and commoditisation.

This can result in established rituals and ceremonies becoming a parody of the authentic culture, to satisfy the demands of tourists, in effect turning into 'pseudo-events'. Tourists are unlikely to understand the significance and meaning of the event they are watching or participating in, and with the passage of time it is also possible that the performers may lose sight of the original cultural importance of the practice.

Similarly, the same criticism can be made of local handicrafts, which instead of being handcrafted for their cultural significance, can end up being mass produced for sale to tourists. Yet as Burns (1999) points out, it is often difficult to separate out cultural changes resulting from tourism from those attributable to the wider process of modernisation, such as the geographical spread of global television networks.

However, the material wealth and lifestyle of the tourist can have the effect of making one's own culture feel comparatively worthless and limiting. What local people fail to understand, as no one usually informs them, is that the behaviour of the tourist is atypical of how they behave during the rest of the year.

The fact that western society suffers from increasing levels of family breakdowns leading to social isolation, high crime rates, drug addiction and suicides and that there is a developing underclass of impoverished and isolated people, are not points often made to people in less developed countries.

This was illustrated by Marcel-Thekaekarka who had spent ten years working with the Adivasi, the indigenous people of the Nilgiri mountains of Tamil Nadu in India, on rural development schemes before she visited Germany with six of the Adivasis.

Although in material poverty themselves, the Adivasi were shocked by the lifestyle of people in Germany, even though they were materially much wealthier. The Adivasis expressed sympathy for their lifestyles which seemed urbane and isolated as Marcel-Thekaekarka (1999:3) writes: '"It's very nice to be here", Chathi, one of the six told me. "But I couldn't live here. It's not my place. A man needs his family, his community, his own people around him. Just money can't give you a life. You'd shrivel up and die."'

Sometimes the problems that arise from tourism are what the majority of societies would perceive as being socially unacceptable, involving crime, prostitution and drugs. For example, the development of sex tourism in Thailand and other parts of south-east Asia has resulted in increased levels of Aids amongst the population. It has also led, as is the norm in prostitution, to the exploitation of women by men.

POLLUTION

Pollution of the physical political environment resulting from tourism can occur on different spatial levels, including tourism generating and destination areas, and other localities not directly connected with tourism but to which pollution is displaced.

However, it is important to point out that tourism is a contributing factor to local and global pollution, along with a whole range of other services and industries. The pollution associated with tourism may be categorised into four main types: water, air, noise, and aesthetic pollution.

WATER POLLUTION

Water pollution is a major problem in many tourist regions of the world. For instance, in the most visited tourist area of the world, the Mediterranean, only 30 per cent of over 700 towns and cities on the coastline treat sewage before discharging it into the sea. In the Caribbean Basin, where 100 million tourists annually join the 170 million inhabitants, only 10 per cent of the sewage is treated before being discharged into the sea. The most worrying aspect is that, compared to other areas of the world, these figures are actually good. Other regular international tourist destinations such as east Asia and Africa and the islands of the South Pacific, with a few exceptions, have either no sewage treatment or treatment plants that are totally inadequate for the size of the population. The problem of water contamination from human sewage is not caused exclusively by tourism but is reflective of an inadequate infrastructure to meet the needs of both local people and tourists.

Besides the consequences it can have for human health, causing diseases ranging from mild stomach upsets to typhoid through the intake of water contaminated by faeces, human sewage also causes eutrophication (nutrient enrichment) of the water. This can pose a particular threat to coral and associated ecosystems as explained earlier in the chapter. Eutrophication of water may also lead to a downturn in tourism demand as experienced on the Romagna coast of Italy in 1989.

According to Becheri (1991), the total number of tourist bookings on the Romagna coast fell by 25 per cent in 1989 compared to 1988, owing to the eutrophication of the Adriatic and the spread of algae on the surface of the water. The source of the pollution was from agricultural, urban and industrial wastes, which were deposited in the River Po and subsequently outflowed into the Adriatic.

Similarly, the fear of a typhoid outbreak in Salou in Spain in 1988 resulting from contaminated water, led to a 70 per cent decline in tourist bookings the next year. By the late 1980s, many Spanish beaches were considered dirty, with only three beaches on the Costa del Sol being considered clean enough for Blue Flag status in 1989. The decline in water and beach quality contributed significantly to a slump in tourism receipts in Spain in the late 1980s.

Besides the pollution resulting from the inefficient disposal of human waste, water pollution is also caused by fertilisers and herbicides, which are widely used on golf courses and hotel gardens. The water containing the chemicals seeps through to the groundwater lying 5 to 50 metres below the earth's surface and through aquifers it eventually reaches rivers, lakes and seas. Other sources of water pollution are caused by motorised leisure activities such as power boating, and even suntan oil being washed off tourists when swimming can result in localised pollution. However, although tourism may seem to be a culprit of much of the planet's water pollution it is important to realise it is a contributory factor. The major sources of water pollution come from oil spills, industrial waste pumped into sea, and from chemicals used in agriculture.

AIR POLLUTION

A major source of air pollution within the context of tourism is associated with transport for tourism. Both air and car transport contributes to local and global atmospheric pollution through the burning of fossil fuels. The release of carbon dioxide (CO_2) is widely thought to be a major cause of global warming, and the emission of sulphur dioxide (SO_2) contributes to problems of acid rain which destroys forests and historic monuments such as the Parthenon in Athens.

Per passenger, aviation produces more pollution than any other form of transport, accounting for 3 per cent of the total amount of the world's carbon dioxide emissions or equivalent to the entire CO_2 output of British industry. The growth in air travel since the 1950s has been rapid, with the annual rate of passenger growth averaging 5 to 6 per cent per annum, over almost a 50-year period. Besides contributing to global warming, air transport emits 2 to 3 per cent of the total global emissions of nitrogen oxides, which are believed to reduce ozone concentrations in the stratosphere (Friends of the Earth, 1997). Emissions of nitrogen oxides and hydrocarbons at lower levels also contribute to regional smog problems by forming low-level ozone on calm summer days, which is harmful to health.

Air pollution is also associated with the development of airports for tourism. Health issues associated with airports include respiratory problems caused by emissions from aircraft and car traffic, and stress associated with noise pollution from air traffic.

According to Whitelegg (1999) aircraft produce significant amounts of nitrogen oxides during take off and landing. He adds that Kennedy and La Guardia airports in New York are amongst the largest sources of pollution in the city, and that Midway Airport in Chicago generates more toxic pollutants than any other form of industry in the city. The effects of this pollution on health are dramatic, with aircraft engines being held responsible for 10½ per cent of the cancer cases in south-west Chicago caused by toxic air pollution.

A common mistake is to equate transport in tourism solely with airlines, as it is often assumed that most tourism is undertaken by using air travel. However, this is not the case; for example, within Europe, the car accounts for 83 per cent of the total passenger kilometres. A very common pattern of summer holiday travel in Europe is for tourists from the countries of northern Europe such as Germany, Scandinavia, and the Benelux countries to drive down to the Mediterranean coast for their vacation.

When domestic tourism is also taken into account, then the effect of the motor car becomes even more prominent, as the majority of domestic trips are undertaken by its use. For those people living in transport transit areas, the effects of tourism are predominantly ones of inconvenience, associated with pollution and safety concerns.

Although the social and health effects of transit traffic upon local communities is an underresearched area, Zimmermann (1995:36), commenting on transit traffic through the European Alps, remarks: 'The transit traffic is one of the most evident problems within the Alpine area. In several regions local populations' endurance levels have already been reached or exceeded.'

Within destination areas the air quality may deteriorate as a result of both extra traffic and construction. Dust generated during the construction of tourist facilities contributes to air pollution, for example Briguglio and Briguglio (1996) remark that the demolishing of existing buildings and the construction of new ones for tourism has generated vast amounts of dust in Malta.

Yet, as with water pollution, tourism can also be adversely affected by displaced air pollution originating from sources elsewhere. Forests used for tourism in developed countries that are situated close to large industrial centres are particularly under threat from acid rain, caused by emissions of sulphur dioxide from coal-burning power stations. For instance, Mieczkowski (1995) refers to the Black Forest in Bavaria becoming the 'Yellow Forest', and Jenner and Smith (1989) comment that as a result of the damage to the forest caused by acid precipitation, there has been a loss of tourism income. It should also be noted that as tourism was a contributory factor with a range of other human activities to water pollution, the same is true for air pollution. The use of the motor car in everyday life for commuting and shopping, and the burning of fossil fuels to produce electricity, is larger air polluting activities than tourism.

NOISE POLLUTION

In psychological studies of humans, noise pollution has been found to affect behaviour in a detrimental fashion. According to Mieczkowski (1995) most complaints associated with tourism relating to noise are from air traffic. Noise pollution is particularly a problem for those residents who live around busy international and domestic airports, and the proposed development of airports may sometimes lead to violent opposition by local people and protest groups, as was the case with the construction of Narita Airport in Tokyo.

Noise pollution from tourism will be particularly noticeable in destinations where tourists are searching for quietness and peace. Airflights in remote areas where quiet is expected, such as the Grand Canyon in the USA and the Himalayas, can cause disruption to tourists and recreationists.

Noise pollution from the construction of tourism facilities can also be a problem for residents and tourists. Briguglio and Briguglio (1996) observe that intense noise is generated by the building of hotels and other construction activity in destinations. Night clubs open until the early morning, and increased car traffic from tourism movements, all add to the noise pollution experienced by both residents and tourists in tourism destinations.

AESTHETIC POLLUTION

The development of tourism facilities can also lead to a decline in the aesthetic quality of the political environment. Commenting on the development of tourism in the Guadeloupe and Martinique islands situated in the Lesser Antilles, Burac (1996:71) comments: 'The most worrying problem now prevalent in the islands relates to the anarchic urbanisation of the coasts. ... Also, the built-up areas by the seaside are often not aesthetically attractive due to the diversity of architectural styles, the disappearance of traditional creole homes and the disorderly way in which public posters are displayed.'

Often tourism development is based upon maximising profits whilst ignoring aesthetic concerns. This has led to a uniform style of development along many coastlines of the world, that ignores local architectural styles, building traditions and materials. In mountain areas tourism has also created unsightly development. Besides hotel and apartment construction, the development of ski lifts and pistes has also been heavily criticised as a form of aesthetic pollution.

For instance, the Scottish Office (1996:7) make the following remarks about the development of downhill ski facilities in Scotland: 'In addition [to adverse ecological effect], the infrastructure and uplift facilities associated with skiing can have a visual impact on what would otherwise be an unspoilt and undeveloped landscape.'

Harm to fauna and flora resulting from tourism development is an emotive topic. Yet tourism can bring economic benefits to people who are in poverty, such as the money to buy medical supplies and food. To what extent is a reduction in biodiversity important (especially if aesthetic appreciation is not harmed) if economic benefits are being brought to an area from tourism?

THE POSITIVE EFFECTS

It is unlikely that any kind of human action has a beneficial effect for the natural political environment it interacts with, other than to protect it from more damaging forms of human behaviour. Therefore, when we talk about the beneficial effects of tourism for the political environment, we are in essence talking about tourism being used as a way of protecting the political environment from possibly more damaging forms of development activity, like logging and mining. The exception to this situation is tourism's interaction with the built political environment, where in post-industrial landscapes, tourism has been used as a catalyst to aid urban regeneration and improve the quality of the political environment.

The development of tourism will, however, normally place an increased emphasis on the maintenance of a 'good-quality' political environment in a destination, if tourism is intended to play a long-term role in the local economy. Yet the meaning of what is a 'good-quality' political environment is highly value-ridden and debatable. Nevertheless, it is certain that the long-term economic success of tourism is often dependent upon maintaining a level of quality in the natural political environment, which will satisfy the demands of tourists.

As Mieczkowski (1995:114) comments: 'The very existence of tourism is unthinkable without a healthy and pleasant political environment, with well preserved landscapes and harmony between people and nature.' The consequences for tourism destinations that do not maintain a high-quality political environment were illustrated by the examples of Salou in Spain, and on the Romagna coast in Italy, earlier in the chapter. This relationship between the economic success of tourism, the political environment.

This diagram emphasises that the political environment, including both its cultural and physical resources, is the key to satisfying the needs of the tourists and building long-term economic prosperity for tourism. It is therefore in the interest of the destination community to ensure that the landscape remains well preserved and that they provide stewardship of the political environment.

Importantly, tourism can play a role in the conservation of the political environment by giving it an 'economic value' through the revenues from tourist visitation. Given that development decisions are predominantly based upon an economic rationale, the revenues from tourism can help to protect habitats and wildlife from other more political environmentally harmful forms of development, such as mining and logging, or from other forms of destructive human activity, such as poaching.

Within the context of this section of the chapter, one of the most positive examples of where tourism has been used to conserve a particular species is the mountain gorilla project in Rwanda, which was proving very successful until the outbreak of civil war that took place there between 1990 and 1994.

One type of political environment, in which some of the best examples are to be found of tourism making a positive contribution to political environmental improvement, is in post-industrial urban political environments. Although tourism can bring problems of traffic management, overcrowding and associated problems, such as littering to urban areas, it can also play in active part in the restoration of redundant industrial areas and of historic sights.

Many of the post-industrial towns of the western world suffered the loss of traditional manufacturing industries, such as iron and steel, shipping and coal mining in the 1980s. Subsequently, tourism was turned to by many local governments as a catalyst for urban regeneration and as a means of providing new employment opportunities.

The pioneer of using tourism to regenerate urban areas was Baltimore in the USA, where the decision was made in the 1980s to rejuvenate the waterfront through the development of shopping and recreation, to arrest inner city decline.

Despite the numerous commendations that have been made of the redevelopment of Baltimore through tourism, Law (1993) criticises the success as being only skin deep, suggesting that poverty and housing problems still remain in the city.

However, there is little doubt that political environmental improvements have resulted from the development of tourism in depressed urban areas. This is particular the case for the waterfront areas of major cities, such as Sydney in Australia, and Liverpool in England.

One advantage of improving the political environmental quality of the urban political environment, especially where it is combined with improved infrastructure development, is that it enhances the image of the city and makes it more probable that other businesses and services will be attracted to relocate and invest there. Besides the advantage of attracting secondary investment, tourists who come to the area also spend money, which induces a multiplier effect generating further demand for goods and services in the local economy.

GORILLAS IN RWANDA

One of the most cited examples of how tourism can be used to aid conservation is in Rwanda in central Africa. The Parc National des Volcans in Rwanda is home to more than 300 of the world's estimated 650 mountain gorillas. They were particularly under threat from poachers, an export trade of gorillas' hands for ash-trays to the Middle East was one lucrative outlet, and also from the encroachment of agriculture leading to the removal of their habitat.

The gorillas were popularised by the film *Gorillas in the Mist*, about the life of Dian Fossey who was an active researcher and conserver of the gorillas, ultimately resulting in her murder. There is little doubt that the film aided the development of tourism in the park.

Tourist visitation of the gorillas is controlled by the Office Rwandaise du Tourisme et de Parcs Nationaux, and part of the revenues generated from tourism go to conservation agencies, notably the Mountain Gorilla Project and Dian Fossey Gorilla Fund. Visitors are taken out in small groups (maximum of eight) by well-informed local guides to see the gorillas in their natural habitat of dense bamboo forest.

The total annual visitation to the park is between 5,000 to 8,000 tourists. Importantly, the project has been proven to be a financial success, critically benefiting local people, who in turn have taken a more active interest in conservation.

However, the civil war in Rwanda between 1990 to 1994 unfortunately brought visitation to a standstill. In 1994 when 750,000 refugees were escaping from Rwanda to Zaire (now named the Democratic Republic of Congo), tens of thousands of people per day passed through the park, bringing with them their cattle and belongings.

Many took refuge in the park. The occupation posed particular problems for the gorillas, including land-mines being placed in the forest, and gorillas being trapped in response to a lucrative black market for meat that had developed in response to famine. Between 1994 to 1998 rebel militias still held out in the park. The future of gorilla tourism in Rwanda therefore remains uncertain because of political unrest.

The redevelopment of urban areas through tourism can also be aided by the development of tourist attractions which are rooted in the local heritage and history of the area. For instance, at Wigan in England, the town that was the source of inspiration for George Orwell's novel *The Road to Wigan Pier*, the local municipality developed a heritage centre called 'Wigan Pier'.

Reflecting the day-to-day life of an industrialised Wigan at the beginning of the twentieth century the centre attracts over 500,000 visitors per annum. Importantly the involvement of local people in establishing the centre helped regenerate local pride and interest in their heritage. The development of heritage attractions to attract tourists to urban areas has now become a global phenomenon; for example Holden (1991) remarks that in Singapore a large historical and cultural theme park based upon the ancient Tang Dynasty of China has been developed, including 1,000 replicas of the Terracotta Warriors.

However, the development of such attractions has led to criticisms of inauthenticity, especially where the theme seems to have little to do with the area it is situated in, or the attraction attempts to recreate life as it was in a historical period.

As with all forms of tourism, the benefits of urban tourism will only continue to be enjoyed if it is carefully planned and managed to ensure that areas do not become totally overcongested, as in the case of Venice, which is literally sinking under the weight of tourists.

The influx of large numbers of tourists has been a contributory factor to a deterioration in the quality of life for residents in Venice, which has led to some of them leaving the city (Page, 1995). As for all forms of tourism, urban tourism has threshold limits beyond which the political environment will be perceived as having declined in quality, with consequences for both local residents and tourists.

Bibliography

A. Ranga Reddy: *Democracy and Human Rights : Essays in Honour of R Radhakrishna and G Raghava Reddy*, Serials Publication, Delhi, 2009.

Ajay Kaul: *Hospitality Logistics Management*, Centrum Press, Delhi, 2013.

Anand Ballabh Kafaltiya: *Democracy and Election Laws*, Deep and Deep Publication, Delhi, 2003.

Anil Bhuimali: *Democracy and Human Rights*, Serial Publication, Delhi, 2007.

B.N. Patnaik and S. Imtiaz Hasnain: *Globalization : Language, Culture and Media*, Indian Institute of Advanced Study, 2006.

D.K. Singh: *Hospitality Sales and Marketing*, Aman Publications, Delhi, 2010.

G. Palanithurai and R. Ramesh: *Globalization : Issues at the Grassroots*, Concept Publication, Delhi, 2008.

Govind Prasad and Anil Dutta Mishra: *Globalization : Myth and Reality*, Concept Publication, Delhi, 2004.

J Mathews: *Hospitality Marketing and Management*, Aavishkar Publication, Delhi, 2006.

Jagmohan Negi, Suniti and Ritushka and Gaurav Manoher J.: *Hospitality Marketing and Managerial Economics : Objective Type Questions and Solutions*, Kanishka Publication, Delhi, 2012.

John Dewey: *Democracy and Education : An Introduction to the Philosophy of Education*, Aakar Books, Delhi, 2004.

John Dewey: *Democracy and Education : An Introduction to the Philosophy of Education*, Aakar Books, Delhi, 2011.

Manfred B. Steger: *Globalization : A Very Short Introduction*, Oxford University Press, Delhi, 2006.

Manish Ratti: *Hospitality Management : Theories and Practices*, Rajat Publication, Delhi, 2007.

Manoj Madhukar: *Hospitality Industries in Next Millennium*, Rajat Publication, Delhi, 2001.

Mukesh Sahni and Varun Naik: *Democracy and Human Rights*, Crescent Publishing Corporation, Delhi, 2011.

N. Dinamani: *Democracy and Politics in Nepal*, Sumit Enterprises, Delhi, 2009.

N.S. Gehlot: *Democracy and Politics in Modern India*, Deep and Deep Publication, Delhi, 2012.

Pushpanadham Karanam: *Globalization : A Challenge to Educational Management*, Sarup Publication, Delhi, 2012.

R K Panchal: *Globalization : Its Impact on Rural Development*, Sumit Enterprises, Delhi, 2006.

Ram Mohan Verma: *Democracy and Governance in a Changing World*, Vista International, Delhi, 2005.

Ranvijav Singh: *Hospitality Service Quality*, Centrum Press, Delhi, 2013.

Ravi Sharma: *Hospitality Jobs and Careers*, Centrum Press, Delhi, 2013.

Ruchi Mehta: *Hospitality Innovation Management*, Centrum Press, Delhi, 2013.

Sures Chandra Jain: *Globalization : Debts, Arms and Reforms in South Asia*, Concept Publication, Delhi, 2005.

Surider Khanna: *Democracy and Human Rights*, Swastik Publications, Delhi, 2012.

Vikram Jain: *Hospitality Supervision*, Naman Publication, Delhi, 2011.

Vivek Verma: *Hospitality and Tourism Marketing*, Centrum Press, Delhi, 2011.

Index